THE
HUMAN PERSON

THE
HUMAN PERSON
ACCORDING TO JOHN PAUL II

Reverend Monsignor J. Brian Bransfield

Pauline
BOOKS & MEDIA
Boston

Library of Congress Cataloging-in-Publication Data

Bransfield, J. Brian.
  The human person : according to John Paul II / J. Brian Bransfield.
    p. cm.
  ISBN 0-8198-3394-0 (pbk.)
  1. John Paul II, Pope, 1920-2005. 2. Theological anthropology--Catholic Church. 3. Catholic Church--Doctrines. 4. Human body--Religious aspects--Catholic Church. 5. Sex--Religious aspects--Christianity. I. Title.
  BX1378.5.B76 2010
  233.092--dc22

                                        2010001471

The Scripture quotations contained herein are from the *New Revised Standard Version Bible: Catholic Edition*, copyright © 1989, 1993, Division of Christian Education of the National Council of the Churches of Christ in the United States of America. Used by permission. All rights reserved.

We acknowledge and thank those publishers whose material, whether in the public domain or under copyright protection, has made this work possible. Every effort has been made to obtain all the proper permissions. But if we have inadvertently not obtained a required permission, we ask the publisher to contact the editor for proper acknowledgment and compensation.

Cover design by Rosana Usselmann

Cover art: Leonardo da Vinci (1452–1519). *Study of Human Proportion: The Vitruvian Man.* Ca. 1492. Pen and ink drawing. Accademia, Venice, Italy. Cameraphoto Arte, Venice / Art Resource, NY.

"P" and PAULINE are registered trademarks of the Daughters of St. Paul.

Published by Pauline Books & Media, 50 Saint Pauls Avenue, Boston, MA 02130-3491.
Printed in the U.S.A.

www.pauline.org

Pauline Books & Media is the publishing house of the Daughters of St. Paul, an international congregation of women religious serving the Church with the communications media.

2 3 4 5 6 7 8 9   17 16 15 14 13

To Mom and Dad,
In Loving Memory

Contents

Part I
TWO CULTURES CLASH

CHAPTER ONE

The Experiences of Wojtyla /
The Experiences of the Twentieth Century

Part II
THE THEOLOGY OF THE BODY, ORIGINAL INNOCENCE, AND ORIGINAL SHAME

CHAPTER SEVEN

The Gifts of the Holy Spirit,
the Beatitudes, and the Virtues

Foreword

It is a great pleasure to introduce *The Human Person: According to John Paul II* by Reverend J. Brian Bransfield, a priest of the Archdiocese of Philadelphia. This work introduces the reader to the fundamental themes in the teaching of the Venerable Servant of God Pope John Paul II on the identity of the human person, the theology of the body, and the mystery of salvation.

Pope John Paul II responded, in heroic fashion, to society's chronic confusion about the identity and meaning of the human person. In his teaching Pope John Paul II repeatedly emphasized that the identity and vocation of the human person are fulfilled in and through the total gift of self in love. Through detailed analysis and simple explanation, *The Human Person: According to John Paul II* spells out and makes accessible to the general reader the teaching on the gift of self as contained in the theology of the body. From the vantage point of key thresholds in the mystery of salvation such as creation, the fall, and redemption, Father Bransfield explains in uncomplicated language the meaning of concepts central to the thought of the Holy Father such as original solitude, original unity, original shame, and original nakedness. The reader will find in these pages a way to understand more deeply and to express more effectively the teaching of the Church for which our world hungers.

The pages that follow appeal, in an easily understandable style, to the teaching of the Fathers of the Church, in particular Saint Augustine and Saint Gregory the Great, as well as to theologians of the twentieth century such as Cardinal Henri de Lubac, Cardinal Jean Daniélou, and Hans Urs von Balthasar. The author demonstrates in everyday terms that the teaching of Pope John Paul II is a rendition of unique caliber, which, at the same time, inherits the tradition in all of its original depth.

The human person, marriage, and the family are the first targets of the culture of death. The teaching of Pope John Paul II stands as a resounding response that sets forth the clear defense and affirmation of the inviolable dignity of the human person, and the splendor of marriage and family. A graduate of the Pontifical John Paul II Institute for Studies on Marriage and Family, Father Bransfield serves as Executive Director of the Secretariat of Evangelization and Catechesis, and as Assistant General Secretary of the United States Conference of Catholic Bishops. He carefully identifies the manner in which the teaching of Pope John Paul II serves the central message of the New Evangelization: the civilization of love will emerge only through the culture of life. I commend this volume as a valuable resource to priests, deacons, seminarians, catechists, and to all the faithful.

CARDINAL JUSTIN RIGALI
Archbishop of Philadelphia

Acknowledgments

I am deeply grateful to the many people who have supported my efforts in writing this book. I am most thankful to Cardinal Justin Rigali, the Archbishop of Philadelphia, for his encouragement of my efforts and his gracious willingness to offer the Foreword to this work. I am very appreciative to Most Reverend Donald Wuerl, the Archbishop of Washington, to Most Reverend Gregory Aymond, the Archbishop of New Orleans, and to Carl Anderson, the Supreme Knight of the Knights of Columbus and Vice President of the Washington, D.C. session of the Pontifical John Paul II Institute for Studies on Marriage and Family, for their kind and thoughtful words regarding these pages.

This book was written while I served as a professor of Moral Theology at St. Charles Borromeo Seminary in Wynnewood, Pennsylvania. I will always be grateful for the invaluable collaboration of my colleagues on the faculty and the attentive support of the seminarians, especially those who participated in the lectures and discussions from which this book arose.

The expert and dedicated staff of the United States Conference of Catholic Bishops has been a source of constant encouragement. In particular, I acknowledge my brother priests at the Conference, most especially Reverend Monsignor David Malloy, the General Secretary, and my colleagues in the General Secretariat and the Secretariat of Evangelization and Catechesis, in particular Mr. Andrew Lichtenwalner. I thank as well those who have assisted with the editing and preparation of this book, including the Daughters of St. Paul and their staff, in particular Sr. Marianne Lorraine Trouvé, FSP; Sr. Maria Grace Dateno, FSP; and Kate Hux. The assistance of Carlos and Elena Tejeda and the generous support of Brian and Joan Gail have gone far to bringing this work to fruition.

On a personal level, I happily express my deep gratitude to the many friends whose support has guided me throughout the preparation of this book. In a particular way, a profound note of thanks goes to Martin and Cynthia Lutschaunig and their sons, Christian, Daniel, and Andrew; to my brother priests Reverend Stephen Dougherty, Reverend Michael Gerlach, Reverend John Pidgeon, and Reverend Eric Gruber; and to Reverend Monsignor Ronny Jenkins for his friendship and example of excellent scholarship.

Lastly, I wish to express my deepest thanks to my family members, to my sister Peggy-Anne and her husband, Michael, my sisters Mary Jane and Paula, and my brother Paul for sharing with me the beauty of family life. Above all, I am forever grateful to my beloved mother and father, who have shared their life and love with me. It is to them and their blessed memory that I dedicate this work.

We wish to express a special word of thanks for the use of the following material listed in this book:

"Autonomous Individualism" by John Kavanaugh. Reprinted with permission of America Press, Inc. © 2007. All rights reserved. For subscription information, call 1–800–627–9355 or visit www.american-magazine.org.

Excerpts from *Athanasius: The Life of Antony and the Letter to Marcellinus*, translated by Robert Gregg, copyright © 1980 by Paulist Press, Inc. Paulist Press, Inc., New York/Mahwah, NJ. Reprinted by permission of Paulist Press, Inc. www.paulistpress.com

Excerpts from *Of Many Things* (May 19, 2008) and *Autonomous Individualism* (January 15, 2007) reprinted with permission of America Press, Inc., © 2007, 2009. All rights reserved. For subscription information, call 1-800-627-9533 or visit www.americamagazine.org.

Excerpts from *Footbridge Towards the Other, Crossing the Threshold of Love*, and *Mysterium Pashale* used by kind permission of Continuum International Publishing Group.

Excerpts from *John Cassian: The Conferences*, Translated by Boniface Ramsey, OP, copyright © 1997 by Boniface Ramsey, OP. Paulist Press, Inc., New York/Mahwah, NJ. Reprinted by permission of Paulist Press, Inc. www.paulistpress.com

Excerpts from *Needful Things* by Stephen King, copyright © 1991 by Stephen King. Used by permission of Viking Penguin, a division of Penguin Group (U.S.A.) Inc.

Excerpts taken from *The Acting Person: A Contribution to Phenomenological Anthropology by Karol Wojtyla*. Published by Springer, copyright © 1979. With kind permission of Springer Science and Business Media.

From SIMPSON. *On Karol Wojtyla*, 1E. © 2001 Wadsworth, a part of Cengage Learning, Inc. Reproduced by permission. www.cengage.com/permissions.

"Generation M: Media in the Lives of 8–18 Year-Olds-Report" (no. 7251), The Henry J. Kaiser Family Foundation, March 2005. The information was reprinted with permission from the Henry J. Kaiser Family Foundation. The Kaiser Family Foundation is a non-profit private operating foundation, based in Menlo Park, California, dedicated to producing and communicating the best possible analysis and information on health issues.

"Of Many Things" by Drew Christiansen. Reprinted with permission of America Press, Inc. © 2008. All rights reserved. For subscription information, call 1–800–627–9355 or visit www.americanmagazine.org.

Permission for "The Family Portrait: A Compilation of Data, Research and Public Opinion on the Family" (2 ed.) granted by The Family Research Council, www.frc.org, 1-800-225-4008, 801 G Street, NW, Washington, D.C. 20001.

Permission has been granted to use material from *The Christian Lives by the Spirit* by Potterie and Lyonnet and from *The Pursuit of Happiness: God's Way: Living the Beatitudes* by Servais Pinckaers (both published by ST PAULS / Alba House).

Reprinted by permission of the publisher from *Abortion and Divorce in Western Law: American Failures, European Challenges* by Mary Ann Glendon, p. 11, Cambridge, MA: Harvard University Press, copyright © 1987 by the President and Fellows of Harvard College.

Taken from *The Beatitudes: Soundings in Christian Tradition*, by Simon Tugwell, published and copyright 1980 by Darton, Longman, and Todd Ltd., London, and used by permission of the publishers.

Taken from *Ways of Imperfection: An Exploration of Christian Spirituality*, by Simon Tugwell, published and copyright 1985 by Darton, Longman, and Todd Ltd., London, and used by permission of the publishers.

The following titles were used with permission: The Catholic University of America Press. Washington, DC. *Interpretation of Genesis: An Unfinished Book* by St. Augustine, *Introduction to Moral Theology* by Romanus Cessario, *At the Center of the Human Drama: the Philosophical Anthropology of Karol Wojtyla* by Kenneth Schmitz, *Sharing in Christ's Virtues: For a Renewal of Moral Theology in Light of* Veritatis Splendor by Livio Merlina, translated by William E. May, *The Self-hood of the Human Person* by John F. Crosby, and *Destined for Liberty: the Human Person in the Philosophy of Karol Wojtyla* by Jaroslaw Kupczak.

The Gift: Creation by Kenneth L. Schmitz. Published Marquette University Press, Milwaukee, Wisconsin. Copyright 1982. Reprinted by permission. All rights reserved. www.marquette.edu/mupress.

Introduction

As Pope John Paul II stepped onto the balcony over Saint Peter's Square on October 16, 1978, he was a man in the middle. He had assumed the papacy midway between two historic events: the Second Vatican Council (1962–1965) and the beginning of the third millennium of Christianity. Either event, taken on its own, could lead to great uncertainty, confusion, stress, and expectation. Both the world and the Church experienced considerable commotion. John Paul II, the 264th successor to Saint Peter, stepped onto the stage with a smile and a vision.

Although some thirty-five years separated the end of the Council and the millennium, Karol Wojtyla, as pontiff, formed the bridge between these two events. His pontificate *embodied* both events and united the Council and the new millennium as if they were one continuous dramatic happening. John Paul II's twenty-six-year ministry on the Chair of Peter was, in a certain sense, the *child* of the unity between the Second Vatican Council and the third millennium of Christianity. John Paul's papacy, understood as the interpretation and implementation of the former, and as the preparation for and inauguration of the latter, leads us to understand his teaching as both the bond and the fruit of history itself, which takes the form of the new evangelization.

The millennium represents the accumulation of the energies of humanity's perennial search for meaning. Humans continually ask fundamental questions about the meaning of their identity and their commitments. Questions slumber along with each person day to day and, at certain times, grow more urgent. The third millennium is quite simply the cry of the world that asks where the meaning of humanity resides after the Enlightenment, the rise of science, and advances in technology. In the face of such realities, what are the meanings of theology, the Church, and faith? The teaching of the Second Vatican Council is the Church's anticipation of and response to man's search-filled cry at the dawn of the third millennium. Catholic identity in the contemporary era is a witness to the encounter of these two cries: the questions of the world and the response of the Church. This book attempts to be a witness, to express the tonality of both cries, which build together to form the continuing event of the new evangelization.

Method

Among the many contributions John Paul II made to the new evangelization, the theology of the body occupies pride of place.[1] The catechesis on the body was one of the early projects John Paul took on as pontiff. In his Wednesday audiences in Rome from 1979 to 1984, he delivered a relatively brief catechesis on this topic to pilgrims from around the world. The theology of the body as a catechesis on Genesis is a novel contribution of the Holy Father to the interpretation of Sacred Scripture, philosophy, and spirituality. The teaching, however, is not an island that can be separated from the wider teaching of John Paul and the teaching of the Church in general. In fact, the theology of the body is adequately understood only within that wider orbit of teaching.

This book is not intended to simply be a commentary on the theology of the body. Instead, the teaching of John Paul will be presented in various sections and then discussed. Additionally, particular categories of

---

1. The catecheses were originally published by Pauline Books & Media as four separate volumes: *Original Unity of Man and Woman: Catechesis on the Book of Genesis* (Boston: St. Paul Editions, 1981); *Blessed Are the Pure of Heart: Catechesis on the Sermon on the Mount and the Writings of St. Paul* (Boston: St. Paul Editions, 1983); *Theology of Marriage & Celibacy* (Boston: St. Paul Editions, 1986); and *Reflections on Humanae Vitae: Conjugal Morality and Spirituality* (Boston: St. Paul Editions, 1984). The catecheses were then published together as one volume under the title, *The Theology of the Body: Human Love in the Divine Plan* (Boston: Pauline Books & Media, 1997). In 2006 Pauline Books & Media published a new edition of the catecheses, translated by Michael Waldstein, under the title *Man and Woman He Created Them: A Theology of the Body*, with an extensive introduction and index. Waldstein's translation is used throughout the present work.

John Paul's teaching will be related to the teaching of the Church and to the thoughts of theologians. The purpose of the book is to help readers more easily understand what the theology of the body is all about.

The work consists of three parts:

Part I: Two Cultures Clash considers the factors that shaped the culture of Karol Wojtyla's early life, and contrasts these with the formation of secular culture in the West.

Part II: The Theology of the Body, Original Innocence, and Original Shame analyzes Wojtyla's teaching on the theology of the body in original innocence and under original sin.

Part III: The Theology of the Body, Life According to the Spirit continues the theme concerning "life according to the Spirit," and relates this to the call of the Second Vatican Council for the renewal of moral theology.

Audiences approach the theology of the body with varying degrees of theological background. Some have very little familiarity with theology or Church teaching. Others know one specific area within theology. The theology of the body easily puzzles many audiences, from the novice to the advanced:

> Indeed, it is no doubt true that the *Talks* [*The Theology of the Body*] would tax the ability of an audience hearing these ideas for the first time ... for the talks make little concession to their hearers.... One finds in the *Talks* the result of years of prolonged meditation upon the deepest aspects of the Christian faith. And so, they are meant to be reread—and reread—for insights that are at once fresh and profound.[2]

---

2. Kenneth Schmitz, *At the Center of the Human Drama: The Philosophical Anthropology of Karol Wojtyla/Pope John Paul II* (Washington, DC: The Catholic University of America Press, 1993), 91. Terrence Prendergast notes the necessity of an understanding "of the principles underlying the interpretation" as requiring one to look "more closely at all the sources grounding John Paul's teaching" ("'A Vision of Wholeness': A Reflection on the Use of Scripture in a Cross-Section of Papal Writings" in *The Thought of Pope John Paul II: A Collection of Essays and Studies*, ed. John M. McDermott, SJ (Rome: Editrice Pontificia Università Gregoriana, 1993, 71). The early councils of the Church relied on philosophy to help clarify the theological distinctions expressed in early conciliar teaching. There is a similar dynamic at work in reading John Paul's teaching. For a description of the impact of philosophy on theology, see Avery Dulles, SJ, *The Splendor of Faith: The Theological Vision of Pope John Paul II* (New York: Crossroad Publishing, 1999), 32–33.

Because readers who seek out the teaching of John Paul have varying backgrounds, this book explains even basic concepts in his teaching to allow the central teaching to be more easily understood. This book will clarify important concepts and terms, presenting them in slow motion. It will also relate these concepts to the wider teaching of John Paul and the teaching of the Church. John Paul's teaching is not a random topic that he simply chose to speak about when he became pope. His work is a strategic development that responds immediately to humanity in crisis.

Pain fills the cry of the third millennium. The pain reverberates from a deeper place: the very identity of the human person. Every day, thousands of people in the United States have their personal information stolen and become victims of identity theft. The thieves steal identity for financial gain, and it can take years to repair the damage. Yet, a far more horrific identity theft has been under way for decades. The theft is not economic but cultural. Human nature is robbed of its dignity and reduced to a mere expression of instinct or business acumen. The anguish of people today flows from several factors. No simple diagnosis has sufficed from a sociological perspective to explain the predicament of humanity in the postmodern age. The prescription of a quick fix brings only further injury.

In remedy, Church teaching and theology seek to reassert true human dignity. Theology typically speaks of the identity of the human person in three distinct periods: in original innocence, before the fall; in sin after the fall; and in the life of grace after sin, which aids man in the battle with sin. In times past, theologians spoke about the human person by using abstract philosophical and theological language. John Paul followed the three-part structure and used traditional language. Yet, he added something. He formulated the traditional truths in an accessible way. This book will trace John Paul's categories through each of the three traditional stages, and refer to the works of theologians to further explain the theological locus as it serves the central mystery.

The first chapter explores one of the remote sources of the theology of the body and the new evangelization, namely, the experiences that shaped its foremost herald, Karol Wojtyla. His experiences are divided into three general groups: personal, intellectual, and pastoral. The picture emerges of a man whose life was formed by remarkable experiences that prepared him on both an internal and an external level to proclaim the culture of life. In themselves, these events were commonplace. But the way in which they came together was quite rare. Karol Wojtyla was a man who suffered many things that could have soured another. But he turned them to his spiritual profit, and they uniquely qualified him to advance the new evangelization as a dramatic response to the signs of the times.

Meanwhile, throughout the twentieth century various factors were forming contemporary culture. Chapter 2 considers the perfect storm formed from three revolutions—the industrial, the sexual, and the technological. Each of these had a significant detrimental impact on catechesis and the sense of Catholic identity. The secular culture that developed contrasted greatly with the life of the young Wojtyla.

Chapter 3 traces John Paul's teaching alongside that of the tradition regarding the identity of the human person based on the first account of creation in Genesis. Chapter 4 continues this analysis by focusing on the second account of creation. This chapter presents in detail John Paul's innovative teaching on the theology of the body and the identity of the human person.

Chapter 5 explores John Paul's teaching on the fall of man and the consequences of original sin for man's identity, including the nature of temptation and the effects of sin. Chapters 6 and 7 present the teaching on redemption and life in the Spirit, which is God's response, in his Son, to human sin. These chapters discuss how God responds point-for-point to temptation, and how the Son of God's action on the cross is the efficacious response from which the Holy Spirit draws the new measure of love. This measure of love forms the basis for the renewal of moral theology that the Second Vatican Council called for. The gifts of the Holy Spirit, the life of virtue, and the Beatitudes are presented as the culmination of the theology of the body and the basis for turning from the culture of death to the culture of life.

Part I

Two Cultures Clash

CHAPTER ONE

The Experiences of Wojtyla /
The Experiences of the
Twentieth Century

A. Formative Experiences

A person gains firsthand experiences in the first third of human life, lives from experience in the second third, and in the final third loves the experiences that have been lived. Experience forms humans, and they are continuously invited to weigh and evaluate their formation. History, in one sense, is a collection of experience. Anticipation is the hope for a fuller experience. Adventure is the high point of experience. Nostalgia is the hunger for the high point.

Candidates seeking employment or a political office need to show what they have achieved. Experience shapes a person's identity. Education, training, redirections, and mishaps as well as successes testify to a nominee's character and suitability. Karol Wojtyla brought to the papacy a personal identity that was formed from a diverse background even before his well-documented professional and pastoral abilities.[1] His resume may be broadly divided into three sets of experiences: his per-

---

1. For a detailed biography of Pope John Paul II see Tad Szulc, *Pope John Paul II: The Biography* (New York: Scribner, 1995) and George Weigel, *Witness to Hope: The Biography of Pope John Paul II* (New York: HarperCollins, 1999).

sonal experiences, his intellectual experiences, and his pastoral experiences. These experiences cross-pollinated and coalesced in a unique way to forge a singular depth within the man who would become Pope John Paul II.

1. Personal Experiences

From the widest perspective, Wojtyla's personal experience consisted in being a son of Poland. This nation has a rich national identity built from a history often marked by invasion and tragedy. Situated between Europe and Russia, Poland was often trampled by foreign armies.[2] Repeated enemy incursions and occupation of their homeland have led the Polish people to develop a culture of resistance to foreign forces that transcends mere rebellion on a military level.[3] Resilience sprouts from the very soil of Poland. Each of its sons and daughters bears an irrepressible resourcefulness. The Polish people have been formed to be recalcitrant, strong, and robust in dealing with hardship. The Polish identity, so durable and lasting, should never be underestimated.

Wojtyla's personal history mirrors the history of his country. Karol was born in the town of Wadowice on May 18, 1920, to Karol and Emilia (née Kaczorowska) Wojtyla. His father, a deeply religious man, fought in the Polish army and earned a commendation in World War I. He retired from military service soon after Poland regained independence on November 11, 1918. Karol had an older brother, Edmund, born August 28, 1906. A sister named Olga, born in 1914, died only a few weeks after her birth.

The future pope's first formations were in the context of marriage and the family. He was raised in an interim period of peace in Poland. The Wojtylas were well versed in competition and excelled in the arts. Their younger son participated in activities ranging from family life, schooling, and sports to Saturday folk nights at a local park, singing and reciting

---

2. George Blazynski, *Pope John Paul II: A Richly Revealing Portrait* (New York: Dell, 1979), 7, 25. Gian Franco Svidercoschi, *Stories of Karol: The Unknown Life of John Paul II* (Liguori, MO: Liguori, 2003), 4.

3. For a synthesis of Polish history in this regard see Raymond Gawronski, SJ, "The Distant Country of John Paul II" in *Creed and Culture: Jesuit Studies of Pope John Paul II*, eds. Joseph W. Koterski, SJ, and John J. Conley, SJ (Philadelphia: St. Joseph's University Press, 2004), 61–74.

poetry around a bonfire.[4] Besides his affection for sports and the outdoors, Karol developed a devotion to the theater. But his personal life, like that of his nation, was to lose its peace in short order.

Aside from the influence of his family life, Karol was formed by suffering, both on a personal and national scale. Karol's mother died on April 13, 1929, at the age of forty-five, when Karol was only eight years old. His older brother, Edmund, a medical doctor, died at the age of twenty-six on December 5, 1932, from septic scarlet fever contracted from his patients.[5] Karol was then twelve years old. He and his father moved to Krakow in 1938 as Karol took up university life[6] and continued his theater activities. Within the year, the German blitzkrieg scarred Polish cities and towns with bombs beginning on September 1, 1939.

The Nazis closed the university and would allow only trade skills to be practiced and learned.[7] Karol and Poland had fallen under the first of two totalitarian regimes. The young Wojtyla worked at a quarry and later at a chemical factory.[8] His theater interests took on a new perspective. He wrote poetry, relying heavily on the themes of Polish history and the spiritual life. He participated in a secret underground theater known as the Rhapsodic Theater. This was a "theater of the spoken word" that kept alive and passed on the integrity of Polish history and tradition.[9] The participants relied upon words and gestures rather than props, costumes, and scenery. Besides being cumbersome, such items, if found, would have made the players liable for deportation to the Nazi death camps.

Amid the pain of family loss and the darkness of war, a light arose in the form of a layman, Jan Tyranowski, a local tailor. He was a man of intense faith who introduced Karol to Carmelite spirituality through the writings of Saint John of the Cross.[10] Tyranowski also introduced Karol to the writings of Saint Louis de Montfort. The influence of faithful lay persons became a third level of formation for Karol. The future pope

---

4. Blazynski, *Pope John Paul II*, 35.

5. Svidercoschi, *Stories of Karol*, 10.

6. Peter Simpson, *On Karol Wojtyla* (Belmont, CA: Wadsworth Publishing, 2000), 1.

7. Blazynski, *Pope John Paul II*, 41.

8. Simpson, *On Karol Wojtyla*, 2.

9. Blazynski, *Pope John Paul II*, 46–47.

10. Blazynski, *Pope John Paul II*, 51; Simpson, *On Karol Wojtyla*, 2; Svidercoschi, *Stories of Karol*, 49–50.

first learned of the laity's mission in the Church not through academic theory but through eyewitness encounter. His later apostolic exhortation *Christifideles Laici* ("Christ's Faithful People") did not spring as much from theological research as it did from the lives and witness of dedicated women and men like Tyranowski.

As Poland's suffering continued, Karol's reached a final height when his father died of a heart attack on February 18, 1942. Karol Wojtyla, now twenty-one, had lost his entire immediate family and had seen the Nazis overrun his homeland.[11] When the war ended on May 7, 1945, the Nazi regime gave way to the tyranny of Soviet communism. The Soviets brought an era of Stalinist terror to Poland, with secret accusations, violence against human dignity, the obscuring of Polish history and identity, and oppression of the Church.[12]

These early losses had a deep impact on Karol, for that which is experienced earliest lasts longest. The deep sensitivity he would show as pontiff to suffering persons, even to the plight of entire nations and cultures, was forged in his own suffering. His eyes and expressions seemed to draw forth and convey extraordinary kindness for the sick and the abandoned. Kindness came naturally to Wojtyla. It was formed in his identity from his earliest personal experiences.

2. Intellectual Experiences

Amid his early losses, Karol turned to the laity, and these men and women pointed him toward the life of the intellect, his fourth layer of formative experience. Wojtyla's intellectual experiences flourished in a life that, despite early pain and hardship, was both vibrantly athletic and devoted to academic study. His academic records, which even show his excused absences from class, are included in *The Making of the Pope of the Millennium: Kalendarium of the Life of Karol Wojtyla*.[13] As a young student, he spoke on behalf of his secondary school graduating class in 1938. His obligatory service in the military was postponed after his graduation. Later that year he entered the Jagiellonian University,

11. Blazynski, *Pope John Paul II*, 50; Svidercoschi, *Stories of Karol*, 38.

12. Svidercoschi, *Stories of Karol*, 129.

13. Adam Boniecki, MIC, *The Making of the Pope of the Millennium: Kalendarium of the Life of Karol Wojtyla* (Stockbridge, MA: Marian Press, 2000).

studying Polish philology in the humanities department. He remained at the university until World War II broke out in September 1939.

With his studies abruptly ended, Karol went to Krakow with his father and began his fifth formational experience, the hard work of a daily laborer. The young Wojtyla worked in a chemical factory and a quarry in the Solvay works near Krakow from 1940 to 1944. His service as a laborer exempted him from exportation to Germany for forced labor. During these years, the religious influence of his father, and later Tyranowski, was fundamental to Karol's life.[14] In addition, the influence of priests and friends led Karol to study theology. During the Nazi occupation he began clandestine studies in the department of theology at the Jagiellonian while still working at Solvay.

Karol's formation followed an unpredictable path. His identity was molded early on by seven sources essential to his faith: marriage, the family setting, the experience of loss and solidarity in the face of national persecution, the strategic influence of dedicated laity, the importance of the intellectual life, the daily work of rigorous labor, and prayerful theology. He was naturally led from those seven formative experiences to theology. This is the early culture of Karol Wojtyla, which formed the man who became John Paul II.

The first targets of the Nazis were not the Polish political, military, or business leaders. Even the Nazis knew that to undermine a people's identity one must first undermine their culture. To do this they attacked Polish intellectuals. The first professionals the Nazis deported were university professors, those who could pass on the historical and cultural identity of the Polish people.

Karol Wojtyla responded to the Nazis by participating in the covert Rhapsodic Theater that sustained the identity of Poland by performing plays essential to its history.[15] In trying to become an actor, he wrote several plays and performed in many more. It wasn't merely chance that drew him to the theater. His attraction for it emerged spontaneously from his experiences of marriage, family, loss, laity, intellectual life, hard labor, and prayerful theology. The stage became the eighth layer of his formational matrix. Meanwhile he began thinking about the priesthood.

---

14. Blazynski, *Pope John Paul II*, 51; Simpson, *On Karol Wojtyla*, 2.
15. Boniecki, *The Making of the Pope*, 81–82; Svidercoschi, *Stories of Karol*, 45.

The influence of religious individuals such as his father and Tyranowski, along with priests he had known from a young age, drew him to it. In October 1942, a year after his father died, Karol entered the clandestine seminary of the Archdiocese of Krakow to study for the priesthood.[16] By now the seeds of what would emerge as his personalist philosophy were sown deeply in his soul. While in the seminary he studied philosophy, which added a further dimension to the developing sense of culture and his appreciation for identity.

Karol Wojtyla was ordained a priest for the Archdiocese of Krakow on November 1, 1946, by the Cardinal Archbishop Adam Stefan Sapieha.[17] After ordination he was assigned to parish ministry and was later sent to Rome for graduate studies at the Pontifical University of Saint Thomas Aquinas. Wojtyla completed his doctoral studies in theology on June 14, 1948, and earned the first of two doctorates. His dissertation, *Doctrina di fide apud S. Ioannem a Cruce*, was published in English as *Faith According to Saint John of the Cross*.[18] After returning to Poland he completed his habilitation thesis, which would give him the credentials to teach at the university level. It was titled *An Evaluation of the Possibility of Constructing a Christian Ethics on the Basis of the System of Max Scheler*, and with it, Wojtyla earned a second doctorate in 1954 from Jagiellonian University.[19] He joined the faculty of the Catholic University of Lublin in October 1954, where he served as professor of ethics.

He taught at Lublin until 1957 and held the ethics chair even after he ascended to the See of Krakow. His lectures while teaching at Lublin include topics such as "Ethical Act and Ethical Experience," "Good and Value," and "The Problem of Norm and Happiness."[20] He did not intend his Lublin lectures to be published. Nevertheless, a German edition was published in 1981,[21] and a Polish text was released in 1986.[22]

---

16. Svidercoschi, *Stories of Karol*, 59.

17. Weigel, *Witness to Hope*, 79.

18. Published in English by Ignatius Press, San Francisco, 1981.

19.Weigel, *Witness to Hope*, 130.

20. Jaroslaw Kupczak, *Destined for Liberty: The Human Person in the Philosophy of Karol Wojtyla / John Paul II* (Washington, DC: The Catholic University of America Press, 2000), 25.

21. Lubliner Vorlesungen Stuttgart: Seewald Verlag.

22. *Wykłady lubelskie*.

The texts are Wojtyla's notes and synopses for the classes.[23] Even as Holy Father, John Paul still held the chair in the department of Christian philosophy at Lublin. He would even serve as reader for student papers and meet with professors for discussion.[24] He continued to hold the chair until his death on April 2, 2005.[25]

Wojtyla's Lublin lectures constitute a major contribution to the field of ethics. The Lublin experience forms a central dimension to Wojtyla's identity. The encounters in the lecture hall allowed him to give considerable attention to what various philosophers thought about the nature of human action and identity. He thus had a professional formation that added to his previous personal experiences.

3. Pastoral Experiences

Simultaneous with his intellectual experiences, Wojtyla gained pastoral experience as a parish priest, university chaplain, auxiliary bishop, and archbishop of Krakow. He brought all of his early formation and culture to his service as a diocesan priest. His early formation in his family, his experiences of loss, the guidance of laity toward intellectual riches, his exacting work as a laborer, and his theological work had been honed in the seminary and offered at ordination. Now Wojtyla brought that rich experience to his pastoral service of the Church in Poland. In 1948 he was assigned as curate at the Church of the Assumption of Our Lady in the village of Niegowi.[26] He was transferred to Saint Florian's Parish in Krakow in 1949, where he also served as chaplain at Jagiellonian University.[27] On September 28, 1958, just a month shy of his twelfth anniversary of priestly ordination, he was ordained auxiliary bishop of Krakow.[28]

His thoughts and teachings as pastor arose not only from his rigorous academic investigation but also from the lived experiences of ordinary people. Besides his regular interaction with his flock, he had a special ministry to some 200 married couples. Together they would go into the

---

23. Kupczak, *Destined for Liberty*, 26, no. 49.
24. Ibid., 26, no. 50.
25. Simpson, *On Karol Wojtyla*, 3.
26. Weigel, *Witness to Hope*, 91.
27. Ibid., 93–95.
28. Ibid., 148.

mountains for prolonged weekends, and Wojtyla would form discussion groups to talk about the challenges of married life. This group of married couples came to be known as *Srodowisko*, a term first suggested by Wojtyla himself in the 1960s. Many continued their friendship with the young bishop in later years. George Weigel notes that this group was one of many "networks of young adults and young married couples with whom Father Wojtyla worked" that "evolve[d] into networks of intellectual conversation."[29] Wojtyla, writing as John Paul II, made reference to this group in *Crossing the Threshold of Hope*.[30] His book *Love and Responsibility* flowed directly from questions that arose in these discussions with young married couples.[31] His pastoral ministry was well grounded in an avid awareness of and concern for his flock. His method was always to meet persons, ask them what they were experiencing, and then to proceed from that knowledge.

Bishop Wojtyla participated in the Second Vatican Council from 1962 to 1965. He was appointed archbishop of Krakow on January 13, 1964, and created cardinal in 1967.[32] In 1972 he published a 400-plus-page book on the implementation of the Council, later translated into English as *Sources of Renewal*.[33]

Even a brief overview of Karol Wojtyla's experiences and background reveals several avenues that enabled him to give prolonged thought to the nature of the human person and identity, and their importance in the formation of culture. As he was passing through these experiences, other events were in motion as well. An extensive storm was forming, one which this young man from Poland would be called upon to engage.

---

29. Ibid., 98.

30. John Paul II, *Crossing the Threshold of Hope* (New York: Alfred A. Knopf, 1994), 122. See also Stanislaw Dziwisz, *A Life with Karol: My Forty-Year Friendship with the Man Who Became Pope* (New York: Doubleday, 2008), 12.

31. Karol Wojtyla, *Love and Responsibility*, trans. H. T. Willetts (San Francisco: Ignatius Press, 1981). This work was originally published in Polish as *Miłość I Odpowiedzialno* (Krakow: Wydamnicto, Znak, 1960). It was first published in English in 1981 by William Collins Sons & Co., London; and Farrar, Straus and Giroux, New York.

32. Weigel, *Witness to Hope*, 184, 187.

33. Karol Wojtyla, *Sources of Renewal: The Implementation of the Second Vatican Council*, trans. S. Falla (San Francisco: Harper & Row, 1980). In Italian: *Alla fonti rinnovamento: Studio sulla realizzazione del Concilio Vaticano II* (Vatican City: Libreria Editrice Vaticana, 1979).

CHAPTER TWO

The Perfect Storm

A. Climate Change

Karol Wojtyla brought his appreciation for experience and culture to the papacy. As Pope John Paul II he noted, "We need to reflect on the dynamics of contemporary culture in order to discern the signs of the times which affect the proclamation of the saving message of Christ."[1] The "dynamics of contemporary culture" are the factors that interact to form the experience that contemporary man undergoes. Pope John Paul II gazed on contemporary culture from the vantage point of his experiences, united with the charism of his office. John Paul listened, as he did with his early experiences of loss, the pain of his nation, the people of Krakow, and the married couples he led into the mountains. He discerned the signs of the times, not just of Poland, or of Europe, but of the world, and in particular, of America.

For the United States, the signs of the times reflect a radical shift in cultural mores in a relatively short period of time. Peter Kreeft reports that a survey of high school principals in 1958 found five main problems among students: 1) not doing homework, 2) not respecting property,

1. John Paul II, "God's Self-Revelation to Humanity" in *Springtime of Evangelization: The Complete Texts of the Holy Father's 1998* ad Limina *Addresses to the Bishops of the United States* (San Francisco: Ignatius Press and Basilica Press, 1999), 41.

3) leaving lights on and doors and windows open, 4) throwing spitballs, and 5) running through the hallways. The results of the same questions in a survey only thirty years later, in 1988, found drastic changes. The top five problems facing school administrators in 1988 were: 1) abortion, 2) AIDS, 3) rape, 4) drugs, and 5) fear of a violent death, murder, guns, and knives in school.[2] Little more than ten years later, on April 20, 1999, violence in the American classroom reached a horrific level when two students massacred twelve fellow students and wounded twenty-three others at Columbine High School in Littleton, Colorado. Kreeft notes that from 1955 to 1995 there was a 500 percent increase in violent crime and a 5,000 percent increase in teenage violent crime.[3]

While the statistics are vivid, the classroom is not the only locus of pain. The American home has been under attack for decades. The change in the rate of divorce in the last hundred years is staggering. Research has shown that the rate of divorce in the United States leapt from 5 percent of all marriages in 1867 to more than 50 percent in the early 1990s.[4] In the forty-one years between 1960 and 2001 the divorce rate almost doubled.[5] "Since 1975, more than one million children have been affected by divorce each year."[6] "The picture remains grim after 2000: a 50 percent chance of divorce would mean that half of all marriages are expected to end in divorce before the marriages break up through death."[7] Recently, Elizabeth Marquardt, in a pioneering national study, has found "close to half of first marriages still end in divorce."[8] The effects of divorce on children are particularly painful. Children of divorce are more likely to suffer from emotional difficulties such as major

---

2. Peter Kreeft, *Making Choices: Finding Black and White in a World of Grays* (Ann Arbor, MI: Servant Books, 1990), 1–2.

3. Peter Kreeft, *Ecumenical Jihad: Ecumenism and the Culture War* (San Francisco: Ignatius Press, 1996), 12.

4. Cf. Andrew J. Cherlin, *Marriage, Divorce, Remarriage* (Cambridge, MA: Harvard University Press, 1992), 22.

5. *The Family Portrait: A Compilation of Data, Research and Public Opinion on the Family*, ed. Bridget Maher (Washington, DC: The Family Research Council, 2004), 102.

6. *The Family Portrait*, 106.

7. National Marriage Project, *The State of Our Unions 2003: The Social Health of Marriage in America*, June 2003, 25.

8. Elizabeth Marquardt, *Between Two Worlds: The Inner Lives of Children of Divorce* (New York: Crown, 2005), 10.

depression, low self-esteem, and higher risk of suicide.[9] The pain and violence that many American young people experience must find an outlet.

Pain is often expressed in promiscuity. The amount of sexual content on television programs increased from 67 percent in 1998 to 77 percent in 2005.[10] In 2006, Meg Meeker writes, "40.9 percent of girls fourteen to seventeen years old experience unwanted sex, primarily because they fear that their boyfriends will get angry."[11] Promiscuity has lasting effects. As Meeker writes, "one in five Americans over age twelve tests positive for genital herpes."[12] Teenagers were five times more likely to have herpes in 2002 than they were in the 1970s.[13] The Centers for Disease Control reported in 2008 that at least one in four teens in the United States has a sexually transmitted disease, or STD.[14] Studies indicate that the higher adolescents' exposure to graphic sexual content in songs, movies, and magazines, the more likely teens are to have sex.[15] Each year 15.3 million Americans contract a new sexually transmitted disease.[16] The relation between teen sex and psychological trauma and distress is greatly underrated.[17] One in eight teenagers is clinically depressed, and rates of completed suicides among teens increased 200 percent from the early 1990s to 2002.[18]

The causes of the growing pain and violence range from the immediate to the remote. Each indicator needs attention. The new evangelization must track the pain to its earliest roots if the healing is to be a cure rather than just an anesthetic. The alienation and the violence of our

---

9. *The Family Portrait*, 112–113.

10. Meg Meeker, *Strong Fathers, Strong Daughters: 10 Secrets Every Father Should Know* (Washington, DC: Regnery, 2006), 14.

11. Ibid., 20.

12. Ibid., 19.

13. Meg Meeker, *Epidemic: How Teen Sex Is Killing Our Kids* (Washington, DC: LifeLine Press, 2002), 15.

14. Study presented at the 2008 National STD Prevention Conference, Chicago, March 11, 2008.

15. Steven C. Martino et al., "Exposure to Degrading Versus Nondegrading Music Lyrics and Sexual Behavior Among Youth," *Pediatrics* 118, no. 2 (August 2006), e430–e441.

16. Meeker, *Epidemic*, 11.

17. Ibid., 63–64.

18. Ibid., 64.

times causes deep-felt pain in our very identity. The later twentieth century, despite all its progress, saw a simultaneous deconstruction of the sense of personal identity that affected even devout Catholics.

1. The Three Revolutions at the Center of the Storm

In the nineteenth and early twentieth centuries a strong cohesion existed among Catholics. The Church provided a necessary and steadfast base that enabled immigrants to stay in touch with their identity in a new culture. The New World was often hostile to various immigrant groups, so Catholics had to band together beyond the natural ties of nationality and faith. Catholic families, ghettos, schools, and associations managed to thrive in an otherwise adverse social climate.

The climate was changing, however. By the end of the nineteenth century the Industrial Revolution was well under way. Innovations of the assembly line, factories, and mass production ushered in a new sense of what it means to be a person. The sexual and technological revolutions were to follow, and would likewise bring tremendous internal changes to the sense of personhood.

a. The Industrial Revolution

In the early 1800s wagons steered west toward the frontier. The perilous journey took months. The settlers used cursory maps and directions to find rumored, elusive landmarks. A little more than a century later the return trip was unnecessary: In mere moments the image of a person on the West Coast could now be beamed to a screen in a living room on the East Coast. The irony is that the latter journey may be more laden with danger than the former. During the first journey the threats came from outlaws who rode horses. In the second journey, the outlaws ride the airwaves. With the beamed images comes advertising, and with advertising comes the race to acquire material things: status above all else. Consumerism becomes a way of life. Consumerism advances profits. The loud voice of profit is rarely questioned.

All seemed well. Catholics in America had arrived by the mid-twentieth century. They had played their part in the Industrial Revolution and answered the call to military service in the Second World War. Prejudice against Catholics had lessened, and they began to take a national position in America. The presidency of John F. Kennedy brought questions of faith-based prejudice to the fore. Each apparent gain as Catholics climbed higher in society, however, came with a high price. As John Paul II wrote, "The capitalism of the early Industrial Revolution did violence to liberty, equality, and fraternity in various ways, allowing the exploitation of man by man in deference to the laws of the market."[19] The shift from immigrant Catholics to sophisticated, mainstream Catholics signaled an ominous transition.

The menacing transition of Catholic identity happened through a cascade of events. By the end of the nineteenth century the United States had changed from a mercantile society to an industrial society in a relatively short time. A series of advances emerged on many levels: The assembly line led to the factory, factories replaced workshops, trains supplanted the stage coach, mass production superseded handmade goods, and regional replaced local.

A new socio-economic model emerged as the factory with its mass production challenged the home-based local tradesman. Profits refereed and declared the Industrial Revolution the winner. People hailed newly invented conveniences as great progress. The harnessing of skill and collective genius was thought to be a stride forward. John Paul said the modern world is "a world which has experienced marvelous achievements but which seems to have lost its sense of ultimate realities and of existence itself."[20] Underneath the apparent progress, new ideas about the human person and the family were taking shape: "The family in industrial communities has changed its form."[21] Men in particular felt the effects: "The Industrial Revolution, in its need for office and factory workers, pulled fathers away from their sons and, moreover, placed the sons in compulsory schools where the teachers are mostly women."[22] The effects soon spread to the entire family:

---

19. John Paul II, *Memory and Identity: Conversations at the Dawn of a Millennium* (New York: Rizzoli, 2005), 109.

20. John Paul II, *Redemptoris Missio*, 2.

21. Lionel Tiger, *The Decline of Males: The First Look at an Unexpected New World for Men and Women* (New York: St. Martin's Griffin, 2000), 97.

22. Robert Bly, *Iron John: A Book About Men* (New York: Addison-Wesley, 1990), 19.

In 1935 the average working man had forty hours a week free, including Saturday and Sunday. By 1990, it was down to seventeen hours. The twenty-three lost hours of free time a week since 1935 are the very hours in which the father could be a nurturing father, and find some center in himself, and the very hours in which the mother could feel she actually has a husband.[23]

The "industrial way of life was one of the most dramatic catalysts ... a real shift, a major jolt, an unexpected array of demands...." on the human person and the human family.[24] The overall effect was visible by the latter half of the twentieth century: "Business's maneuver to substitute themselves for the parents has worked."[25] When fathers left the home, they were less likely to find fulfillment in the workplace. They simply became victims of a "state of materialist violence."[26] The workplace fared no better:

> American business made a decision some years ago to be "competitive" in the fast market as opposed to keeping promises to workers and supporting their communities. From 1973 to 1991, the average hourly wage for production and nonsupervisory workers steadily fell. From 1980 to 1993, the Fortune 500 companies shed more than one quarter (4.4 million) of all the jobs they had previously provided. Meanwhile, during that same period, these companies increased their assets by 2.3 times and their sales by 1.4 times. The major CEOs increased their annual compensation by 6.11 times.[27]

Just as industry was pressuring the father out of the home, Karol Wojtyla was being formed by the immediate presence of his father and dedicated lay persons such as Jan Tyranowski. Even though his family experiences were marked by loss and civil turbulence, they would strengthen the depth of his awareness and sensitivity. While one part of the world, in the midst of prosperity, was losing the cultural importance of family, Karol's Poland, in the midst of persecution, was relying on family and community for its very identity.

Fatherlessness has been a silent, steady killer in marriage, family, home, and workplace. Its ill effects have compounded over the decades

---

23. Robert Bly, *The Sibling Society* (New York: Addison-Wesley, 1996), 36.

24. Tiger, *The Decline of Males*, 105.

25. Bly, *The Sibling Society*, 33.

26. Ibid., 28.

27. Ibid., 35.

like an "anti" trust fund from which love continues to leak. In the 1990s, "only one hundred and forty years have passed since factory work began in earnest in the West, and we see in each generation poorer bonding between father and son, with catastrophic results."[28] In the mid 1990s commentators realized "about 40 percent of American children will go to sleep in homes in which their fathers do not live.... Fatherlessness is the most harmful demographic trend of this generation ... It is also the engine driving our most urgent social problems."[29] Fatherlessness does not end with a whimper on a lonely pillow at night. Rather, it emboldens some of the most graphic sociological signals of our time: "Fatherlessness ... contributes to a decline of character and competence in children.... For boys, the most socially acute manifestation of parental disinvestment is juvenile violence. For girls, it is juvenile and out-of-wedlock childbearing."[30] The pervasive effects of fatherlessness cause substantial harm.[31] While profits rolled off the assembly line, the deep costs of fatherlessness led to unimaginable losses in the American family.

Our earlier agrarian or mercantile lifestyles formed an identity marked by specific values. These longstanding values bore fruit in person-to-person association, transgenerational trust in families, reliable products, and sound traditions. They formed a foundation for absorbing Catholic teaching and truths. Yet these lifestyles are giving way. Catholics are becoming absorbed into a more industrialized society *at the expense of* rather than *with* the Catholic identity that had been such a part of their early experiences in the New World. The cost was not noticed at first because the recognizable or ceremonial aspects of the identity remain: national parishes, Catholic education, and celebration of rituals. Things look the same on the outside, but a shift has occurred on the inside. The cost to our Catholic identity, however, is like a bill that comes due when there is no money in the bank. A personalist atmosphere is being replaced by a secular focus on humanism. Given the prevailing winds, which

---

28. Bly, *Iron John*, 94.

29. David Blankenhorn, *Fatherless America, Confronting Our Most Urgent Social Problem* (New York: Basic Books, 1995), 1.

30. Ibid., 45.

31. Steven E. Rhoads, *Taking Sex Differences Seriously* (San Francisco: Encounter Books, 2004), 79.

would combine to form the perfect storm, the loss of our moorings dealt a serious blow to the ship of Catholic life.

b. The Sexual Revolution

A second system emerged as the harmful effects of the Industrial Revolution continued to grow. The sexual revolution and the exaltation of privacy eroded people's willingness to commit themselves in marriage. The sexual revolution refers to a phenomenon of the mid-twentieth century characterized by the loosening of traditional moral strictures as regards sexual activity. The center of human sexuality shifted from the family to the individual. John S. Grabowski cites several forces that led to this shift: the change of social attitudes regarding sex caused by Margaret Sanger's birth control campaign and the pansexualism in the thought of Sigmund Freud, as well as the post-World War II consumer culture that treated sex as a commodity. The symptoms included the rise of pornography, which spread even farther in the technological age.[32] Four effects of the sexual revolution emerged that run counter to Wojtyla's early formation and become the caldron of woes he would one day address as the successor of Peter: disregard for women, the spread of cohabitation, the rise in divorce, and the growing trend of fatherlessness.

1) The Effect on Women

Even in the later years of the Industrial Revolution, contraception was regarded as something decent people avoided and did not discuss. Traditional practices such as withdrawal and barrier methods were routinely regarded as immoral and unbecoming. During the 1950s Margaret Sanger's contraception campaign and scientific discoveries about the female fertility cycle did much to extinguish the common wisdom of the ages. The birth control pill promised to equalize the struggle between the sexes. "The appearance of the long-awaited birth control pill and the signs of the times had spurred re-examination of traditional attitudes

---

32. John S. Grabowski, *Sex and Virtue: An Introduction to Sexual Ethics* (Washington, DC: The Catholic University of America Press, 2003), 4–9.

toward sexuality and sex roles."[33] The pill all but assured that women could "control pregnancy and thus could regard sex as recreational...."[34] Women, freed from the "fear" of pregnancy, could now be on a par with men in their personal relationships and careers. The first ironic result was that women, in order to reach "liberation," followed the same troubled path men had taken in the Industrial Revolution: They left the home and the family. That route has not treated women any better than it did men. Society needed men, as husbands and fathers, to return closer to the family. It didn't need women, as wives and mothers, to abdicate their place as well. Men had been suffering due to their estrangement from the home. Now women began to suffer more from it as well, and the family, especially children, paid the price.

A second irony was that the era of the pill actually permitted "more access to women's bodies by more men; what it actually achieved was not a great deal of liberation for women but a great deal of legitimacy for male promiscuity...."[35] Sanger's attitude toward the pill along with the pansexualizing focus of Freud tended to portray sex as a familiar and nondescript event. Casual or recreational sex means sex without commitment, personal investment, or affection.[36] As a result, sex took on features of anonymity rather than relationship.[37] This led to higher depression rates, particularly among women.[38]

The pill, promiscuity, and depression weaken the capacity of a Catholic to trust his or her faith and lead to confusion. In this confused and depressed state, people turn back to casual sex as a way to feel good again. This vicious cycle begins when society dismisses the Church's teaching on contraception as naïve. It then claims that unfulfilled desires and a sense of guilt cause depression and that the way out is sexual "liberation." In this way society normalizes a lifestyle of contraception and pansexualism.

---

33. Mary Ann Glendon, *Abortion and Divorce in Western Law: American Failures, European Challenges* (Cambridge, MA: Harvard University Press, 1987), 11.

34. Rhoads, *Taking Sex Differences Seriously*, 96.

35. Sally Cline as quoted in Rhoads, *Taking Sex Differences Seriously*, 97.

36. Rhoads, *Taking Sex Differences Seriously*, 100, 102.

37. Ibid., 106.

38. Ibid., 107.

2) Cohabitation

Cohabitation is the natural result of casual sex. "Maintaining a relationship is far less dramatic and exciting than the tournament of courtship, and it [courtship] requires deliberate and thoughtful decisions."[39] Recreational sex does not prepare people for marriage, because such sexual relations do not require commitment. Cohabitation actually reinforces noncommitment, and avoids "deliberate and thoughtful decisions." All this undermines the notion of the dignity of the person as taught by the Church.

Those who follow the Church's teaching are caricatured as naïve and childish, while those who choose the lifestyle of the world are portrayed as enlightened and advanced. In this atmosphere it is difficult to maintain or establish the Catholic heritage. Instead of a solid rampart of secure identity, many choose the passing images and hyped promises of the world.

The reasons for cohabitation range from supposed convenience to economic feasibility to a trial run for marriage. These reasons seem to make sense on the surface, but the statistics do not support the logic. Cohabitation is notoriously unstable. "Only about one-sixth of cohabitating relationships last as long as three years."[40] Those who cohabit before marriage remain at high risk: "Couples who live together before marriage actually have a 50 percent greater chance of divorce than those who don't."[41] The logic is simple: How can one "practice" for a permanent commitment, i.e. marriage, by not being committed? How will those who neglect the moral obligation of celibacy before marriage fulfill the moral obligation of fidelity in marriage?

Behavioral traps multiply when a couple live together instead of getting married. It may seem to make sense economically. Their combined salaries enable them to pay living costs that would be too high for a single young adult. The danger is that fear, rather than commitment, keeps them together. When—not if—a sensitive issue arises in their

---

39. Tiger, *The Decline of Males*, 97.
40. As in Rhoads, *Taking Sex Differences Seriously*, 119.
41. Bishops of Pennsylvania, *Living Together: Questions and Answers Regarding Cohabitation and the Church's Moral Teaching* (Harrisburg: Pennsylvania Catholic Conference, 1999), 5.

relationship, they are less likely to discuss it. If his drinking bothers her, or her shopping bothers him, the issue may not be dealt with directly. Cohabitating couples stonewall one another more easily and threaten to move out rather than face the stress of confrontation and change of behavior. In the face of the threat of abandonment and huge financial obligations, the complaint is often dropped and the offending behavior goes "underground" in the relationship. If the matter is pursued and the offender leaves, one or both may need to go home to Mom and Dad and hear those four terrible words: "I told you so."

Persons who choose cohabitation often define marriage itself in vague and psychological language. Ironically, the emptiness of such language surfaces when ignored issues come up later, after the vows, infected with an untold amount of anger and resentment that corrodes marriage and family life.

Karol Wojtyla's experiences were the exact opposite of cohabitation and casual sex. He enjoyed the stability of marriage and family in his own home. He saw the dedicated witness of his father, who as a widower devoted his energy to rearing Karol. Wojtyla also benefited from befriending lay persons who were dedicated to their history and identity, who united against a terrorist regime. They did not devote their energies toward their own interests, but to those of their community and nation.

3) Divorce

The promiscuous lifestyle promoted by the sexual revolution is an illusion. When the illusion fails to satisfy, the revolution itself is not blamed. It is too impacted in the culture. The person, the spouse, the father, the mother, the son or daughter, marriage, or the family must absorb the cost. The payment comes due in divorce. The Second Vatican Council enumerated "The plague of divorce, so-called free love … selfishness, hedonism, and unlawful contraceptive practices"[42] among the evils facing marriage at the time of the sexual revolution. Historian Paul M. Johnson asserts that "the decisive single development in America during the second half of the twentieth century [was] the

---

42. Second Vatican Council, *Gaudium et Spes*, 47.2.

decline of the family and of family life, and the growth in illegitima-cy."[43] Divorce and its effect, fatherlessness, are direct descendants of the sexual revolution.

Elizabeth Marquardt has published the revealing results of a national study on adult children of divorce. Early data on the effects of divorce was skewed by an "adult-centered vision" of its effects. Through the 1970s and 1980s, research on the effects of divorce on children was based on interviews with their caregivers. Psychologists, parents, and teachers spoke for the children of divorce because the children were thought to be too young to have a voice.[44] During their childhood years after the divorce, these children were subject to pressure from their own desire to please their caregivers. They would "say the right thing." The second-hand reports left the impression that divorce could somehow benefit the child. Instead of having one home in which two people fought or argued, now the child had the diversity of two homes. Instead of two parents, they could have as many as four, with promises of diversity, more resourc-es, and enrichment. The popular adult-centered thinking was: Keep the divorce "good" and the children can actually reap benefits. A good divorce was seen as better than a bad marriage.

The first generation of children who underwent the effects of divorce on a wide scale are now adults. The Marquardt studies reveal that con-trary to earlier reports, regardless of its tenor, "divorce powerfully chang-es the structure of childhood itself."[45] The adult children of divorce report ongoing conflict not only after the divorce, but *because* of the divorce. They report consistently having to deal with two separate identi-ties, complex inner negotiations, confusion, and recurrent burdens, all at the level of identity. Initially we can conclude that the notion of a "good divorce" is really a fable. It may actually be better for the children if hus-band and wife who are in a relatively low-conflict marriage remain in the marriage rather than divorce. Approximately two-thirds of all divorces are relatively low conflict.

---

43. Paul M. Johnson, *A History of the American People* (New York: HarperCollins, 1998), 971. For the overall effect of the sexual revolution on Western society, see Don S. Browning, *Marriage and Modernization: How Globalization Threatens Marriage and What to Do About It* (Grand Rapids, MI: Wm. B. Eerdmans, 2003), esp. 15–19.

44. Marquardt, *Between Two Worlds*, 16.

45. Ibid., 12.

4) Fatherlessness

Divorce, cohabitation, and promiscuity are directly related to father-lessness. The absence of the father from the home that began in the Industrial Revolution was taken to a new height by the sexual revolution. Now, rather than being gone for most of the day, the father is simply *gone*. Rather than being missed, he is never known. Fatherlessness does not plague only one economic sector or racial group: The effects of fatherlessness are seen "in the aggression of fatherless gangs among the disadvantaged, and the presence of depressed and passive youngsters among the advantaged."[46]

Practically, without a father present, "people remain in adolescence long past its normal span."[47] Ironically, fatherlessness has a way of per-petuating itself: "[B]ecause children of divorced parents are themselves twice as likely to divorce in adulthood, fatherlessness resulting from divorce will often be perpetuated in the next generation."[48] The effects of fatherlessness reverberate deep in the child's soul: "Few sons now share a toolbox with their father. The son experiences the father only in a world of longing."[49]

Again, Karol Wojtyla's formation was diametrically opposite that of divorce and fatherlessness. His mother's devotion, her early death, his father's sustained dedication, and the mature bearing of laypeople such as Jan Tyranowski greatly enriched Wojtyla's life. These gave him a pro-found sense of the value of faithful presence and the drastic effects of a chosen absence. His instinct for presence showed itself to the married couples with whom he regularly journeyed into the mountains of Poland while under Soviet occupation. He was a present father.

c. *The Technological Revolution / Mass Media*

A third system to join the gathering storm in the mid-twentieth cen-tury was the technological revolution, including the mass media. Television and cable network entertainment and news have spread every-

---

46. Bly, *The Sibling Society*, 37.
47. Ibid., 45.
48. Rhoads, *Taking Sex Differences Seriously*, 80.
49. Bly, *The Sibling Society*, 51.

where, transmitting values to an entire generation. Many young people spend time passively watching television instead of picking up a book, and this depresses their faculty for creative, imaginative thinking. The effect is sometimes downright traumatic: "[T]alk shows tell all the secrets before the child has learned to trust life...."[50]

Previously, media was an element of culture, a way in which families remained in touch with world events as well as national and local news. While television may keep people informed, it can also keep them more isolated. When combined with the effects of divorce and fatherlessness, electronic media can express the anger of lost relationships. It then "tends to radiate an aggression that is diffuse, nondirectional, and inconsolable. The names of some rock bands describe the situation very well. They call themselves Suicidal Tendencies, Porno for Pyros, Crash Test Dummies, Urge Overkill, and Arrested Development."[51]

Ever since the 1960s, in order to enter into "relation" children need only press a button, turn a channel, and stare at a screen. Relationship skills atrophy in the process. More and more treat one another like televisions, turning each other on and off, so to speak, when the entertainment level decreases. Debate has become flush with opinion rather than thought. The average citizen now experiences the unending maze of an unmanageable "internal conflict" between the two volatile extremes society offers for acceptance: the contemporaneous need to be an individual and the need to conform.[52] Many are stretched so thin they need to escape. The hours spent each day watching television or other media are an indication of the extent to which the tendency for evasion has engulfed Americans. Bringing the television into the bedroom has tended to further erode relationships. The advent of the personal computer and cell phone has only compounded this: "Kids spend, on average, 6.5 hours per day with media. Twenty-six percent of the time, they are using more than one device. This means that 8.5 hours' worth of media exposure per day is packed into 6.5 hours. (This is equivalent to a full-time job.)"[53] Robert Bly points out, "In fact, our children get most of

---

50. Ibid., 133.
51. Ibid., 51.
52. Nancy J. Dougherty and Jacqueline J. West, *The Matrix and Meaning of Character: An Archetypal and Developmental Approach* (New York: Taylor & Francis, 2007), 93.
53. Meeker, *Strong Fathers, Strong Daughters*, 22.

their values from music, videos, and films, and even though we regret that situation, we have not yet found a way to change it."[54] Mothers and fathers, brothers and sisters, sons and daughters, teachers and students, and even friends and enemies can retreat to impersonal media instead of direct personal relationships.

Karol Wojtyla was shaped in a far different ethos. He had no easy buttons to press. His cultural bearing was molded in a much more robust and ancient form of communication: the theater. He also learned relationship through hard labor in the chemical factory and the quarry. By studying philosophy he learned the importance of ideas and how to communicate them. Instead of sitting before a screen, he learned the natural importance of a gesture and the cadence of words.

Before the mainstreaming effects of television and electronic media, the phenomenon of entertainment relied on personal, familial, and local creativity. A keyboard used to refer to a part of a musical instrument that produced beauty. Families and groups of friends gathered around a piano as talent poured forth and community was strengthened. But today, the computer keyboard has replaced the piano keyboard. The computer exchanges community for efficiency, beauty for a mere search for pleasure, and talent for profit and isolation. The technological age is the era of "instantaneous infotainment."[55] The news media has become in large measure entertainment. This has reduced the need for personal creativity. The piano communicates personal talent; the computer communicates only information, and reduces the personal to the informational.

Faster computer chips may also speed up loneliness. The video game was the midpoint between television and personal computer. Video games, Web chats, and streaming video can easily replace the direct nature of person-to-person relationships, and they have introduced an automatic fantasy style of low-grade loneliness as recreation. Recreation has dwindled into amusement. The kitchen table has become a place not to gather, but to drop mail and book bags on the way to the television or computer. Every need, it seems, can be met by a screen.

The three revolutions have joined forces in a perfect storm that threatens to drown the notion of personhood. The storm has a direct

---

54. Bly, *The Sibling Society*, 32–33.
55. Drew Christiansen, SJ, "Of Many Things," *America*, May 19, 2008, 2.

impact on personal identity. The Industrial Revolution ravaged personhood with the idea that persons are what they produce, consume, spend,
and profit from. Such values lead people to that envious glance to see
who has "made it" and who hasn't. What do the neighbors drive? Do
they have a shore house? What do their parents do? How much do they
make? What academy's jacket does their son wear? Education becomes
simply a race to get grades, extracurricular points, and awards so the
student can go to a private high school, get into an Ivy League university, graduate with honors, and make double the parents' salary. This is
what a "person" has become.

The sexual revolution quickens the storm. The pursuit of pleasure
becomes the primary focus along with the portfolio. Whatever feels good
rules the day. Marriage, family, and children are obstacles to pleasure, so
they are dispensed with. This is what it is to be a human person—accu-
mulating things and pleasures. Unless you have those, you are less a
person, and your personal identity is incomplete. Unless you are "feeling
good" you are not a full person.

The technological revolution surged in on top of the first two systems. To "you are what you acquire" and "you are what you feel," it adds
the steroidal rush of "now do it all as quickly as you can." The greed of
the Industrial Revolution and the hedonism of the sexual revolution now
ride the wave of speed and efficiency. "Personhood" is assigned on the
basis of how closely you can conform to a "social construct based on the
compelling presence of certain qualities that we determine to be necessary" rather than on inherent capacities.[56] Remember that five-star portfolio and the blond goddess or handsome hunk on your arm? Those
things now have to be available immediately, all the time. Everything has
to be one click of a button away. If you have to wait for anything, you are
not a person in the real sense. Your identity is somehow diminished or
lessened. The contemporary view of human nature itself is skeptical and
was limited "to a narrow sectarian perspective" by some of the most
influential thinkers of the past one hundred and fifty years.[57] A great

56. Martin R. Tripoli, SJ, "John Paul II the Countercultural Pope," *Creed and Culture: Jesuit Studies of Pope John Paul II*, ed. Joseph W. Koterski, SJ, and John J. Conley, SJ (Philadelphia: Saint Joseph's University Press, 2004), 44.

57. Carl Anderson, *A Civilization of Love* (New York: HarperOne, 2008), 27.

reversal takes place at the heart of secularism. John Paul made clear that the contemporary secularist mentality that has crept into the attitudes and behavior of Christians is an "acute pastoral concern."[58] People now desire much less than God and his life: "What they desire is not eternal life at all, but this present life, for which faith in eternal life seems something of an impediment . . . more like a curse than a gift."[59]

2. Catechesis

The threefold surge of the perfect storm washed over the twentieth century with devastating force. Anything incompatible with accumulation, pleasure, and efficiency was laid waste and declared inconsequential. The times had spoken. The mission of the Church must bear directly on the signs of the times. Since the early Church, catechists have formed a unique and irreplaceable rampart of the Church's mission. Cardinal Jean Daniélou, a French Jesuit scholar, noted that catechesis underwent great development and organization in the second century and the beginning of the third.[60] Origen, a great theological writer and early catechist, described the catechist's task as teaching both doctrine and morality.[61] During the Second Vatican Council, the perfect storm had a great impact on catechists. Pope Benedict XVI writes that in the midst of growing secularism, faith is not denied outright, but is "displaced onto another level—that of purely private and otherworldly affairs—and at the same time it becomes somehow irrelevant for the world."[62] Many schools, religious education programs, and youth groups remained on the front lines and handed on to children and adolescents the basics of the faith. The perfect storm, however, was wreaking havoc on the supply lines that supported catechists.

An immediate effect of the perfect storm raging against Catholic identity in the mid to later twentieth century was the decline in catechesis. In June 1997 an oral report delivered to the General Assembly of

---

58. John Paul II, *Veritatis Splendor*, 88.
59. Benedict XVI, *Spe Salvi*, 10.
60. Jean Daniélou, *Origen* (New York: Sheed & Ward, 1955), 10.
61. Ibid.
62. Benedict XVI, *Spe Salvi*, 17.

U.S. Bishops described "a relatively consistent trend of doctrinal incompleteness and imprecision" or "doctrinal deficiencies" in various catechetical materials.[63] The decline and deficiencies were not in style, but in content. The report noted that insufficient attention was given to the Trinity. The texts obscured the centrality of Christ in salvation history, especially by an insufficient emphasis on his divinity. Further deficiencies concerned the understanding of the identity of the human person and the teaching of moral theology. The moral theologian Livio Melina observed:

> [A]n ever increasing number of the faithful and of pastors, while not openly contesting "official" teaching, keep their distance from it … Thus a diffuse resignation prevails, as it were, in preaching: it is better not to preach morality, above all morality in regard to certain hot topics, so as not to disturb the consciences of the faithful. Refuge is sought in the *kerygma*, or talk is limited to vague exhortations regarding love….[64]

Like all teaching, catechesis depends on an adequate foundation. Ordinarily, Catholic education has flourished by laying a foundation of the basic truths of Catholic identity in the lower elementary level. A major difficulty, however, is that the intermediate grade curriculum tends to repeat the foundational material rather than build on it. Thus seventh-grade students, for example, often review foundation material under a new heading. But Catholics at this age are better able to deal with abstract thinking and more conceptual notions. Catechesis at this level must begin to address difficult questions and skepticism, rather than mainly reviewing material of previous years. The latter leads to frustration and disappointment with explanations of the faith, leaving a teenager more easy prey to secularist or fundamentalist approaches. Faith in Christ is replaced by secularism's "programmatic vision" of faith in material and scientific progress.[65] Christianity is then reduced to sentiment:

---

63. Excerpted from Archbishop Daniel M. Buechlein's oral report to the General Assembly of Bishops, June 1997.

64. Livio Melina, *Sharing in Christ's Virtues: For a Renewal of Moral Theology in Light of* Veritatis Splendor, trans. William E. May (Washington, DC: The Catholic University of America Press, 2001), 16.

65. Benedict XVI, *Spe Salvi*, 17.

"How often do we hear it said that to be a Christian it is enough to live honestly and to follow one's own conscience!"[66]

Catholic parents are often dismayed when their children stop practicing the faith or even abandon it for another church or no church. The U.S. Religious Landscape Survey found that overall "the proportion of the adult population that identifies itself as Catholic has held fairly steady, at around 25 percent."[67] Commentators took little comfort in the survey from the Pew Research Center's Forum on Religion & Public Life. According to an analysis of the survey, the fuller truth of the calculation is "that Catholicism has lost more people to other religions or to no religion at all than any other single religious group. These losses, however, have been offset partly by people who have switched their affiliation ... but mostly by the significant number of immigrants who have immigrated to the U.S. in recent decades."[68] The survey goes on to note that the Catholic Church has experienced the greatest net loss due to change in religious affiliation by adults.[69] Out of 31.4 percent of adults who say they were raised Catholic, only 23.9 percent continue to identify with the Catholic Church.[70] These numbers must be clarified, however. According to the Center for Applied Research in the Apostolate (CARA):

> The Catholic Church has lost many members in terms of total population but it is important to remember that the Catholic Church is also the single largest faith in the United States. Proportions matter. As sizeable as the losses have been, they would be even larger if Catholics were losing their young members at the same rate as every U.S. [mainline] Protestant denomination. The Pew Study indicates

---

66. Melina, *Sharing in Christ's Virtues*, 22.

67. The Pew Research Center's Forum on Religion & Public Life, *U.S. Religious Landscape Survey* (Washington, DC: Pew Research Center, 2008), 19; The Knights of Columbus, *An American Perspective* (New York: Marist College Institute for Public Opinion, 2008) found that 26 percent of Americans identify themselves as Catholic.

68. *U.S. Religious Landscape Survey*, 19.

69. Ibid., 23.

70. Ibid. "The study also shows the Catholic Church has been hardest hit by these shifts, but that the influx of Catholic immigrants has offset the loss ... roughly 10 percent of all Americans are former Catholics. Almost half of these former Catholics joined Protestant denominations, while about half do not have a religious affiliation and a small percentage chose other faiths" (*America*, March 10, 2008, 7).

that none of these other faith groups has had as much success as the Catholic Church in keeping those raised in the faith in the pews as adults. Pew reports that the Catholic Church has retained 68 percent of those who grew up Catholic … It is also important to understand that the Catholic losses that have occurred are not the result of any recent mass Catholic exodus.…[71]

Equally important, "social scientists have long understood that some who no longer consider themselves to be a member of the faith in which they were raised, especially those who say they are 'unaffiliated,' will return to that faith later in life."[72] While the interpretation of surveys, methodology, and terminology may be in dispute, what is not in dispute is that the Church is called in every age to a robust and eager proclamation of the faith. While the retention rates of the Catholic Church are high, other studies have noted "broad-based concern"[73] over trends associated with commitment of Catholics in the contemporary American scene.

3. The 2008 CARA Study

Georgetown University's Center for Applied Research in the Apostolate conducted a national study in 2008. The study, "Sacraments Today: Belief and Practice among U.S. Catholics," was commissioned by the department of communications of the U.S. Conference of Catholic Bishops. It surveyed 1,007 adult Catholics in the United States regarding their participation in the sacramental life of the Church. The survey attempted to gauge beliefs, attitudes, practices, commitment, knowledge, and level of agreement behind the participation levels of adult Catholics.

The study shows that a fertile field has emerged for evangelization and catechesis. More than 77 percent of adult Catholics agree that they are proud to be Catholic. The results further show strong areas of commitment: Catholics, even those who practice only somewhat or not as

---

71. "CARA Reflections on the Pew Religious Landscape Survey," *The CARA Report* 13, no. 4 (Spring 2008), 2–3.

72. Ibid., 2.

73. William V. D'Antonio, et al., *American Catholics Today: New Realities of Their Faith and Their Church* (Lanham, MD: Rowman & Littlefield, 2007), 6.

often, are aware of and seek to adhere to the discipline of Lent (60 percent). A large number (80 percent) find strength in the beliefs of the Creed regarding the Trinity, the Blessed Virgin Mary, and the Incarnation. The report gives firm basis to congratulate and be thankful for dedicated Catholic priests, catechists, and teachers who have passed on the teachings of the faith for decades. With great personal sacrifice over many years, catechists remained after school to teach in religious education programs. Many were proud to teach in Catholic schools, making sacrifices to do so. Besides teaching, many stood in the rain and the cold to guide children to and from school as they waited for cars and buses. We are proud of them, and thankful. The report shows again what we already knew: that the noble efforts of those committed to Catholic education show a level of vocational commitment. The pride of over 77 percent of adult Catholics testifies clearly to this.

At the same time, consistent with the past years, 23 percent of Catholics attend Mass at least once a week. Another 10.3 percent attempt to attend once a week. This means that on any given Sunday more than 31 percent of Catholics may be in attendance. The open field is obvious: Between the 77 percent who are proud to be Catholic and the 23 percent who practice regularly, there is a highly fertile 54 percent who are accessible and within immediate reach. Some of these are very close to frequent practice. This highly fertile region is the field of the new evangelization. Catechesis and outreach to this proximate 54 percent can leaven the remaining 23 percent who say they are less than proud to be Catholic.

The results confirmed the ongoing need for catechesis, particularly about the Eucharist, attending Mass on Sundays and holy days of obligation, and the relationship between the sacrament of Penance and the Eucharist. Renewed efforts are needed to transform commitment into action, and belief into practice. Catechesis at the elementary grade level forms the basis that can be built on in high school and college. These latter present challenges of their own: the need to outwit today's skepticism, to show the true relationship between science and faith, and to strengthen the foundations already in place.

A new bud also appears within the field of data. When asked which sacrament is personally "most meaningful" to them, the Vatican II generations cite Baptism and the Eucharist. This shows that good catechesis has taken place on the Council's call to holiness. Within this context, 43 percent of Millennials (those who were ages 18–26 in 2008) identify Marriage as the sacrament most meaningful to them. Born right in the middle of Pope John Paul II's catechesis on the theology of the body, they are called to embody his teaching and are showing signs of doing so.

The CARA research gives a direction for Catholics. Some will point pessimistically to the CARA data, thinking it is meant to show outcomes only. But the CARA research is more like an x-ray before treatment than a post-op report after treatment. The report is not meant to stir up nostalgia for the way things used to be; rather, it is an invitation to the new evangelization. The x-ray reveals where the effects of the secular culture have impacted our people. We now know better where the healing needs to be aimed.

Culture change takes a long time. It is not automatic or command-based. Pope Benedict XVI, when he was Cardinal Ratzinger, wrote: "… certainly, God does not count in large numbers…."[74] Catholics as a whole tend to identify with their faith and find meaning in their identity as Catholics, but at the same time they easily claim to be less committed to the moral teaching of the Church.[75]

The decreased practice of the faith is due to many factors. Believers hunger for truth, but too often they are given abstract ideas that cannot fill their hunger, living as they do in a very concrete world. Lukewarmness begins to spread. In the midst of feelings of inadequacy, reducing faith to a series of formal ideas makes it more vulnerable to doubts and skepticism. Because they are intangible, ideas can be easily dismissed. Students are confused about their identity due to the ravages of the perfect storm of the three revolutions. The "technical progress" of the twentieth century was "not matched by corresponding progress in man's ethical formation, in man's inner growth" and was not really progress at all, "but a threat for man and for the world."[76] The twentieth-century notion of personhood supports nothing but the self-sufficient self. This is a burden to students and teachers alike.

---

74. Joseph Ratzinger, "The New Evangelization: Building the Civilization of Love," http://www.ewtn.com/new_evangelization/Ratzinger.htm.

75. D'Antonio, *American Catholics Today*, 26.

76. Benedict XVI, *Spe Salvi*, 22.

Often, adolescents cannot answer their own difficult questions. They need answers that can shed light on what it means to be a human person, despite the effects of the perfect storm that work to obscure it. Those who stop practicing their faith may return one day, when the responsibilities of raising a family make them think about passing on the faith. This return is a profound opportunity to reintroduce the adult Catholic to the content of the Catholic faith. Whether such Catholics remain or return later, the basic situation remains the same: adult Catholics tend to live their faith at the last scholastic grade level they completed. The level of their religious education could be at a sixth grade, eighth grade, or secondary school level. The ten specific areas identified in 1997 as being doctrinally deficient in catechetical series used in the United States show where catechists need to focus their efforts. Faith formation requires that the central realities of the faith be clearly explained. Major areas of concern include the Trinity as the central mystery of the faith, the centrality of Jesus Christ, ecclesiology, Christian anthropology, emphasis on the primacy of God's initiative, grace, sacraments, the teaching on sin, the moral life, and eschatology.[77]

4. The Impact on Identity

The initial impact of the three revolutions was a decline in the receptivity toward catechesis. Over time, the new toys and possibilities diverted Catholics from the mystery of faith. New pursuits took precedence. The thriving economy instigated a rush after things in full-throttled materialism and acquisition. The emphasis on privacy to protect the newly won toys was enshrined through individualism. John Paul warned, "Taken to its extreme consequences, this individualism leads to a denial of the very idea of human nature."[78]

The thrill that comes with status and pleasure is a highly calibrated hedonism. The revolutions touched down in full-fledged ideologies that swept in with silent stealth until turning back seemed impossible. The ideologies converged and acted as an extended-release sedative on the

---

77. Excerpted from Archbishop Daniel M. Buechlein's oral report to the General Assembly of Bishops, June 1997.

78. John Paul II, *Veritatis Splendor*, 32 (cf. John Paul II, *Evangelium Vitae*, 19).

sensitivities of Catholics. The resultant storm on identity was made up of pressure systems that favored a shift from the resilience of an immigrant faith to a surface-level sophistication that reduced Catholic identity to edification and ceremony.

Think of your own identity. Drop the censure and examine what comes first to your mind with this question, "Who am I?" What was the first description you thought of? Some variation of nationality or your position in the family (husband, mother)? Or your occupation, job, schooling, trade ... white collar, blue collar? Some gravitate to the bottom line, defining themselves by their financial statements, grades, promotions, or latest bonus. Others cling to an ideology: Democrat, Republican, hawk, or dove. Still others adhere to the rules of a clique, or favor a sharp wit, a critical nature, humor, the shine on their car. They may see themselves as pleasers, cheerleaders, self-starters. Daniélou points out the importance of detecting our "fundamental attitudes to existence."[79] If these attitudes "are radically falsified from the start it is absolutely impossible to arrive at any solution."[80] We must begin by evaluating what constitutes the fundamentals and essentials of what it means to exist.

The immediate danger when we consider our identity, what we think of ourselves in our innermost accessible place, is that we will end up hating, unhappy, in denial—and the denial itself begins to be an identity. Denial forces us to the surface and inflates us with helium so we are not grounded and do not sound like ourselves. For a large part of our life our identity tends to come from the external, the labels, the things around us.

Maturity includes a person considering the formation of his or her identity. The onrush of adolescence is the first time we become self-reflective on identity in a prolonged way. The teen years are made up of frequent and often critical self-examination. On the surface teens may appear to avoid rumination on their sense of self. In fact, adolescents often overindulge in rumination about what they do, who their friends are, what others may think of them. The pattern of deliberation and being acquainted with internal questions of identity is crucial. Again at midlife, self-reflection on identity opens in a momentous way. Self-questioning returns at major times of transition: the loss of a loved one, a move or transfer. Transition or any passage evokes an immediate refer-

---

79. Jean Daniélou, *Myth and Mystery* (New York: Hawthorne Books, 1968), 59.
80. Ibid., 59.

ence to one's identity. Questions of identity and selfhood are prominent and persistent. A realistic sense of self depends on knowing the starting point for identity.

Another phase finds people searching exclusively in the internal, finding "their" truth. The danger is that we may become obsessed with ourselves; we become our own project. We obsess over the puzzle of ourselves rather than the mystery of Christ. Preoccupied with ourselves and our perceived problems, we filter all we hear or read, trying to make ourselves better. This becomes a distraction in itself. All the dead ends we are left with as we contemplate identity are the inheritance of the three revolutions: we are children of the technological revolution, grandchildren of the Industrial Revolution, and siblings of the sexual revolution.

The erosion of Catholic and personal identity does not arise from chance or random collision of these elements. The fuel behind the displacement of identity had deep roots in philosophical systems. Josef Seifert, rector and professor at the International Academy of Philosophy in the principality of Liechtenstein, notes:

> In no century have more millions of persons been murdered than in the Twentieth Century.... [T]he victims of Auschwitz and the Gulag and countless other places have to a large extent not been killed by a relapse to animal passions or on account of dark feelings of national pride or vengeance, but *by a mere logical application to politics and private life of ideas about man which highly respected scientists and philosophers have taught for decades at the most prestigious universities around the globe.* These ideas about man, when carried out in practice, killed and are killing millions of human lives when they are translated and transposed into political ideologies.[81]

Human actions do not arise in a vacuum. They arise from the depths of the person. A mistake in an action can be traced back to the notions

---

81. Josef Seifert, "Philosophy and Science in the Context of Contemporary Culture," in *The Human Search for Truth: Philosophy, Science, and Theology / The Outlook for the Third Millennium.* Proceedings of the International Conference on Science and Faith, May 23–25, 2000 (Philadelphia: Saint Joseph's University Press, 2002), 25. Maria Antonia Bel Bravo notes that the twentieth century "was the most cruel century in history" (Maria Bel Bravo, "Introduction: Christianity and the Advancement of Women" in Pontifical Council for the Laity, *Woman and Man: The* Humanum *in Its Entirety,* Proceedings on the Twentieth Anniversary of John Paul II's *Mulieris Dignitatem* (1988), International Congress, Rome, February 7–9 (2008), 145.

in the person's particular understandings. If the understanding of what it is to be human is askew, then the actions will be offset, and may ultimately result in tragic outcomes: "Mistakes about the human being prompt mistakes in ethics."[82] The "ideas about man" of which Seifert writes are that one human can look at another and say, "He is not a human; he is not deserving of being treated as a human person." The ideologies of the three revolutions, turned to their highest decibel, proclaim the same message: the only person is the supreme individual who can acquire things, profit, and money, and can use the same to enhance pleasure. Those who fall short of this measure, the vulnerable, the infirm, the child, the unborn child, the elderly—these are not members in full.

The task of the new evangelization in America is to confront the effects of the three revolutions. Karol Wojtyla was alert to the signs of the times. Already in the late 1960s he was absorbed in the response. In a letter to the French Jesuit Henri de Lubac, Wojtyla wrote that he was involved in writing

> a work [*The Acting Person*] that is very close to my heart and devoted to the metaphysical sense and mystery of the person. It seems to me that the debate today is being played out on that level. The evil of our times consists in the first place in a kind of degradation, indeed in a pulverization, of the fundamental uniqueness of each human person.... To this disintegration planned at times by atheistic ideologies, we must oppose, rather than sterile polemics, a kind of "recapitulation" of the inviolable mystery of the person.[83]

The field that studies the personal identity of human nature is known as philosophical anthropology. The term can be confusing to the North American mind. Kenneth Schmitz explains the difference between anthropology and philosophical anthropology:

> Up until very recently in North America the term "anthropology" has been more or less restricted to the discipline or set of disciplines within the special sciences with which our university departments acquaint us: physical anthropology draws upon paleontology, physiol-

---

82. Romanus Cessario, OP, *Introduction to Moral Theology* (Washington, DC: The Catholic University of America Press, 2001), 22.

83. Henri de Lubac, *At the Service of the Church: Henri de Lubac Reflects on the Circumstances that Occasioned His Writings* (San Francisco: Ignatius Press, 1989), 171–172.

ogy, and related disciplines, and cultural anthropology draws upon archaeology, sociology, psychology, linguistics, and related disciplines. This is still the common usage of the term in North America. One of the European senses of the term, however . . . takes into account these positive scientific studies, but the sense of the term is above all philosophical, and appears also within theology as a branch of that study.[84]

The strength of Catholic identity and the level of commitment born from that identity are an urgent consideration for the Church.[85] A range of factors influences the response of Catholics to a variety of issues. The overriding theme is a separation or gap in the attitudes of Catholics on beliefs and practices. Beyond the more evident influences of generation, ethnicity, schooling, gender, and controversies, there is a factor that, while remote, nevertheless exerts considerable strength. Pope John Paul II writes:

> I have become more and more convinced that the ideologies of evil are profoundly rooted in the history of European philosophical thought.... In order to illustrate this phenomenon better we have to go back to the period before the Enlightenment, especially to the revolution brought about by the philosophical thought of Descartes.[86]

The contemporary separation in beliefs and practices is rooted in the ideologies of separation, which go back centuries. Along with the more current factors, catechesis must consider these remote but highly effective philosophical influences so that catechesis itself can guide the overall shaping of Catholics.

The starting point for the new evangelization is the place of pain: the pain of the totalitarian ideologies that have burned through the twentieth century in Europe and Asia, and the ideologies sprung from the three revolutions that have crossed America. The place of pain is the identity of the human person. The Industrial Revolution told us that to be a person we *acquire things*; the Sexual Revolution told us that to be a person we *acquire pleasure*; the Technological Revolution told us that to be a person we must *acquire pleasure quickly*.

---

84. Schmitz, *At the Center of the Human Drama*, 30–31.

85. D'Antonio, et al., *American Catholics Today* provides empirical data concerning these questions. See also The Pew Forum on Religion and Public Life, *U.S. Religious Landscape Survey 2008* (Washington, DC: Pew Research Center, 2008).

86. John Paul II, *Memory and Identity*, 7–8.

B. The Forecast

1. The New Evangelization

A unique door opened in the latter half of the twentieth century, a door connecting the Second Vatican Council and the beginning of the third millennium of Christianity. Either of these events, massive in its own right, could take decades to digest and internalize. The alignment of the two opened a unique pastoral window that only the eye of a pastor could discern: the new evangelization.

Contrary to popular thought, the phrase "new evangelization" did not originate during the papacy of John Paul II. In his book *Crossing the Threshold of Hope*, John Paul acknowledged that the phrase came from Paul VI: "The expression *new evangelization* was popularized by *Evangelii Nuntiandi* as a response to the *new challenges that the contemporary world creates for the mission of the Church.*"[87]

Evangelii Nuntiandi called for a new evangelization a year after the Third General Assembly of the Synod of Bishops in 1973, which was devoted to evangelization. Paul VI issued the document on the feast of the Immaculate Conception, December 8, 1975, the tenth anniversary of the close of the Second Vatican Council. Pope Paul stated that the bishops at the Synod

> decided to remit to the Pastor of the universal Church, with great trust and simplicity, the fruits of all their labors, stating that they awaited from him a fresh forward impulse, capable of creating within a Church still more firmly rooted in the undying power and strength of Pentecost a new period of evangelization.[88]

a. Feliciora Evangelizationis Tempora

The phrase "new evangelization" originates from various translations of Paul VI's phrase, rendered in English as "a new period of evangeliza-

---

87. John Paul II, *Crossing the Threshold of Hope*, 114.

88. Paul VI, *Evangelii Nuntiandi*, 2 (cf. Paul VI, *Address for the Closing of the Third General Assembly of the Synod of Bishops* [26 October 1974]: AAS 66 [1974], 634–635, 637).

tion." Other translations also use the word "new," for example, the Spanish *tiempos nuevos de evangelización,* and the Italian *nuovi tempi d'evangelizzazione.* The official text, the *editio typica,* however, is the original Latin of the document: *feliciora evangelizationis tempora.* The Latin does not use the typical word for new, *nova.* Instead, it uses *feliciora,* which translates more literally as "an *abundant season* of evangelization." *Feliciora* comes from *felix,* or happy. *Feliciora* connotes abundance, something that is nobler, propitious, flourishing, more auspicious, fortunate, or bountiful in an agricultural sense. The choice of the Latin word indicates how the new evangelization is "new." The new is not opposite what was in the past, or opposite "old." The new is not synonymous with contemporary or current. Rather, the new evangelization is new in the sense that evangelization is to be a noble, bountiful, flourishing of abundance. While the word "new" is a suitable adjective for "evangelization," the quality of the newness should be understood in the sense of *feliciora.*

The Church uses various approaches in this new evangelization. One form involves an exchange between a believer and another person. It may begin with a question or a discussion of some particular teaching. The ensuing conversation can be like a tennis match. Point is matched by counterpoint. Various levels are dragged onto the theological court: history, ideas, and emotions. The goal is to argue in a way that finds flaws in the other's logic, discovers an error, or defends one line of reasoning as more likely or believable. In this type of discussion, believers present their knowledge and seek to convince the other. The formal name for this approach is "apologetics."

But there is a richer form of evangelization. In a more original form, evangelization takes on the character of a sign. This sign shows that the believer lives from a source that informs his being and direction in the world. Living from this source enables the believer to slowly, gradually, and repeatedly peruse the truth, goodness, and beauty associated with the intelligible mystery of the faith. As Carl Anderson writes, we have a responsibility "to radically transform culture, not by imposing values from above, but through a subtler yet more powerful process—living a vocation of love in the day-to-day reality of our lives."[89]

---

89. Anderson, *A Civilization of Love,* 5.

The believer presents himself as someone who knows Someone, and is now describing this Person. The believer wants to introduce this Person to another. In this view, apologetics is a tool, not the structure. What then is the starting point to describe a Person? Begin with what the Person has to say about himself. The Christian faith recognizes that this Person, God, has spoken about himself in Sacred Scripture. God has chosen to begin speaking about himself by speaking about the human person.

Evangelization is the antidote to the poison that has found its way deep into the heart of modern man. The perfect storm has left the wreckage of a social construct of what it is to be a person, with all the pain and errors that flow from this false caricature. The new evangelization must start at the very beginning, at the original experiences of man. As Karol Wojtyla did, we must start with the experience of our capacity to reason and to enter into relationship. In this manner, the healing serum of truth may sink deeply into the human heart, extinguishing the pain and reconstructing the beauty of the human person.

The experiences that formed Karol Wojtyla contrast greatly with the experiences that form much of secular culture. He was formed within a multileveled alliance of marriage, family, loss, laity, intellect, hard labor, and theological exploration. His pastoral ministry focused in a unique way on marriage and family. Besides all this, he experienced the effects of two of the most vicious totalitarian regimes in history. His experiences led him to appreciate *communio*, communion, at every turn. The secular culture, instead, has been formed from within the perfect storm of separation, consumerism, materialism, hedonism, and utilitarianism. These states emerge from the pain of divorce, cohabitation, fatherlessness, and contraception, all claimed under apparent freedom that is, in reality, autonomous isolation. This isolation may prove to be more oppressive than history's worst dictators. A fragmented identity emerges.

Wojtyla's communion, on the contrary, forms the basis for the culture of life and the civilization of love. Secularism's cruel matrix forms the foundation for the culture of death. The new evangelization offers an alternative to the culture of death by forming true personal identity.

With the new evangelization, John Paul II bequeathed not only a fresh restatement of the content of the faith, but also an invigorating method to explore the content. His *method* is, in a sense, his first *content*.

The new evangelization is not simply a reaction or a means of being relevant, but it is a relationship that communicates Christ to others through our living in communion with Christ.[90] Truth is not an abstract opinion, but a divine Person, Jesus Christ. The subsequent chapters of this book will distill John Paul's teaching, in both content and method. The hope is that this will provide access to the new evangelization and offer all a shelter from the perfect storm, a path from death toward life. The perfect storm told us that to be a person we must *acquire pleasure quickly*; the opposite is the truth: to be a person we must not acquire but *give*, we must not acquire pleasure, but *give beauty*, we must not acquire pleasure quickly *but give beauty slowly*.

90. Christian A. Mugridge, SOLT, and Marie Gannon, FMA, *John Paul II: Development of a Theology of Communication* (Rome: Libreria Editrice Vaticana, 2008), 31.

Part II

The Theology of the Body, Original Innocence, and Original Shame

CHAPTER THREE

―――⌒∾⌒―――

The Beginning

A. The Evolution Debate

During the past century and a half scientists made unprecedented advances and developed various theories of evolution. The force of this empirical data seems to leave behind the Genesis accounts as mere bedtime stories that we ought to quickly outgrow. Catholics are sometimes suspicious, shy, and even a little apologetic about the Book of Genesis.[1]

The "sarcasm of the worldly-wise" proceeds:

> [D]o you expect us to believe, we men of the Twentieth Century, we who belong to the age of atomic energy, of planetary exploration, of evolution, that the first woman was made from a rib of the first man and the old evil in the world came about because she munched on an apple? How can you expect us to believe that God created the world in six days, when we know that it was the result of millions of years of evolution?[2]

Such objections, however, are based on false conceptions about Genesis. Jean Daniélou notes that to explain the early chapters of Genesis, we must first eliminate the obstacles to understanding the relationship between faith and science.[3] During his Wednesday catechesis

---

1. Walter Kasper, *Transcending All Understanding: The Meaning of Christian Faith Today* (San Francisco: Ignatius Press, Communio Books, 1989), 79.

2. Jean Daniélou, *In the Beginning ... Genesis I–III* (Baltimore: Helicon, 1965), 14.

3. Ibid., 13.

of April 16, 1986, Pope John Paul quoted and reiterated the teaching of Pope Pius XII in his 1950 encyclical *Humani Generis*: "The magisterium of the Church is not opposed to the theory of evolution being the object of investigation and discussion among experts. Here the theory of evolution is understood as an investigation of the origin of the human body from preexisting living matter, for the Catholic faith obliges us to hold firmly that souls are created immediately by God (DS 3896)."[4]

The Church has long acknowledged the proper domains of science and those of faith. Each discipline must respect the proper domain of the other. Science has valid contributions to make to the understanding of man and his identity. The empirical sciences deal with what we can observe and measure. Scientists who explore the roots of the identity of the human person can only investigate what is visible and quantifiable about the emergence and identity of humans. Science is able to measure and approximate *how* and *when* man was created. The Church is not opposed to the discussion of various theories of evolution among experts, that is, discussion on the way the human body emerged from preexistent living matter.

Theology, on the other hand, does not concern itself primarily with *how* and *when* man was created. Rather, theology probes the questions of *who* created man and *why* man was created. These questions directly involve man's soul. Because science deals with the visible, physical, observable, and measurable, it is simply not equipped to deal directly with *who* created man and *why*. Because theology is based on revelation and reason, it deals precisely with the latter two questions and leaves the *when* and *how* to science. When each discipline retains its own proper method, "there is no opposition whatsoever between the truths revealed in these [Genesis] texts and the truths established by science."[5] The responses from theology and science are not contradictory: "The complete man is one who is able to have a scientific approach to reality, and on the other hand to have a religious approach to the same reality."[6]

---

4. John Paul II, *God, Father and Creator: A Catechesis on the Creed* (Boston: Pauline Books & Media, 1996), 1:229.

5. Daniélou, *In the Beginning*, 14.

6. Daniélou, *Myth and Mystery*, 16.

B. Preamble of Truths About the Identity of the Human Person

John Paul was alert to the "principal message" of Scripture "which is a religious message."[7] In his catecheses on the theology of the body, he examined the Genesis text to uncover from the verses the truth of the identity of the human person. John Paul's analysis is a patient, step-by-step consideration that interprets the tradition in a novel manner.

1. Two Creation Accounts

The Book of Genesis contains two accounts of the creation of the world. These texts reflect a Near Eastern mentality, which depended on the science of the times.[8] The author's description differs from the cosmogonic myths of the time,[9] and each account contains a story of the creation of man. At one time, the presence of two accounts of man's creation was met with skepticism, with some scholars asserting that the mere presence of two accounts means that neither is accurate. It was thought more likely that both arose from purely fictitious sources and hence were not reliable. But just as when two persons who witness the same event may describe it from different angles, the event described is clearly the same. Each creation account describes the same created world and the same being of man, albeit from a different perspective and style. Hans Urs von Balthasar notes, "Contrary to the plain words of the text, people have continually tried to separate the first account of creation from the second."[10]

John Paul affirms that the presence of two accounts serves to highlight the identity of man from two complementary directions. As John

---

7. James Swetnam, SJ, "A Vision of Wholeness: Response," *The Thought of Pope John Paul II: A Collection of Essays and Studies*, ed. John M. McDermott, SJ (Rome: Editrice Pontifica Università Gregoriana, 1993), 94.

8. Daniélou, *In the Beginning*, 28.

9. Ibid., 29.

10. Hans Urs von Balthasar, *Theo-Drama II: Dramatis Personae: Man in God* (San Francisco: Ignatius Press, 1990), 370.

Paul points out several times, to ask which account is more accurate is to miss the genre of the text, because the two accounts are compatible. The truth presented in Genesis concerning the identity of the human person is neither lost in myth nor constrained by material evolution. The accounts are rich in content concerning the identity of the human person. John Paul's interpretation unseals these layers of meaning. In the theology of the body, John Paul shows no embarrassment for his repeated appeal to the two creation accounts in Genesis.

2. Myth

Early in his analysis of the creation accounts, John Paul gives prolonged attention to their style. The accounts are not simply the artifact of an early attempt of religion to monopolize what we think. He acknowledges that the accounts are myth, but not in the rationalist sense of a fable. It is crucial to understand the significance of Genesis as a myth in the traditional sense of myth: a myth is not the same as a fable or fairy tale that tells a story to convey a true notion. Henri de Lubac, the French Jesuit scholar, writes, "On the other hand, *fabula* (tale, fable) (μνθος [myth]), in the singular, does not always indicate that it is a question of a false story, of events that did not happen."[11] Rather, myth in the classical sense tells a truth about the human person through an event that is so true it cannot fit under a microscope. The rationalist emphasis of the nineteenth century attempted to relegate myth to fantasy. The stories of the past were branded as not true, made up, false—fantastic tales with no truth in them. As a category of human expression, however, myth is deeper.

The Genesis accounts are the classic myth: the accounts are in a sense "more than true"; they convey a truth too dense to fit in a fact.[12] Myth is not about fiction or the unreal, but the *more than real*. In fact, in light of the truth about man contained in the myth, the modern approach to the human person and marriage is unveiled as the fabrication. Rather than read as fantastic, out-of-date stories, the first chapters of Genesis

---

11. Henri de Lubac, *History and Spirit: The Understanding of Scripture According to Origen* (San Francisco: Ignatius Press, 2007), 134.

12. John Paul II, *Man and Woman He Created Them*, 138, no. 4, cf. p. 157.

must be understood as prophetic history[13] extending into the "dateless past" of an anteroom of history, "a region beyond memory," whose reality is nonetheless accessible.[14] The author of the first book of the Bible is expressing a truth about man that has a different consistency from a mere series of factual notes.

John Paul points out that "the rationalism of the nineteenth century" regarded myth as a "product of the imagination or what is irrational."[15] He then goes on to describe the classical sense of myth as discovering "the structure of reality that is inaccessible to rational and empirical investigation."[16]

Several commentators note that time, in the context of myth, likewise is mysterious, "bent to theme and purpose, a kind of prime matter of religious history."[17] Myth is made of a solidity and compactness that appeals to "spiraling time, not linear time."[18] The nature of time has a unique itinerary in myth: "Time as a mere sequence cannot convey the larger callings and renegings, the sins, disruptions, and interventions that have shaped and misshaped our past—and inevitably, our present."[19] The myth communicates "the inward reality of history" and the "real purpose of history" from the standpoint of a "deeper stratum of human experience than man ever sounded before."[20] Kenneth Schmitz points out that the purpose of the myth is to "communicate the original and ultimate meaning of things and to provide human life with a guiding pattern" and "to take its hearers back to the primordial time, into the presence of those archetypal founding events in order to be renewed by their power."[21] The past time of the myth is "the first time, the time of

---

13. Simon Tugwell, *The Beatitudes: Soundings in the Christian Tradition* (Springfield, IL: Templegate, 1980), 49.

14. Gaston Bachelard, *The Poetics of Space: The Classic Look at How We Experience Intimate Places* (Boston: Beacon, 1994), 57, 143.

15. John Paul II, *Man and Woman He Created Them*, 138, no. 4.

16. Ibid.

17. Daniel Berrigan, SJ, *Genesis: Fair Beginnings, Then Foul* (Lanham, MD: Rowman & Littlefield, 2006), 67.

18. Ibid., 80.

19. Ibid., 69.

20. Jean Daniélou, *The Lord of History: Reflections on the Inner Meaning of History* (Cleveland: World Publishing, Meridian, 1968), 101.

21. Kenneth Schmitz, *The Gift: Creation* (Milwaukee: Marquette University Press, 1982), 2, 6.

beginnings.... The time is so remote that it is utterly unlike these present times ... measured by a different temporal rate."[22] Time, in the myth, never grows old.

The skeptical approach tends to measure the Genesis text as the out-dated and stale view of prescientific man. The same microscope that opened up worlds beneath the appearance of matter now closes the world of the text with suspicion and attempts to move on to supposedly more rational matters. But that which is rational is not always reasonable. The skeptics make a misstep when they assume that the author of Genesis was trying to convey scientific facts. The author's intention was never to do that, but rather to show transcendent truth: the "very telling of the myth is meant to provide . . . a sort of narrative bridge that is to take its hearers back to the primordial time, into the presence of those archetypal founding events in order to be renewed by their power ... to communicate the freshness of that beginning...."[23] The Genesis accounts do not attempt to simply gather the secular lineage of human facts into a pure sequential chronicle of temporal history. Rather, the texts account for the panoramic design of "the hidden glories of charity ... the nakedness of history."[24] The creation accounts have something to offer that cannot be obtained anywhere else. They relay the events that reveal the deep meaning of the identity of man.

3. The First Account

The first account of creation (Gen 1:1–31) differs from the second (Gen 2:4–25), especially regarding the way that God created the human person. On each day of creation, God issues a series of imperative com-mands: "Let there be...." The commands take on a crisp, rapid structure as the creation of the visible world unfolds—until the sixth day.

God seems to pause on the sixth day and draw within himself. This drawing within is not the prolonged rest of the seventh day. God's inward turn signals a break in the staccato structure. On day six, God's method of operation changes. He says, as if pondering, "Let us make man in our own image. Let them have dominion...." (Gen 1:26). No

---

22. Ibid., 4–5.
23. Ibid., 6.
24. Daniélou, *The Lord of History*, 103.

explicit planning is mentioned for creation other than man, whereas the creation of the human person results from God's pondering within himself. God looks for a blueprint for man's identity and turns within himself to find it. "The first account puts the creation of the first human couple at the end of an ascending process of creation."[25] Hans Urs von Balthasar notes that this pondering takes on a character of deliberation, as if God is considering and turning over in his mind the prospect and risk of creating a being with free choice—of a being who could reject his love. God decides, and he creates man: "God created man in his own image, in the divine image he created him, male and female he created them" (Gen 1:27). Placing the creation of man in the midst of the visible world shows man's relation to the rest of creation, while the manner of his creation makes explicit man's relation to God, a relation that draws man above the visible world, yet in the midst of it. It remains that "[o]ne must establish an appropriate relationship between God the Creator and man the created being" from within the accounts.[26] Both male and female are created at the same time, and the text explicitly mentions that the human person is created in the "image and likeness of God" (Gen 1:27).

Analysis of the first verse of Genesis shows that it carries substantial meaning. "In the beginning, when God created...." reveals not only that God is the Creator, but also the significance of God's act of creation. This meaning is captured by a series of classical terms: *bara'*, *ex nihilo*, and *dabar*. These terms refer to the immediacy of the creation (*bara'*) of the world by the word (*dabar*) of God out of nothing (*ex nihilo*). These terms converge in a way that gives us an initial vantage point from which to understand the identity of the human person. This trio of Latin (*ex nihilo*) and Hebrew *(bara', dabar)* terms assembles the foundational truths concerning God as Creator and the human person as creature.

a. Bara'

Bara' appears immediately in the Genesis text. John Paul calls attention to the first words of Genesis: "*'Beresit bara'*!—In the beginning he

---

25. Balthasar, *Theo-Drama II*, 369.
26. Andrew N. Woznicki, *A Christian Humanism: Karol Wojtyla's Existential Personalism* (New Britain, CT: Mariel, 1980), 3.

created …' The circumstantial adverbial phrase 'in the beginning' indicates God as the One who exists before this beginning, who is not limited either by time or space, and who 'creates,' 'gives a beginning' to everything that is not God.…" [27] God's creation is universal; there is no "independent matter that escapes his creative power."[28]

John Paul II points out that "The word 'created' is a translation from the Hebrew *bara'*, which describes an action of extraordinary power whose subject is God alone."[29] While man can *make* music, or *build* a table, God alone can *bara'*. Jean Daniélou points out, "'Created' is *bara'* in Hebrew; this word is of particular interest. The Old Testament uses it only when referring to God and therefore it belongs to a sacred vocabulary. It is not a profane analogy such as 'to manufacture' or 'to construct.'"[30] Rather, *bara'* "implies a divine action."[31] Kenneth Schmitz notes that the Hebrew word *bara'* "denotes a special exercise of divine power, and is attributed to God alone. Such creative action is exclusively and uniquely divine."[32] Schmitz notes that "Our making is limited by what is given prior to our making."[33] God's is not.

Appeal to the Jewish tradition reveals:

> [T]he Hebrew verb *bara'* does not simply signify "create," in the sense of "produce," but rather derives from a root whose meaning is "expel outside." In this case God would have "expelled creation outside himself," he would have "given birth" to the world by a creative expulsion. This separation gives birth to a "non-God," a creature who acquires a real existence and subsists from then on by itself. It can thus accept or refuse the alliance that God proposes to make with it.[34]

---

27. General audience, November 29, 1978, *Talks of John Paul II* (Boston: Daughters of St. Paul, 1979), 361–362.

28. Schmitz, *The Gift: Creation*, 16.

29. John Paul II, *God, Father and Creator*, 1:201.

30. Daniélou, *In the Beginning*, 33.

31. Daniélou, *The Lord of History*, 149.

32. Schmitz, *The Gift: Creation*, 16. See, among others, J. L. McKenzie, "Aspects of Old Testament Thought," in *The Jerome Biblical Commentary*, ed. R. E. Brown, et al. (New Jersey: Prentice Hall, 1968), no. 77, para. 54, p. 745b. Cf. Greek *kitzo*, Latin *creo*, causative of *cresco*, and sanskrit *kshi*: to establish; cf. Kenneth Schmitz, *The Recovery of Wonder: The New Freedom and the Asceticism of Power* (Montreal: McGill-Queen's University Press, 2008), 36.

33. Schmitz, *The Recovery of Wonder*, 5 no. 7.

34. Xavier Leon-Dufour, *To Act According to the Gospel* (Peabody, MA: Hendrickson, 2005), xi.

The notion of "expel outside oneself" does not imply that the world or human beings are pieces of God. *Bara'* does not imply pantheism, as if we were all little pieces of God and therefore autonomous gods in some measure. Neither does *bara'* imply that man is an emanation from God.[35] God's presence to us is unlike any other presence in the universe. He is present as Causal Agent. God, as part of his creative power, continues to hold creatures in existence. It is from this perspective that Daniélou can state, "The word *bara'* then designates those things which only God can accomplish, works truly divine. This is of prime importance. The entire Bible will simply be a development of it...."[36]

We can begin to grasp an initial meaning of God's presence in creation through an analogy with a piece of art. My two cousins, Patty and Colleen, are three years apart and have both enjoyed art and painting from an early age. When Patty was about four years old, I visited their house and saw a picture she had painted on poster paper displayed prominently on the refrigerator door. The picture was awash in light blues across the page. The long, leisurely strokes showed the brush had been heavy with paint as she moved it slowly across the surface. The density of the powder blue liquid at the bottom of the work made it look like an ocean depth. The lighter, less dense powder blue at the top made it look like the initial twenty feet of ocean water penetrated by the sun's light. Evidently, after she had applied the blue, she had dipped her brush in plain white and slowly moved it in the air over the print as white drops in dots and lengths spotted portions of the blue. The picture looked like an ocean depth with huge white whales swimming through it as white air bubbles ascended to the surface. I immediately claimed it and had it framed.

When I visited again some time later, after Colleen had turned four, one of her works was now prominently displayed. Colleen had chosen red and green for her work. Instead of long, slow lines of leisurely stroked depth, it had blotches of round, red full circles. Each circle covered a portion of another. Some green paint was dotted through the red here and there in a circular fashion. This painting looked like an impressionist work of a basket of apples. I claimed it and had it framed as well.

---

35. John Paul II, *God, Father and Creator*, 206 (cf. Balthasar, *Theo-Drama II*, 118, 137). See also, Jean-Pierre Torrell, O.P., *Saint Thomas Aquinas: Spiritual Master*, vol. 2 (Washington, DC: The Catholic University of America Press, 2003), 62.

36. Daniélou, *In the Beginning*, 33.

If I show the two framed works to anyone who knows Patty and Colleen, he or she can easily identify the artist of each work. Patty's is the long, leisurely blue, with gradations of white. Colleen's is the eye-catching red in quick circles. The movement in these pictures reveals something about each artist. Patty is leisurely, gradual, and flexible, while Colleen is immediate, decided, and direct. They are present to their work, but obviously not by composition. They are present as the agent of cause. Their work reveals them. God is present in analogous fashion in creation.

All that has been said about the creation of the world (*bara'*) also applies to the creation of man: "God created man in his own image; in the divine image he created him, male and female he created them" (Gen 1:27). In the first verse of Genesis *bara'* is used only once in general reference to the creation of the world. John Paul notes that "In this phrase the triple use of the verb 'created' (*bara'*) is striking. It seems to give a particular importance and 'intensity' to the creative act."[37] The intensity alludes to intimacy: God "drew man from the mystery of his own Being."[38]

Both the meaning of *bara'* and its repetition are significant.[39] In the act of creating man, "God is the exclusive and direct principle of the new being, to the exclusion of any pre-existing matter."[40]

To think about God the Creator in a mechanistic way prevents us from having a mature sense of his presence. God is "anything but a God of total and tactless manifestation."[41] His presence to me is thus dynamic and concrete, not static or abstract. The image of God as an accountant who watches to catch any misstep must yield to a more energetic and primary image. God is present to us as the one who has caused things to be. We sense this intimate presence the way we can tell the artist by the art. God is present to us, but not such that we can control him or he us. His presence is closer than that. God alone freely creates the world and

---

37. John Paul II, *God, Father and Creator*, 222.

38. General audience, December 6, 1978, *Talks of John Paul II*, 397.

39. The word and its repetition occur again in Genesis 5:1–2 (Angelo Scola, *The Nuptial Mystery* [Grand Rapids, MI: Wm. B. Eerdmans, 2005], 32).

40. John Paul II, *God, Father and Creator*, 202.

41. Bruno Forte, *To Follow You, Light of Life; Spiritual Exercises Preached before John Paul II at the Vatican* (Grand Rapids, MI: Wm. B. Eerdmans, 2005), 84.

man in time, and God alone maintains creation by continually holding it in being.[42] Creation (*bara'*) is "an integrally divine act that arouses existence out of nothingness and not simply the unfolding of eternally existent being."[43] The truth of creation is not in the first instance an impulse to explain things so that everyone will believe the same thing. Rather, it is meant to prepare us for the truth about human nature. The first truth about human nature is that we do not cause ourselves to exist.

b. Ex Nihilo: *The World Is Not Reducible to the World*

The significance of *bara'* gives depth to the original question about what it means to be a human person. The question requires a "downward arrow" technique that proceeds from the initial experience and continues to uncover the foundations of our existence.

Creation (*bara'*) is the notion that God created the world "out of nothing," that is "*ex nihilo sui et subjecti* or simply *ex nihilo.*"[44] To be created from nothing means there was no preexistent matter out of which the world emerged. John Paul points out, "An initial view ... is offered by the first page of Sacred Scripture, which indicates the moment when God's creative power made the world out of nothing...."[45] In addition to the layers of meaning established by *bara'*, John Paul draws attention to "the first lines of Genesis when creatures, summoned by the powerful Word of the Creator, spring from the silence of nothingness."[46] If we search all the way back beyond evolution, beyond the amoebas, beyond the intrinsic moments that lead from instinct for survival to sacrificial love, what was there? "Prior to the fact of creation, there was only God and nothingness. Creation meant the birth of every being except God."[47] Creation out of nothing emphasizes the truth that God alone is God: he needs nothing else and depends on nothing else: "In the act of creation, God is the exclusive and direct principle of the new being, to the

---

42. John Paul II, *God, Father and Creator*, 205.

43. Jean Daniélou, *God and the Ways of Knowing* (San Francisco: Ignatius Press, 2003), 38.

44. John Paul II, *God, Father and Creator*, 201.

45. John Paul II, *The Trinity's Embrace: God's Saving Plan, A Catechesis on Salvation History* (Boston: Pauline Books & Media, 2002), 308.

46. Ibid., 311.

47. Woznicki, *A Christian Humanism*, 1.

exclusion of any preexisting matter."[48] There was a time beyond time, a "time" when there was only God, which is to say "eternity": "The truth of creation expresses the thought that everything existing outside of God has been called into existence by him."[49]

The interconnection of *bara'* and *ex nihilo* continues throughout Scripture: "Look at the heavens and the earth ... God did not make them out of things that existed. So also mankind came into being" (2 Mac 7:28). The New Testament also testifies to creation of the world out of nothing: "Abraham believed in God who gives life to the dead and calls into existence the things that do not exist" (Rom 4:17). Creation out of nothing means that "everything was created by God. Therefore, nothing existed before creation except God."[50]

When we realize that "God depends on nothing else," we come to the essential awareness of our creaturehood, a reality from which modern man is in the long flight of denial. We would rather think that we are so important we give God a hand. But God is outside of created being. He chooses out of his generosity and love, not out of any necessity, to create those things that exist outside himself.[51] At one point within his eternity, God decides to create, because of his own generosity. His creation emerges on the basis of his overflowing love, from which he makes a gift of self in time and space. While based on eternal love, this love in time and space has both a similarity and a dissimilarity with the proportions of eternal love. "[T]he creature has its origin fully and completely from the power of God."[52] When we reason to God's presence from the beauty and order of the created world, we can better realize that we are not God.[53] Creation out of nothing protects us from pride by reminding us where we come from.

According to Balthasar, "The (essentially unrefined) formula, 'creation out of nothing,' has been current since the first Christian centuries."[54] For

---

48. John Paul II, *God, Father and Creator*, 202.
49. Ibid., 201.
50. John Paul II, *The Trinity's Embrace*, 4.
51. John Paul II, *God, Father and Creator*, 203. See also, Torrell, O.P., *Saint Thomas Aquinas: Spiritual Master*, 62, 176, and 234.
52. John Paul II, *God, Father and Creator*, 202.
53. Balthasar, *Theo-Drama II*, 273.
54. Ibid., 264.

Schmitz, the world, and ultimately humans, do not emerge "out of chaos, or out of a primordial sea, or from a mythical monster, or out of any pre-existent material."[55] The ultimate ground of origin for the identity of the human person is not reducible to the world. The teaching that the world was created out of nothing has a consistency with science and certainly philosophy. The human person can emerge only from what is *personal*.

The coalition of *bara'* and *ex nihilo* may appear technical, but it has implications for the way we understand the human person to be related to God. Each of us reasonably understands "there was a time when I was not." I did not exist before my parents came together in an act of love. Science can trace my beginnings from a physical-genetic perspective back to the meeting of the gametic cells in the fallopian tube of my mother. Even here science has mysteries it cannot penetrate. Scientific investigation can describe the physiological effects of the attraction my parents felt to each other. Various disciplines can comment on the emotional and relational nature of the love between my mother and father. But no microscope can enter that love itself, which led them to make a gift of self through a two-in-one-flesh union that bore fruit in the union of the gametic cells from which I came to be. Science can describe the physiological environment that accompanies my coming to be, but it cannot make the leap to the inner nature of love from which I came to be. Scientific truth and religious truth come together to respond to the question of meaning.

John Paul emphasizes that "The Creator is he who 'calls to existence from nothing' ... *because he is love* (1 Jn 4:8).... As an action of God, creation thus means not only calling from nothing to existence and establishing the world's existence, but, according to the first account, *beresit bara'*, it also signifies *gift*...."[56] Creation "'from nothing' makes something to be where there was nothing before and does this by the power of the agent alone (*ordinaliter post*)."[57] All man is has been *given* to him. Man is a gift.

Creation out of nothing reveals that the world came from a gift of love and reinforces that I come from love. No matter what my parents may have done after I was born, no matter how many times they may

---

55. Schmitz, *The Recovery of Wonder*, 27.
56. John Paul II, *Man and Woman He Created Them*, 180.
57. Schmitz, *Creation: The Gift*, 28.

have dropped me on my head afterward, they did the first thing right. They loved. At some point, they loved, no matter how fallen they may have been after that. Even in cases of assault, in the extremely rare circumstance that a sexual assault results in pregnancy—where there was no love between mother and father—in keeping the child, the mother's love redeems the horrific act of the father. The mother's love makes the origin of the child to be an act of love. What existed prior to the love from which I came? The love of my grandparents, and so on back: love, forgiven many times.

When you and I observe things and the world, they say to us that they did not cause themselves. At one level we more readily realize that we did not cause our individual selves to be, but we have a difficult time understanding that the human race itself as well as the entire cosmos is contingent. It is not so much that we want to deny God's existence, but that we want to deny our contingency, our dependence upon God. We want God to be there, but we want him to be measurable and predictable. Yet love, in its most rare vintage, is immeasurable.

God did not create to enhance his divinity. He did not get bored one day and just try something new. He did not construct us as part of a project at God-school. No. Creation out of nothing protects us from thinking ourselves as fated to be here, part of mere genetic destiny. While this teaching protects us from pride, it also protects us from anonymous despair. Creation out of nothing means God *calls us* into being. This call into existence reinforces that we are created out of love. Our creation is not just a static and routine event. At some point man is called forth from nothingness.[58] Science can approximate this given the nature of contingent reality. John Paul points out that contingent beings depend on the Absolute Being.[59] We emerge from the love of God himself. And love creates simply because it is good: "God did not hope to find in them [creatures] a completion of His own perfection. God's unconditioned fullness of being and goodness ... cannot be supplemented."[60] The truth about God's fullness has a reflection in a truth about the beauty of the world: "God's nature shows itself to be 'absolute love' by giving itself

---

58. John Paul II, *God, Father and Creator*, 197.

59. Ibid., 199.

60. Woznicki, *A Christian Humanism*, 1.

away and allowing others to be, for no other reason than this (motive-less) giving is good and full of meaning—and hence is, quite simply, beautiful...."[61]

The first truth of our existence and the first truth of maturity are the same: I did not cause myself. The human race did not cause itself. The world did not cause itself. This is the starting point of true poverty. To be called into existence from nothingness is to be poor in the richest sense: "Poverty means being open to the surprises of the Eternal, and so it also means refusing to manage one's life on one's own ... ready to give up every security already attained, accepting to live by the ever surprising fidelity of God, who clothes the lilies of the field and feeds the birds of the air."[62]

The attribution of creation to God says something about *man*. "Creation comes *from* God by way of agency, but the divine production is *from nothing* by way of material causality, i.e., it issues from no material substrate."[63] The fabric of man's identity, in its most basic weave, is from two directions: "[T]hough man is created in the image and likeness of God, he is formed from the dust of the earth. Though he is called to be the highest, the nearest to God, he is by origin the most lowly."[64] His lowliness is a built-in direction toward humility: He cannot forget or deny "his condition of not-being-God, the nothingness of his origin."[65]

Creation out of nothing also tells us something about the world in which we live. The world has a structure within that reveals something of God's love. The world is not only *from* love, it is *for* love. Therefore we must receive it rather than impose upon it. We so easily try to recreate the world for our own purposes through frenetic activity, rather than receive it with God's purpose. Creation *ex nihilo* reminds us God was here first and we follow his plan: "Anyone who penetrates into the mysteries of God recognizes more and more that the world as a whole is

---

61. Balthasar, *Theo-Drama II*, 273.

62. Bruno Forte, *The Essence of Christianity* (Grand Rapids, MI: Wm. B. Eerdmans, 2003), 72.

63. Schmitz, *Creation: The Gift*, 29.

64. Hans Urs von Balthasar, *The Christian State of Life* (San Francisco: Ignatius Press, 1983), 67.

65. Ibid.

created 'for nothing,' that is, out of a love that is free and has no other reason behind it...."[66]

The commingling of the notions of *bara'* and *ex nihilo* as truths of revelation is also harmonious with human experience. Man's fundamental experience is to be utterly dependent on God for existence itself. At the same time, man experiences his permanence. The coalescence of *ex nihilo* and *bara'* account for this experience of man. In his contingency-permanence, man can only be a gift. The doctrine of creation "is based upon a feature in things that required a creator: namely, the utterly radical contingency inherent in the finitude of things."[67] Creation is not necessary for God, but it is necessary for man in his identity as experienced by him. For God, creation is an unnecessary generosity. For man, the generosity is most necessary.

c. Dabar

All that has been said thus far about creation via *bara'* and *ex nihilo* coalesces around the Hebrew notion of *dabar*, the word. God *bara's* the world *ex nihilo* through the speaking of his word, *dabar*. The Genesis account of creation takes the form of a series of commands. John Paul emphasizes that on each individual day a new event is spoken by God and it comes to be: "The expression recurs: 'God said: Let there be....' Through the power of this word of the Creator—'*fiat*, let there be,' the visible world gradually arises."[68] The Psalmist repeats this: "It was the LORD's word that made the heavens" (Ps 32:6).

The mentality of the Old Testament understood there is power in the word of a person. Today, contracts are full of abstract legalese in fine print, just waiting for a lawsuit. Words are detached, malleable instruments of technical information and confusion. Infomercials proclaim we can "lose twenty pounds in twenty days" with the latest exercise machine. But then we see a small white line below the machine. If we get to the screen before it quickly disappears, we find it reads, "Results not typical."

---

66. Balthasar, *Theo-Drama II*, 260.
67. Schmitz, *The Recovery of Wonder*, 36.
68. John Paul II, *God, Father and Creator*, 204.

Unlike advertising that has to cajole, persuade, and entice, God's word is "effective in itself. God speaks and it is."[69] With God there is no small print. In Old Testament times, the word and the event were one. This unity of word and event is expressed in the Old Testament word *dabar*.[70] The word did not promise an action to come: The word was the action.[71]

The truth that creation comes from God does not give Christians a monopoly on the world so that they can establish an unbroken line of authority over earthly affairs. The Genesis description of creation is not a mechanical event that God oversees from a distant throne as another sheer exhibition of his power. Christianity does not say: "Look how much power God has. He created all of this leisurely by his word. You'd better listen to him, because if you don't, you may find yourself on the wrong side of his power." If God wanted to show raw power he would just conquer the world as it is. Instead, God shows the unique power of love by creating in such a way that he leaves evidence that points to his love as Creator and Father.

Creation arising from the word of God shows closeness to that power. Creation is an event that is close to God. While rocks, plants, trees, animals, and people are not God, they are close to him. This closeness to God is not a mere sentimental disposition or benign familiarity. In creating the world God speaks a word that proceeds from his generosity. He creates beings outside himself out of the love that is within himself.

Creation via the *dabar* of God is significant for the identity of the human person. God calls man out of nothingness (*ex nihilo*) through love (*agape*) in such a way that God is present to man (*bara'*) in an immediate though noncontrolling manner. God does this not by some remote command, but by intimacy. This kind of closeness—without man's absorption into God, in which the greater overtakes the lesser—is guaranteed in the means by which God chooses to create. God is present to me as the one who speaks a word (*dabar*). God is an event of love. From this love, he freely moves to create a world outside himself.

---

69. Yves Congar, *The Word and the Spirit* (San Francisco: Harper & Row, 1986), 10.
70. Balthasar, *Theo-Drama II*, 106.
71. Congar, *The Word and the Spirit*, 10.

d. Exitus-reditus

God creates as *bara'*, that is in a nondistant, attentive manner, and does so *ex nihilo*, out of nothing, with his *dabar*. This places a unique momentum within creation. The meanings of *bara'*, *ex nihilo*, and *dabar* are collectively inherited in the schema known as *exitus-reditus*. The Latin term *exitus* means "to go forth from." The term *reditus* means "to return to." The *exitus-reditus* schema highlights the generosity of God within the continuous movement of all creation coming forth from his word as origin and returning to him as source. John Paul teaches that "the capacity to love infinitely, to give oneself without reserve or measure, belongs to God."[72] The *exitus-reditus* demonstrates the structure of this love.

Through the *exitus-reditus* pattern, the *dabar* of God that creates *ex nihilo* has the character of an effusive movement of love that proceeds from God. *Dabar* creates and sustains continuously that which is created (*creatio continua*),[73] and finds its return to God, the source of love. Just as the Persons in the immanent Trinity eternally pour forth love among themselves, God also pours forth in time and space his creative love. God is the origin and goal of all that exists outside himself in time. The eternal processions of the Persons in the Trinity is the source of God's gift of existence to the world and to man.[74]

The *exitus-reditus* allows theology to speak of the presence of God as a unique form of presence with unmatched characteristics. The invisible, infinite God lacks nothing and chooses out of his generosity to create a visible, finite world outside himself in such a way that he can be recognized in his works.[75] This recognition is based on a unique manifestation of God's power. God's presence to his creation is not a mere tag of ownership or oppressive possession. God's presence is not remote, nor does it smoother us and prevent our free will. The presence of God to man is a relationship enacted by God sending his Word: "through him all things were made; without him nothing was made that has been made" (Jn 1:2).

---

72. John Paul II, *The Trinity's Embrace*, 183.

73. Pontifical Biblical Commission, *The Bible and Morality: Biblical Roots of Christian Behavior*, 2008, 9. See also, Torrell, O.P., *Saint Thomas Aquinas: Spiritual Master*, 55, 56, 58, 60, 63, 90, and 177–178.

74. John Paul II, *God, Father and Creator*, 212.

75. Balthasar, *Theo-Drama II*, 138.

The *exitus-reditus* depicts how God's *dabar* creates *ex nihilo* through *agape* in such a way that God remains present to the free creature without being absorbed into the makeup of the creature. The creature comes forth (*egressus*) from its God and at the same time begins its return (*regressus*) to God.[76] It is the process by which man comes to be, and the movement of his freedom, ie., his nature, "is forever distinguished from God in that it comes from him and goes to him."[77]

God is present not as a distant judge or consultant who watches from a safe haven with all the answers well within reach while we scramble around trying to figure out the game of life. He is not a mere silent bystander. He is not present in the world by composition with it, as if we could somehow touch him when touching a leaf or water. Two extreme tendencies must be avoided. Pantheism is the idea that God is present to creation by composition. Deism is the belief that God is so remote from creation that his presence is merely a mechanistic beginning after which God is, for the most part, absent to the creature. God's presence is much more sublime and dramatic.

The concept of *exitus-reditus* is drawn from the categories and schema of Saint Thomas Aquinas. The concept helps us to understand the unique way in which God is present to creation, especially to human persons. The schema is animated by the image of the breath of God as seen in Psalm 104: "How many are your works, O LORD! In wisdom you have made them all.... You hide your face, they are dismayed; you take back your spirit, they die, returning to the dust from which they came. You send forth your spirit, they are created; and you renew the face of the earth" (Ps 104:24, 29–30). God's breath makes way for his wisdom: "his almighty wisdom penetrates all things: 'unique, manifold, subtle, active, incisive, unsullied, lucid, invulnerable ... unperturbed, almighty, all-surveying, penetrating all intelligent, pure and most subtle spirits' (Wis 7:22–23)."[78] God's presence is both the origin and destination of all creation.[79] His presence is the most significant for man, for only man

---

76. Ibid., 290.

77. Ibid., 237.

78. Ibid., 244.

79. Cessario, *Introduction to Moral Theology*, 3, 7, 9; see also Romanus Cessario, OP, "What the Angels See at Twilight," *Communio* 26:3 (Fall 1999), 587.

has the capacity to relate to God in and through conscience. The *exitus-reditus* demonstrates that God is present as none other is present. Even those we have loved for many years are not, and cannot be, present in the unique way God is present—though they may participate in the way that God is present to us.

The *exitus-reditus* explains how a Trinitarian structure informs the created world. Love is always in motion. The unique quality of God's love, *agape*, brings forth a twofold movement in creation: a continuous *exitus* in creating (*catabasis*) and at the same time a *reditus* (*anabasis*) in the same creating. God creates through a pouring forth of love through the Word. John Paul notes that "God is *agape*, that is, the gratuitous and total gift of self which Christ proved to us, especially by his death on the Cross."[80] God's seeking for man has one purpose. He seeks for us in order to lead us, and bring us back to his house, "the unfathomable region of the Trinity."[81] *Agape* is "the climax of the action of the divine agape in seeking for man to lead him into the realm of the Trinity."[82]

The *exitus-reditus* also establishes the twofold movement of revelation: God's descent to man and man's ascent to God. Man's ascent begins with his desire for God, who has first reached out for man. Man's ascent "consists in his training by the Word, who accustoms him with God's ways as the Word is accustomed with man's" through the Incarnation.[83] The human person was created by God, for God. All of history is thus the history of this twofold movement and is the plan of salvation.

The teaching on creation does not fall into undifferentiated emanationism or pantheism that the *exitus-reditus* model could suggest. Instead, the schema postulates a going out from and a going back to God, who is the cause of creation, not part of it. The teaching on creation gives us a correct understanding of God's agency in the world: God is both transcendent and immanent to his creation. His transcendence, however, does not prevent him from being in relationship with us. Nor does his relationship entail a blurring with or absorption by the creature. The

---

80. John Paul II, *The Trinity's Embrace*, 183; see also 308–309.
81. Daniélou, *Christ and Us* (New York: Sheed & Ward, 1961), 46.
82. Ibid., 146.
83. Ibid., 96.

created world truly expresses the meaning of God's truth without exhausting it. The human being is set between God as origin and goal.

The preamble of truths concerning creation is drawn from the Genesis accounts and based upon the teachings of John Paul in his *Catechesis on the Creed*. The correct understanding of myth and the ensemble of *bara'*, *ex nihilo*, *dabar*, and *exitus-reditus* form a springboard from which to better internalize his theology of the body and to understand the identity of the human person.

CHAPTER FOUR

The Theology of the Body and the Two Creation Accounts

As a priest and bishop Karol Wojtyla regularly escaped from the Communist regime into the mountains of Poland. Once there, he and a rotating base of 200 married couples kayaked, hiked, and talked.[1] They did not plan any diplomatic intervention or military coup to counter the regime. Instead, they resisted and opposed the occupying power by talking about the true nature of the identity of the human person and the authentic meaning of marriage. The mountains gave them the freedom to converse about these truths.

Some thirty years later, Wojtyla, as Pope John Paul II, conversed with a worldwide audience. He gave a series of lectures not in the countryside but at the Vatican in Rome, almost every Wednesday from 1979 to 1984.[2] The occupying powers this time were secularization, materialism, and the unbridled pursuit of pleasure. His plan of attack was the same: He taught the "theology of the body" to describe the identity of the human person and of marriage. This teaching is badly needed because the three revolutions have badly battered the institution of marriage.

As a result, false ideas abound for persons entering marriage today. The modern focus on consumerism translates into: "The more I get the

---

1. John Paul II, *Crossing the Threshold of Hope*, 122.
2. John Paul II, *Man and Woman He Created Them*, 137.

happier I'll be." The concentration on materialism and usefulness translates into "I am what I own." Materialism holds that the identity of a person is the product of "economic conditions."[3] The emphasis on feeling good translates into "If it feels good do it." These ideas infect marriage and the sense of the human person. Couples begin to "run their marriages" as a business rather than a bond of love. But Genesis gives us a different picture.

The Pope chooses to begin his teaching from three conjoined perspectives. The theology of the body is at once christological, scriptural, and anthropological. The teaching begins with the words of Christ in Scripture and is about the human person.

John Paul starts with the words of Jesus in the nineteenth chapter of Saint Matthew's Gospel. The Pharisees meet Jesus and they ask him,

> "Is it lawful for a man to divorce his wife for any reason?" And he answered them, "Have you not read that from the beginning *the Creator created them male and female*, and said, 'For this reason a man will leave his father and mother and unite with his wife, and the two will be one flesh'? So it is that they are no longer two, but one flesh. Therefore, what God has joined let man not separate." They objected, "Why then did Moses order to give her a certificate of divorce and send her away?" Jesus answered, "Because of the hardness of your heart Moses allowed you to divorce your wives, *but from the beginning it was not so*." (Mt 19:3–8, emphasis in *Man and Woman He Created Them*)

In asking Jesus a question about divorce, the Pharisees are not interested in a legal opinion, but in trapping Jesus. If he says, "Yes, follow the law of Moses and permit divorce," then the Pharisees can say he is not serious about the love he is talking about. If he says, "No, divorce is not permitted," then they can claim they have evidence that Jesus departs from the law of Moses.

John Paul points out that "Christ does not accept the discussion on the level on which his interlocuters try to introduce it; in a sense, he does not approve the dimension they tried to give the problem."[4] The Pharisees present an ethical question to Jesus, but he simply will not

---

3. Benedict XVI, *Spe Salvi*, no. 21.

4. John Paul II, *Man and Woman He Created Them*, 132. See also 219.

accept it the way they word it. He does not give a yes or no response. He says that to adequately answer an ethical question about man's behavior, one must examine the anthropological dimension and see who man is. One cannot simply go back to Moses. One must return to "the beginning."

A. "The Beginning"

Following the direction of Jesus, John Paul goes back to "the beginning."[5] The beginning is the moment of man's creation. If we want to know what man should do, we have to go back to the meaning for which man was created. Jesus refers to "the beginning" twice. John Paul notes that Jesus wants the Pharisees to turn to the "mystery of creation," to "man was formed precisely as 'male and female,'" in order to understand correctly the normative meaning of the words of Genesis."[6] It is as if Jesus is addressing every ethical question that could ever be asked. Contemporary responses to ethical questions such as human embryonic stem-cell research, same-sex marriage, and euthanasia often consider a limited or narrow perspective. A situation, a set of rights, legal precedent, or custom are simply not enough to fully grasp the dignity of humans. Each question faced about human behavior has to go back to probe the identity of the human person.[7]

The response of Jesus refers to both creation accounts of Genesis. Jesus says, "From the beginning the Creator made them male and female." This is a reference to the first account of creation (Gen 1:27). Jesus then adds a verse from the second account: "For this reason a man shall leave his father and mother and cling to his wife, and the two will be one flesh" (Gen 2:24). Jesus thus invests Genesis with his own authority.[8] John Paul frequently repeats that the two accounts of creation in

---

5. "From this reply on the part of Christ, John Paul looks back with the authoritative light of Christ to the beginning, to the moment of creation, before sin came into the world" (Schmitz, *At the Center of the Human Drama*, 92).

6. John Paul II, *Man and Woman He Created Them*, 133. (Cf. Hans Urs von Balthasar, *The Glory of the Lord: A Theological Aesthetics VII, Theology: The New Covenant* [San Francisco: Ignatius Press, 1989], 119.)

7. John Paul II, *Man and Woman He Created Them*, 133.

8. Ibid., 132.

Genesis must be read side by side in order to adequately understand the identity of the human person. In fact, "the two accounts complement each other, each shedding somewhat different light upon our mysterious origin."[9]

B. Original Innocence

The first part of the theology of the body describes the identity of the human person in the state of original innocence. John Paul is describing the *status naturae integrae*, or state of integral nature. This state is also called the state of original innocence or the prelapsarian state.[10] John Paul also refers to this state as "man's theological pre-history."[11] Human nature as we experience it today is wounded by original sin, but not destroyed by this wound.

We can dimly reason back to approximate what the dimensions of original innocence were. This "primordial time is inaccessible, yet the second time is rooted in ... this first, inaccessible time."[12] Revelation assists us with this task.[13] It is difficult for the reader to grasp fully the notions John Paul presents. All persons except Jesus and Mary are born into the *status naturae lapsae*, or state of fallen nature, also known as postlapsarian. John Paul refers to this state as the time of "historical man."[14] In our fallen state, it is very difficult to look back into the state of unfallen nature or original innocence and discern what that was like. The Swiss theologian Hans Urs von Balthasar notes: "Because man's primitive state [original innocence] was a simple one in which those characteristics had not yet been differentiated (rich-poor, free-obedient, fruitful-virginal) that would later split it into a multiplicity of states, it resists every attempt to reconstruct it clearly."[15]

In the state of fallen nature, man can only look abstractly at best and encounter those times in a dreamlike partial remembrance because he

---

9. Schmitz, *At the Center of the Human Drama*, 93.

10. John Paul II, *Man and Woman He Created Them*, 141.

11. Ibid., 143.

12. Earl C. Muller, SJ, "The Nuptial Meaning of the Body," *John Paul II on the Body: Human, Eucharistic, Ecclesial* (Philadelphia: Saint Joseph's University Press, 2007), 88.

13. Schmitz, *At the Center of the Human Drama*, 99.

14. John Paul II, *Man and Woman He Created Them*, 143.

15. Balthasar, *The Christian State of Life*, 18.

always has the effects of original sin that inject some measure of selfishness. Though man has lost his original innocence, John Paul writes, the answer of Jesus is "decisive and clear": The "normative conclusions" of original innocence regarding man's identity and dignity are still in force and must be considered essential in the discernment and evaluation of man's ethical behavior.[16] Though fallen from original innocence man is still "rooted" in his theological prehistory.[17] It is difficult to imagine a state, a time of existence that was only "the original synthesis of love."[18] We still detect, in the dreamlike fog of some distant memory, the momentum of original energy, like some long ago afterburn that proceeded from the high stature of the original innocence for which each of us was meant. More often, we directly experience, through the hard reality of suffering and pain, that we have fallen from that original paradise through sin and its effects. The interpretative key for the first part of the theology of the body is the contrast "between God's original plan of creation and the present situation of fallen humanity and sin."[19] The roots of our existence "plunge well beyond the history that is fixed in our memories."[20]

1. The First Account of Creation

John Paul proceeds to examine the first account of the creation of man in Genesis. This account presents the six-day cycle of creation, with God resting on the seventh day. On the first five days God creates parts of the visible cosmos through a direct divine command: "Let there be..." (Gen 1:3, 6, 9, 14, 20, 24). At the end of the third, fourth, fifth, and sixth days God sees that what he created "was good" (Gen 1:10, 12, 18, 21, 25, 31). The volley between the numbering of the days, to God's command, to the daily affirmation "it was good" infuses the account with a crisp, familiar staccatolike rhythm and structure.

---

16. John Paul II, *Man and Woman He Created Them*, 141–142.

17. Ibid., 143.

18. Balthasar, *The Christian State of Life*, 18.

19. William S. Kurz, SJ, "The Scriptural Foundations of *The Theology of the Body*," *John Paul II on the Body: Human, Eucharistic, Ecclesial* (Philadelphia: Saint Joseph's University Press, 2007), 37.

20. Bachelard, *The Poetics of Space*, 33.

The first account is actually the more recent of the two accounts.[21] One of the predominant features of this account is that it begins to formulate the "essential truths about man" created as "the image of God."[22]

a. The Creative Pause of God

In the first account of the creation, the world comes to be through a series of God's commands: "Let there be light, let there be a dome, let there be creeping things, let there be a light in the heavens…" and so on. God creates the world immediately through a direct utterance. Each day God speaks and it is made. He speaks, and it happens! Except for the creation of man. Except for the sixth day.

On the sixth day all the commands stop. They are checked at the door. God becomes almost reflective and meditative: "Let us make man in our own image and after our likeness. Let him have dominion over the birds of the air and the fish of the sea. And so God created man in his own image, in the image of God he created him, male and female he created them" (Gen 1:26–27). It is as if God is putting his hand to his chin, considering the creation of a being like himself. John Paul says that prior to the creation of man God withdraws into himself in a moment of creative pause:

> In the cycle of the seven days of creation, a precise step-by-step progression is evident; man, by contrast, is not created according to a natural succession, but the Creator seems to halt before calling him into existence, as if he entered back into himself to make a decision, "Let us make man in our image, in our likeness." (Gen 1:27)[23]

John Paul repeats similar sentiments in his *Letter to Families*:

> [B]efore creating man, the Creator withdraws as it were into himself in order to seek the pattern and inspiration in the mystery of his being, which is already disclosed here as the divine "we." From this mystery the human being comes forth by an act of creation.[24]

---

21. John Paul II, *Man and Woman He Created Them*, 134.
22. Ibid.
23. Ibid., 135.
24. John Paul II, *Letter to Families*, no. 6.

Kenneth Schmitz points out the significance of the "pause" of God: "[M]an's creation is announced with a certain fanfare that is absent from the creation of other creatures. It is as though God had stopped to deliberate before undertaking the risk of creating this being who is to be like him in a way no other creature is."[25] God emphasizes the difference between man and the rest of creation in the moment of the creation. The world arises from a command, but man comes into being after an intimate consultation in *communio*.

b. The Imago Dei

When Saint Jerome translated Genesis 1:27 from the Hebrew into the Vulgate, that is, the Latin translation of the Scriptures, he translated the phrase "image of God" as *imago Dei*.[26] This Latin phrase has come to denote the classical notion of human identity that sets human persons apart from the rest of the visible world, and thus serves as the basis of their particular dignity. The *imago Dei* is the basis of the personal, inherent, and inviolable dignity of every human person. John Paul teaches that "unconditional respect" is due to "the insistent demands of the personal dignity of every man."[27] The Holy Father points out that the Sacred Congregation for Education regards development of the theology of the *imago Dei* as a task within moral theology: "moral theology will acquire a deep spiritual dimension in response to the need to develop fully the *imago Dei* present in man."[28]

According to Cardinal Avery Dulles, the concept of *imago Dei* is central to the Pope's anthropology, which in turn is crucial for his thought on culture: "Behind all of the Pope's thinking about culture stands the theological anthropology that underlies the Pastoral Constitution *Gaudium et Spes*, and is amplified in works of John Paul II's catechesis on the Book of Genesis. Central to this teaching is the idea

---

25. Schmitz, *At the Center of the Human Drama*, 95.

26. See also Sirach 17:1–14 and Wisdom 2:23.

27. John Paul II, *Veritatis Splendor*, 90; cf. "The biblical text [of the *imago Dei*] is concerned to emphasize how the sacredness of life has its foundation in God and in his creative activity. 'For God made man in his own image' (Gen 9:6)" (John Paul II, *Evangelium Vitae*, 39).

28. John Paul II, *Veritatis Splendor*, 111.

that every human person is created in the image of God (GS 12) and is therefore endowed with inalienable freedom and personal dignity."[29]

Male and female are created together on the sixth day in the crisp and concise style of the first account of creation. These verses, to which Jesus refers, have yielded a series of truths about the identity of the human person. John Paul points out that the explicit mention of the *imago Dei* is a major contribution of this first account. While man is created in the midst of the visible world, his identity cannot be reduced to the visible world.[30] Jean Corbon states, "For we are a whole, a unique, disconcerting, polymorphous whole which cannot be reduced to any one of its component parts."[31] Man's likeness is to God, not to the world. Man "is not just another part of the organic creation but has a vocational dimension inscribed into his being which is intrinsically tied to the nature of God."[32] The Pharisees must consider these truths as they examine the legitimacy of divorce.

c. Classical Theology and the Imago Dei

The early Fathers of the Church and the Scholastics gave considerable thought to what comprises human dignity. They asked, "What constitutes the image of God in the human person?" Man and animal share certain characteristics: Each has a somatic structure, moves about, relies on continual nourishment, reproduces, and has instincts. There are various categories of existence and life in the visible world, most generally, mineral, vegetable, animal, and human. Each possesses some of the qualities of the former, but each dramatically transcends the former as well.[33]

Saint Augustine looked for that in the human person which corresponds to the nature of God. The doctrine of the Trinity attests that

---

29. Dulles, *The Splendor of Faith*, 118.

30. John Paul II, *Man and Woman He Created Them*, 135.

31. Jean Corbon, *Path to Freedom: Christian Experiences and the Bible* (New York: Sheed & Ward, 1969), 4.

32. Joseph C. Atkinson, "Nuptiality as a Paradigmatic Structure of Biblical Revelation," *Dialoghi sul mistero nuziale*, eds. G. Marengo and B. Ognibeni (Rome: Pontifica Università Lateranense, 2003), 21.

33. This type of classification is known as a Porphyrean Tree. William J. O'Malley, SJ, *Building Your Own Conscience* (Allen, Texas: Tabor Publishing, 1992), 20–21.

there are three persons in one God. Augustine sees three powers within man's rational capacity: memory, understanding, and will. Yet these three powers are in the one substance of the mind. Augustine saw in this the image of the Trinity in man.[34] Saint Leo the Great and Saint Thomas Aquinas inherit and affirm the teaching of Augustine that the image of God in the human persons resides in the rational capacity.[35]

Classical theology teaches that man is the image and likeness of God in the capacity to know and to love. Hans Urs von Balthasar notes: "For a long time people ... sought man's image-character in what raises him above the animals: self-consciousness, reason, free will, personality, responsibility and then in his dominant position in the cosmos, which is explicitly highlighted (Gen 1:28)."[36]

He continues: "'Image of God' remains, therefore, an attribute of man: He is created different from the other beings and is placed in a particular 'relation' to God, just as he is, that is, as a whole, living body-soul being."[37]

Balthasar notes that the teaching on the human person created in the image of God was given little attention in twentieth century theology: "It must be said, however, that this topic, which was central in the patristic period and still received adequate attention in Scholasticism, scarcely plays any part in works of the more modern dogmatic theologians ... "[38] In contrast, the Second Vatican Council and the teaching of Pope John Paul II integrate the *imago Dei* as a central teaching. The International Theological Commission notes:

> Especially since Vatican Council II, the doctrine of the *imago Dei* has begun to enjoy a greater prominence in magisterial teaching and theological research. Previously, various factors had led to the neglect of the theology of the *imago Dei* among some modern Western philosophers and theologians.[39]

---

34. Augustine, *De Trinitate*, 6:22; 14:3–4.

35. Thomas Aquinas, *Summa Theologiae* Ia q. 35, a. 2 ad. 3, and q. 93, a. 1 ad. 2; Leo the Great, *Sermons*, no. 12:1 (PL 54, 168; Nicene and Post-Nicene Fathers, 12, 121).

36. Balthasar, *Theo-Drama II*, 318.

37. Ibid., 320.

38. Ibid., 317.

39. International Theological Commission, "Communion and Stewardship: Human Persons Created in the Image of God," *Origins* 34:15 (September 23, 2004), 235.

d. Capax Dei

John Paul's teaching on the creation of the human person reveals that man exists from the first moment in dynamic relation to God. The sequence of *bara'*, *ex nihilo*, and *dabar*, within the *exitus-reditus* schema, reveals that the human person is created in the image of God with a capacity to know and to love in a relationship of communion. John Paul's detailed treatment of the concepts behind the creation of man reveals that God is not simply a divine being who fluctuates in transcendent distance. Rather, God's transcendence has immediate implications for intimacy with the human person.

In creating man, God has opened himself up to man for relation: "If God opens himself to man in his Spirit, man, on the other hand, is created as a subject capable of accepting the divine self-communication. As the tradition of Christian thought maintains, man is *capax Dei*: capable of knowing God and of receiving the gift he makes of himself."[40] Man is capable of God; that is, of all that man can do and achieve within the visible world, there is one relation that fulfills man like none other. The coordinates of this relation are deep within man, emerging from his origin, and calling him to fulfillment in God alone.

2. The Second Account of Creation

When Jesus referred to "the beginning" (Mt 19:4, 8) he also referred to the second account of creation (Gen 2:4–25) known as the Yahwist account.[41] John Paul notes that this account has a "different character" from the crisp, cyclic, and explicit tone of the first account.[42] In contrast, the second account "gives a more pictorial account of human creation."[43] It proceeds almost in slow motion as it describes the inner dimensions of man's consciousness.[44] John Paul considers the text at length, as Kenneth Schmitz notes: "[T]he pope—as much poet and dramatist as he is theo-

---

40. John Paul II, *The Trinity's Embrace*, 105.
41. John Paul II, *Man and Woman He Created Them*, 137.
42. Ibid.
43. Kurz, "The Scriptural Foundations of *The Theology of the Body*," 41.
44. John Paul II, *Man and Woman He Created Them*, 138. (Cf. Hans Urs von Balthasar, *Theo-Drama V: The Last Act* [San Francisco: Ignatius Press, 1998], 139, 146.)

logian and philosopher—is attracted to [the second account] precisely because of its strongly anthropological ... character."[45]

John Paul bases much of his teaching on a mysterious interval between the creation of man and that of woman (Gen 2:7; 2:22).[46] This interval forms the basis for a series of meanings, or original experiences, about the internal identity of the human person and the relation of man to woman.[47] John Paul's reference to "original experiences" has a particular meaning. He does not mean "original" merely in the sense of first. Rather, he is moving to "reconstruct the constitutive elements of man's original experience."[48] The popular meaning of "original" is first in a series, or a privileged and rare beginning whose originality then fades. John Paul uses the term more in the sense of original versus artificial.[49] "Original" seeks to show not just what comes first in time, but more so how human nature is grounded in an experience that each person undergoes. The quality of that experience never diminishes no matter how much is known about it. These elements are not time-bound: "They are always at the root of every human experience" and, as such, are "essential experiences" for every person regardless of his or her condition.[50] The primordial experiences, while described on the basis of biblical revelation, are also accessible to right reason. Such reflection shows why man is different from the entire visible world and created *imago Dei*, in the image of God.

a. Original Solitude

The first original experience is original solitude.[51] The popular notion of solitude is a calm, silent retreat at a monastery on a hill. This is not the solitude to which John Paul refers. Original solitude is John Paul's term for the internal, spiritual identity of the human person. As

---

45. Schmitz, *At the Center of the Human Drama*, 93.
46. John Paul II, *Man and Woman He Created Them*, 139.
47. Ibid., 147.
48. Ibid., 169.
49. Hans Urs von Balthasar, *Theo-Drama IV: In the Action* (San Francisco: Ignatius Press, 1994), 16.
50. John Paul II, *Man and Woman He Created Them*, 170.
51. Ibid., 146ff.

such, original solitude has two meanings.[52] The first derives from the very humanity of the person. The second meaning is based on the first meaning and is the search outside the self to be in relation[53] that characterizes this humanity.[54]

1) The First Meaning of Original Solitude

John Paul bases the meaning of original solitude on the Genesis text: "It is not good for the man to be alone; I want to make him a help similar to himself" (Gen 2:18). The "aloneness" of man is not in the first instance a feeling of depression. The solitude describes man in his very humanity, in the very structure of his being.[55] The "aloneness" of his solitude is man in the very nature of his personhood, his identity. It is not good for man to be isolated in his identity. The identity of man is not complete so long as he is only one. Man's "aloneness" is revealed in his circumstances. He has been created and placed in the garden. There, he has a series of "tasks" or a specific "test" before God and himself.[56] The test or series of tasks consists of tilling the soil (Gen 2:5), naming the animals (Gen 2:19),[57] and respecting God's command regarding the tree (Gen 2:17). The first aspect of how man is in the image of God is about to emerge.[58]

2) Consciousness

The experience of his solitude brings forth man's capacity to experience consciousness, and on this basis the "first self-definition" of man emerges. Several things take place as man tills the soil. Exteriorly, he digs furrows and rows and prepares the ground. Interiorly, he experiences something of his own *internal identity*. Man has heard the command to till the soil. When he begins to do so, he *realizes* that he is tilling soil. He is *conscious* of himself tilling the soil. He is *conscious of himself being*

---

52. Ibid., 147.
53. Ibid., 149.
54. Ibid., 162.
55. Ibid., 151.
56. Ibid., 148.
57. Ibid., 152.
58. Ibid., 151.

conscious of the command to till the soil and then carrying it out. This otherwise seemingly incidental relay is an original experience man has of his identity. Man "can realize his own existence only by relating to and communicating with other beings," in this case the otherness of the visible world.[59] The fact that man "distinguishes himself" as a being of consciousness is a hallmark of John Paul's philosophy.[60] Balthasar notes a point of philosophical reflection at work in such experiences:

> When I grasp some finite thing that is true or good, this act is accompanied by a self-awareness containing something inseparably twofold: the consciousness of being present to myself ... Present to myself in this way, I know not only that I exist but in the same knowledge I am open to all being since, in this consciousness that I *am*, I have touched the farthest possible horizon ... a light that discloses the first principles of all being ... unveiled in my own presence to myself.[61]

Man's presence to himself is one in which he is "aware" of his aloneness.[62] Jean Corbon explains that man is "interior to his own reflection on himself."[63] This consciousness and self-awareness is not merely a cerebral relay among neurons, however. How does man till the soil? He does so in and through his body. Man's bodily activity makes him aware of his own consciousness as he carries out God's command. Something is revealed to man in this awareness. No other being is carrying around a rake. Only man. Because man only becomes aware of this through his body, the meaning of his body is revealed. His body can engage in an activity that the bodies of animals do not. He is different from the rest of the visible world. Adam experiences his existence in and through his body.[64] He tills the soil and is self-aware that his body has a meaning in this human activity: His awareness of the meaning of his body in this activity reveals a structure to his consciousness.[65] The consciousness of which John Paul speaks is not a higher consciousness in a New Age

---

59. Woznicki, *A Christian Humanism*, 6–7. (Cf. Hans Urs von Balthasar, *Theo-Drama V: The Last Act* [San Francisco: Ignatius Press, 1994], 99–100.)

60. John Paul II, *Man and Woman He Created Them*, 150.

61. Balthasar, *Theo-Drama II*, 207–208.

62. John Paul II, *Man and Woman He Created Them*, 152.

63. Corbon, *Path to Freedom*, 6.

64. John Paul II, *Man and Woman He Created Them*, 154.

65. Ibid., 153.

sense. The consciousness of man is not a "simple 'self-consciousness,'" but one in which priority is given to man as a "substantial entity."[66]

3) Self-awareness

The meaning of original solitude is founded on man's experience of existence and being. This experience conveys something to him: He has self-awareness within this visible world. As he turns to name the animals (Gen 2:19) this internal process repeats itself. He is aware that "in naming the animals, [he] is truly sharing in God's creativity."[67] In tilling the soil and naming the animals, man is acting. For Wojtyla, "[Action] reveals the person, and we look at the person through his action ... Action gives us the best insight into the inherent essence of the person and allows us to understand the person most fully."[68] Man's consciousness can "educe" something of his identity "from the experience of action."[69]

Man is aware of the meaning of his body. In this he is aware of his fundamental difference from the animals. He identifies and names them on the basis of their bodies. "A human person ... establishes contact with all other entities precisely through the inner self...."[70] He knows he is different from them. While both man and animals have a body, man's body reveals a truth to him: he is not like the animals. Something about his body conveys to his self-awareness that he transcends the animals that live merely by instinct. He deduces through an intuition the meaning of his body, realizing that it is different from all the bodies of the animals. Only his body expresses a person.[71]

John Paul points out:

> The first "man" carries out the first and fundamental act of knowledge of the world. At the same time this act enables him to know and distinguish himself, "man," from all other creatures, and above all from

---

66. Woznicki, *A Christian Humanism*, 10.

67. Tugwell, *The Beatitudes*, 46.

68. Karol Wojtyla, *The Acting Person*, trans. Andrzej Potocki; ed. Anna-Teresa Tymieniecka. *Analecta Husserliana* 10 (New York: Reidel, 1979), 11.

69. John McNerney, *Footbridge Towards the Other: An Introduction to the Philosophy and Poetry of John Paul II* (New York: T & T Clark, 2003), 2.

70. Karol Wojtyla, *Love and Responsibility*, 23.

71. John Paul II, *Man and Woman He Created Them*, 153–154.

those which as "living beings"—endowed with vegetative and sensitive life—show proportionally the greatest similarity with him, "with man," who is also endowed with vegetative and sensitive life.[72]

John Paul interprets the tilling of the soil and the naming of the animals as the moments that reveal to man the solitude of which Genesis 2:18 speaks: "It is not good for man to be alone ... " The aloneness conveys that man is a being who possesses consciousness and self-knowledge through self-awareness. In the first meaning of original solitude, man experiences his acts as his own through "the reflexive function of consciousness. It is a natural and immediate turning back upon the subject so as to make the subject of the mirrored acts aware that it is the subject and that these acts are its own."[73] John Paul points out that this development corresponds to the first account of Genesis: "have dominion ..." (Gen 1:28).[74] The same sentiment is expressed by the psalmist: "Yet you have made him little less than a god; with glory and honor you crowned him, gave him power over the works of your hand, put all things under his feet" (Ps 8:5–6).

4) Self-determination

John Paul next turns his attention to the third task or test: the command regarding the tree. "The LORD God gave man this order: 'You are free to eat from any of the trees of the garden except the tree of knowledge of good and bad. From that tree you shall not eat; the moment you eat from it you are surely doomed to die'" (Gen 2:16–17). As with the tilling of the soil and the naming of the animals, the command regarding the tree will reveal the features of the first meaning of original solitude, the internal spiritual identity of the human person.

This command brings Adam to repeat his experience of consciousness, self-awareness, and self-knowledge. He knows that the tree is a boundary. If he moves to the tree and relates to it with his body, that is,

---

72. General audience, December 6, 1978, in *Talks of John Paul II*, 401.

73. Simpson, *On Karol Wojtyla*, 24–25. John McNerney points out, "It is of course Wojtyla's philosophical belief that we can reach the ultimate truth about the human person if we pause and reflect upon human action" (McNerney, *Footbridge Towards the Other*, 5).

74. John Paul II, *Man and Woman He Created Them*, 148.

eats from it, he will undergo a new experience, an experience he has yet to have: death. He does not know what it is "to die."[75] He has never done that. But he is conscious and aware that an action in regard to this tree can result in a new experience. He can change the state he exists in: Man has the power of "self-determination."[76] A further meaning of the body is thus revealed in relating to that tree within the bounds set by God. As Adam carries out the tasks God has given him he learns not only about his own identity, but also that the task "given to man by God is a conditional superintendence and use of nature in accordance with the original intention of God...."[77]

5) On the Basis of the Body

Adam realizes his internal, spiritual identity on the basis of his body: He is a being who has the capacity for consciousness and for self-knowledge through self-awareness and self-determination.[78] Karol Wojtyla noted that the philosopher can "pause in the process of reduction, which leads us in the direction of understanding the human being in the world (a *cosmological* type of understanding), in order to understand the human being inwardly. This latter type of understanding may be called *personalistic.*"[79] John Paul has introduced to theologians a new consideration of the meaning of the body: "The body expresses the person." Donald Asci notes, "As a constitutive element of the person, the structure or design of the body tells us something about the nature of personhood."[80] Asci explains, "The human body differs from other bodies because, rather than being something entirely exterior, 'the human body is the exteriorization of something that is essentially interior.'"[81] Corbon also accents the importance of the body in the identity of man: "[O]ur own bodies ...

---

75. Ibid., 155.

76. Ibid., 151.

77. Schmitz, *At the Center of the Human Drama*, 96.

78. John Paul II, *Man and Woman He Created Them*, 149.

79. Karol Wojtyla, "Subjectivity and the Irreducible in the Human Being" in *Person and Community: Selected Essays (Catholic Thought from Lublin)*, trans. Theresa Sandok, OSM, (New York: Peter Lane, 1994), 213.

80. Donald P. Asci, *The Conjugal Act as a Personal Act: A Study of the Catholic Concept of the Conjugal Act in the Light of Christian Anthropology* (San Francisco: Ignatius Press, 2002), 132.

81. Ramon Lucas Lucas, *L'uomo spirito incarnate* (Torino, Italy: Paoline, 1993).

are our most intimate point of contact with the cosmos.... [O]ur body also has a meaning all its own."[82] Corbon notes that man can discern this meaning inherent in the body.[83]

Man has the capacity to experience his interior life, an attribute proper to him; he can manifest this self-reflection in his choices.[84] In other words, the choices man makes reflects who he is as a person. Original solitude begins to describe the manner in which the human person "is distinguished from even the most advanced animals by a specific inner self, an inner life, characteristic only of persons."[85] Wojtyla's philosophy is that man is "a dynamic subject, which is constituted *of* human acts, through which an individual man manifests his own inner-self."[86] This is the first meaning of original solitude, how man is "alone" through his own humanity.[87] Kenneth Schmitz notes:

> The original solitude certainly marks man off from the rest of creation: it registers a radical difference between him and the other visible creatures, and seals his distinctive nature. For *'adam* alone of all visible creatures has been created in the image and likeness of God ... John Paul remarks that the root of self-knowledge is to be found here in this solitary awareness, which senses both the privilege of the solitude that sets man apart from other creatures, and the incompleteness that attends *'adam* as he faces the rest of the visible creation.[88]

No other being engages the internal sequence that marks the identity of man. John Paul points out that the "'invisible' determines man more than the 'visible.'"[89]

6) Subjectivity

When John Paul speaks of a subjective nature he is not referring to subjectivism. Subjectivism is the assertion that the individual is autono-

---

82. Corbon, *Path to Freedom*, 45.
83. Ibid.
84. Wojtyla, *Love and Responsibility*, 23, 24.
85. Ibid., 22.
86. Woznicki, *A Christian Humanism*, 11.
87. John Paul II, *Man and Woman He Created Them*, 151.
88. Schmitz, *At the Center of the Human Drama*, 100. (Cf. Balthasar, *Theo-Drama IV*, 473; Hans Urs von Balthasar, *Theo-Logic I: Truth of the World* [San Francisco: Ignatius Press, 2001], 37, 44; and Hans Urs von Balthasar, *Theo-Logic II: Truth of God* [San Francisco: Ignatius Press, 2004], 36.)
89. John Paul II, *Man and Woman He Created Them*, 155–156.

mous in his or her existence and hence may give each reality its own meaning as the individual decides. In subjectivism, existence is emptied of any normative meaning. John Paul traces subjectivism to Cartesian philosophy.[90] Subjectivism results from a philosophy that

> has made a separation between body and soul ... Consciousness then becomes the autonomous subject of acting and existence while the body, which is regulated by the determinism of biological laws, is relegated to the periphery. In this philosophy, person is identified with consciousness and is the subject of interior experience ... Such a view destroys the integrity of the human composite.[91]

John Paul's use of the term "subjectivity" is intended to show the objective depth in every man. Subjectivity differs from subjectivism. Subjectivity emphasizes the capacity of the person to grasp and internalize the objective meaning of existence, a meaning knowable by all. Karol Wojtyla's method reflects philosophical background and depth:

> "Consciousness allows us not only to have an inner view of our actions (immanent perception) and of their dynamic dependence on the ego, but also to *experience these actions as actions and as our own.*" Thus, consciousness enables man to experience the intimate relationship between himself and his acts, thereby enabling him to take responsibility for his own acts and to share in the moral quality of the act as its subject.[92]

Knowing himself and the objective meaning of his actions, man can take responsibility for his actions. The experience of the capacity for consciousness reminds the person of the beginning: "Consciousness rejuvenates everything, giving a quality of beginning to the most everyday actions."[93] For all of the wonder of his being, however, something yet eludes man. John Paul points out that man, in his paradise, still experiences a disappointment at this early stage: "How very significant is the

---

90. John Paul II, *Crossing the Threshold of Hope*, 51.

91. Mary Shivanandan, *Crossing the Threshold of Love: A New Vision of Marriage* (Washington, DC: The Catholic University of America Press, 1999), 47.

92. Wojtyla, *The Acting Person*, 42, emphasis in Asci, *The Conjugal Act as a Personal Act*, 317–318. See also Richard M. Hogan and John M. LeVoir, *Covenant of Love: Pope John Paul II on Sexuality, Marriage, and Family in the Modern World* (New York: Doubleday, 1985), 40: "Our consciousness not only allows us to determine ourselves, it is also the source of our self-knowledge ... This latter function of consciousness is the source of self-knowledge."

93. Bachelard, *The Poetics of Space*, 67.

dissatisfaction which marks man's life in Eden as long as his sole point of reference is the world of plants and animals (cf. Gen 2:20)."[94]

7) The Second Meaning of Original Solitude

Man has discovered the meaning of his identity on the basis of consciousness. He has come to self-knowledge through self-awareness and self-determination, all on the basis of the body. This discovery is not a static event in man's being. As the first meaning of original solitude is consolidating, man simultaneously discovers a second meaning and "finds himself from the first moment of his existence *before God* in search of his own being ... one could say ... 'identity.'"[95] All of the activities regarding tilling the soil, naming the animals, and obeying God's command regarding the tree take place in the dynamic momentum of a search. That search reveals who man is (a being who possesses consciousness, self-knowledge through self-awareness, and self-determination all revealed in and through the body), and who he is not: "It is not good for man to be alone, I shall make a helper fit for him" (Gen 2:18).

Of course, there is no evil in paradise, so what does "not good" mean? "Not good" means that man's identity is not yet complete: "but the man did not find a help similar to himself" (Gen 2:20). Schmitz points out:

> Something essential is missing; something more is still needed to round out and to complete the origin and nature of man ... [T]he person of *'adam* was not fulfilled in this solitude, though it had not yet become ... loneliness. The original solitude is not sufficient; man—that is to say, the human being—is not meant to be alone.[96]

The helper is not a helper to till the soil or to name the animals. The helper is the helper in terms of the man's very identity.[97] Man does not identify with the other living beings in an essential way. This nonidentification reveals that his search goes further than consciousness, self-awareness, self-knowledge, and self-determination. The body reveals meaning and identity and includes the search outside himself in openness to another in relation.[98]

---

94. John Paul II, *Evangelium Vitae*, 35.
95. John Paul II, *Man and Woman He Created Them*, 149.
96. Schmitz, *At the Center of the Human Drama*, 100–101.
97. John Paul II, *Man and Woman He Created Them*, 163.
98. Ibid., 149.

b. Original Unity

In discovering the identity of the human person as presented by the second account of creation, original solitude is a prelude to original unity.[99] Male and female were created at the same time in the first account of creation (Gen 1:27). In the second account, man is created prior to the woman (Gen 2:7). Recall that John Paul sees no contradiction between the two accounts. Both texts seek to explain the deeper content of the identity of the human person. The details differ, but the truth of the identity of the person is the same, and made even clearer by different features of the two accounts. John Paul notes that the mysterious interval between the creation of male and female in the second account actually begins to explain the *imago Dei* of the first account.[100]

The second original experience, original unity, reveals the meaning of the human person created always as either masculine or feminine.[101] Joseph Murphy notes: "John Paul [says] that male and female are two incarnations of the same solitude, two ways of being a body, of being human, two complementary dimensions of self-consciousness and self-determination. That is, femininity finds itself in the presence of masculinity and masculinity is confirmed through femininity."[102]

John Paul bases his description of original unity on the verse, "It is not good that the man should be alone; I want to make a help similar to himself" (Gen 2:18). The features of the identity of man as presented in original solitude are not enough to portray the deep meaning of man. Schmitz explains, "The original solitude is not sufficient—man, that is to say, the human being—is not meant to be alone."[103] When no being is discovered to be fit for man, "the LORD God caused torpor [or a state of unconsciousness] to fall upon the man, who fell asleep; then he took one of his ribs and closed the flesh again in its place. With the rib that the LORD God had taken from the man he formed a woman" (Gen 2:21–22).

---

99. Ibid., 156.

100. Ibid., 157.

101. Ibid., 156 ff.

102. Joseph Murphy, SJ, "Human Solidarity and the Church in the Thought of John Paul II" in *The Thought of Pope John Paul II*, ed. John M. McDermott, SJ (Rome: Editrice Pontificia Università Gregoriana, 1993), 132.

103. Schmitz, *At the Center of the Human Drama*, 101.

The sleep of Adam and the creation from the rib are central to the meaning of man's identity in original unity. The insufficiency of the animals demonstrates that man is not fulfilled by what is extrinsic to him. Rather, the solitude of man is to be fulfilled from within.[104]

1) The Sleep of Adam / Creation from the Rib

Adam's sleep is no ordinary nap. For John Paul, the sleep precedes the great action of God, as when Abraham fell into a sleep or trance before encountering God; as did Jacob, Saint Joseph, and the apostles.[105] The sleep is Adam's return to nonbeing, to the moment preceding his creation.[106] The sleep reveals that Eve is created by God alone. The sleep is an annihilation of Adam's conscious existence.[107] Saint Augustine referred to the sleep as a kind of visionary contemplation.[108] Balthasar likewise notes, "The LORD gives sleep to his own, the sleep of peaceful, 'abiding' love and contemplation."[109] As such the sleep of Adam enriches his existence: "The man retains a primacy while at the same time, at God's instigation, he steps down from it in a *kenosis*; this results in the God-given fulfillment whereby he recognizes himself in the gift of the 'other.'"[110] This gift brings something to man that nothing else in the visible world could afford: "It is through being overpowered in a 'deep sleep' and robbed of part of himself, near to his heart, that man is given fulfillment."[111]

Created from the rib, Eve shares the same humanity as Adam.[112] The creation of woman from the side of man shows again the manner in which man is the image of God:

---

104. Ibid.

105. John Paul II, *Man and Woman He Created Them*, 158, no. 12.

106. Ibid., 159.

107. Ibid.

108. Augustine, *On Genesis: Two Books on Genesis Against the Manichees*, trans. Roland J. Teske, SJ (Washington, DC: The Catholic University of America Press, 1991), 113.

109. Hans Urs von Balthasar, *Explorations in Theology II: Spouse of the Word* (San Francisco: Ignatius Press, 1991), 13.

110. Balthasar, *Theo-Drama II*, 373; Balthasar notes the sleep is a form of the gift of self (cf. Balthasar, *Theo-Drama IV*, 188).

111. Balthasar, *Theo-Drama II*, 373. See also, Jean Daniélou, *Advent* (New York: Sheed and Ward), 31.

112. John Paul II, *Man and Woman He Created Them*, 160.

The removal of the rib was for Adam an infinitely ennobling grace: the grace of being allowed to participate in the mystery of the Father's self-giving to the Son, by which the Father empties himself of his own Godhead in order to bestow it on the Son who is eternally of the same nature as he is. It was a wound of love that God inflicted on Adam in order to initiate him into the mystery, the lavish self-prodigality, of divine love.[113]

The creation of woman "from the side" highlights God's action: "I called to the LORD in my distress; he answered and freed me. The LORD is at my side, I do not fear ... The LORD is at my side as my helper ... " (Ps 118:5–7). All distress that man can encounter in life hearkens back to the original distress of not finding a helper in his humanity. The creation of woman from Adam's side shows that God is at the side of man, working and freeing him. This freedom casts out fear.

Upon awakening, Adam does something we have not yet seen him do. He speaks for the first time. He had seen the tremendous beauty of what God created. Yet none of this caused him to speak. Now, he exclaims, "This, at last, is bone of my bone and flesh of my flesh. She shall be called woman, because she has been taken from her man" (Gen 2:23). God has produced another being "who possesses that same mark of solitude."[114] Adam shows "joy and even exultation, for which he had no reason before, due to the lack of a being similar to himself."[115] Corbon declares, "[A] relationship with another human being is a new experience of creation."[116] Balthasar notes, "The highest point, therefore, that an eye is able to attain is to look into another eye that sees. Two clarities, two separatenesses sink into one another and coincide without being blended together."[117]

The joy of Adam is based on his recognition of one similar to himself. Adam recognizes her on the basis of her body. "The communal oneness of Adam and Eve was thus the oneness of Adam's flesh, which became by grace the source of the duality of male and female."[118] In naming her,

---

113. Balthasar, *The Christian State of Life*, 228.
114. Schmitz, *At the Center of the Human Drama*, 101.
115. John Paul II, *Man and Woman He Created Them*, 161.
116. Corbon, *Path to Freedom*, 52.
117. Balthasar, *Explorations in Theology II*, 475.
118. Balthasar, *The Christian State of Life*, 227.

he reveals something about himself: until now in the Genesis text he has been called the general "adam" or "man." Yet when he names her, "woman," he names himself "male."[119] This is a significant point, "In naming her, *'adam* himself assumes a new name: her presence 'matching him' is a revelation of who both of them are in relationship."[120] Her identity unlocks his, and vice versa. "[F]emininity in some way finds itself before masculinity, while masculinity confirms itself through femininity."[121] As Balthasar says, "[A]lthough potentially and unconsciously he bears the woman within him, he cannot give her to himself."[122] The meaning of her identity for his own fills his consciousness, self-awareness, self-knowledge, and self-determination, and vice versa.[123]

The previous dimensions of original solitude remain: man encounters woman, and woman encounters man in their consciousness. "A new reciprocity is born within humanity—it is the internal reciprocity of solitudes—and with this inner reciprocity, humanity now acquires its essential completeness."[124] Whereas before man was conscious and had self-knowledge through self-awareness and self-determination through the process of tilling, naming, and the stewardship regarding the tree, now the same cognitive capacities and features are used. Except this time those features are filled with a new content, a new consciousness, a new self-knowledge through self-awareness. The man and the woman are now conscious of each other. They have a self-knowledge through the awareness of the self as they each look upon the other. And they each possess a self-determination to act in a certain way with this other—the only one with whom they have a "shared unity."[125] This includes "the new consciousness of the meaning of one's body ... with a deep consciousness of human bodiliness and sexuality."[126] The cry of exultation

---

119. John Paul II, *Man and Woman He Created Them*, 139, 147.

120. Francis Martin, "The New Feminism: Biblical Foundations and Some Lines of Development," in *Women in Christ: Toward a New Feminism*, ed. Michele M. Schumacher (Grand Rapids, MI: Wm. B. Eerdmans, 2003), 148; see also Grabowski, *Sex and Virtue*, 99, no. 11.

121. John Paul II, *Man and Woman He Created Them*, 166.

122. Balthasar, *Theo-Drama II*, 373.

123. See John Paul II, *Man and Woman He Created Them*, 165.

124. Schmitz, *At the Center of the Human Drama*, 102.

125. Ibid.

126. John Paul II, *Man and Woman He Created Them*, 165.

(Gen 2:23) is a cry of identity. The consciousness and knowledge they have revealed in the cry of exultation is the observation that "the 'definitive' creation of man consists in the creation of the unity of two beings," the human person created male and female.[127]

2) The Openness

John Paul has been developing a sketch of the identity of the human person. He has analyzed at length the sequence of consciousness, self-awareness, self-knowledge, and self-determination. All of this shows how man was distinct from the animals and the created world. Then this prior analysis launches further into the identity of the human person as a search for the other who is different from myself—yet this difference is a call to unity. This concept is detailed in the analysis of the sleep and the creation of woman from the rib. All of this is background to a pre-dominant feature: This search reveals that man is distinguished from the rest of creation by his *openness* to another like himself, though different: There is a "difference of body, a difference in the way each—the man and the woman—holds their shared humanity."[128]

The meaning of the identity of the human person is revealed through a series of complex experiences. The human person is a being with the capacity for consciousness, in which self-knowledge comes through self-awareness and self-determination. All of that is revealed in and through the body. As illustrious as each feature is by itself or when combined with the others, it is still not enough. Together, these features reveal the most essential element of the identity of the human person: the capacity to find fulfillment only in and through relation to a being like himself. The fulfillment in this relation is the "help" of which the Creator spoke: "It is not good that the man should be alone; I want to make a help similar to himself" (Gen 2:18).

Man's difference from the rest of the creatures is experienced as openness to another like himself. John Paul emphasizes this dynamic: Man's *distinction from* all other beings primarily reveals his *openness to* another.[129] The Holy Father lingers over the nature of this openness: "This

---

127. Ibid., 161.

128. Schmitz, *At the Center of the Human Drama*, 103.

129. John Paul II, *Man and Woman He Created Them*, 162. (Cf. Balthasar, *Theo-Logic I*, 44.)

opening is no less decisive for man as a person, in fact, it is perhaps more decisive than the 'distinction' itself."[130] In fact, this openness is more crucial to the identity of man than all the features that have led to it, even his distinction from the rest of creation.[131]

Prior to his election as Pope Benedict XVI, Cardinal Joseph Ratzinger noted that the aloneness of Adam and the creation of woman from his side as he slept demonstrate two points. First, as one of "the great archetypal images the Bible gives us," this passage allows us to glimpse the common nature of man and woman.[132] Second, "the other point is their being turned toward each other. This is shown in the wound, which is present in all of us and which leads us to turn to each other."[133] Ratzinger emphasizes an interpretation similar to that of John Paul II. The human person possesses a nature with the central capacity to turn toward another. Ratzinger refers to this capacity as a "wound." This wound is not an effect of original sin. This wound is not a deficit or an evil, but a positive wound in the classical Latin sense of a *vulnerability*, or a true openness that allows for relation. This is not the vulnerability of the modern age that is more synonymous with porous passivity, but rather an ontological vulnerability that places relation at the very center of identity. The openness is fulfilled in "the discovery of an adequate relation 'to' the person, and thus as opening toward and waiting for a 'communion of persons.'"[134]

3) Communion of Persons

The term "communion of persons," or *communio personarum*, has a precise meaning for John Paul. The Holy Father greatly developed the meaning of *personarum* throughout his discussion of original solitude and original unity. *Communio* is part of being a person: *"It indicates precisely the 'help' that derives in some way from the very fact of existing as a person 'beside' a person."*[135] The "help" recapitulates all that has been said about

---

130. John Paul II, *Man and Woman He Created Them*, 162.

131. Ibid.

132. Joseph Ratzinger, *God and the World: A Conversation with Peter Seewald* (San Francisco: Ignatius Press, 2002), 80.

133. Ibid., 80.

134. John Paul II, *Man and Woman He Created Them*, 162.

135. Ibid.

the identity of the human person in original solitude and original unity and develops it. The help is "reciprocity in existence."[136] This help is not mere manual assistance. John Paul points out that "the woman must 'help' the man—and in his turn he must help her—first of all by the very fact of their 'being human persons' … [which] enables man and woman to discover their humanity ever anew and to confirm its whole meaning." This existing "beside a person" is directed toward "the unity of the two": "In the 'unity of the two,' man and woman are called from the beginning not only to exist 'side by side' or 'together,' but they are also called *to exist mutually 'one for the other.'*"[137]

As Archbishop of Krakow, Karol Wojtyla wrote *Sources of Renewal* to help implement the Second Vatican Council in the archdiocese. He noted, "The Latin word *communio* denotes a relationship between persons that is proper to them alone; and it indicates the kind of good that they do to one another, giving and receiving within that mutual relationship."[138] He noted that this union signifies more than community (*communitas*): it is a communion (*communio*).[139] In the Wednesday audiences John Paul carefully distinguished between community and *communion*: "One could also use the term 'community' here, if it were not so generic and did not have so many meanings."[140]

4) Rehabilitation of the *Imago Dei*

Classical theology has given considerable attention to the *imago Dei* as abiding in the intellectual capacities of man's rational soul. On the basis of this tradition of the "rational" *imago Dei*, John Paul develops the teaching regarding the relational *imago Dei*. He teaches that while the second account of creation does not explicitly mention the concept of "image of God" as does the first account, the second account helps us understand "the trinitarian concept of the 'image of God.'"[141] Francis

---

136. Ibid.

137. John Paul II, *Mulieris Dignitatem*, 7.

138. Wojtyla, *Sources of Renewal*, 61.

139. Ibid. Wojtyla develops this further: "*Communio*, which is essentially an *I-other* relationship inwardly maturing into an interpersonal *I-thou* relationship, should be clearly distinguished from *communitas*, which embraces a larger number of persons" (Karol Wojtyla, "Participation or Alienation?" in *Person and Community*, 204).

140. John Paul II, *Man and Woman He Created Them*, 163.

141. Ibid., 164.

Martin points out that the second account actually does testify to man being the image and likeness of God, though in poetic fashion:

> The text states three things: first that man is formed directly by God; second, that he is a mysterious unity of matter and breath; and third, that in common with other creatures he is a "soul alive" and yet achieves this status in a unique way: being endowed with the very breath of God. Thus the more humanistic tradition [of the second account] with which we are dealing here, rather than having recourse to the abstract notion of "image," portrays 'adam as endowed with the vital quality of God, his breath.[142]

The identity of man in the communion of persons "reveals that the complete and definitive 'creation' of man (subject first to the experience of original solitude) expresses itself in giving life to the 'communio person-arum' that man and woman form."[143] John Paul concentrates on this theme: "Man is the 'image of God' not only through his own humanity, but also through the communion of persons . . . he becomes an image of God not so much in the moment of solitude as in the moment of communion."[144] The Holy Father notes that the *Catechism of the Catholic Church* includes the teaching that the union of man and woman in marriage represents a particular manifestation of the *imago Dei*: "With the *Catechism of the Catholic Church* we can draw this conclusion: 'The divine image is present in every man. It shines forth in the communion of persons, in the likeness of the unity of the divine Persons among themselves' (no. 1702)."[145]

The theme of the union of man and woman as the image of God is a major theme within the Wednesday audiences on the theology of the body. "[M]an, in the mystery of creation, was 'the image of God,' in his personal 'I' as much as in his interpersonal relationship, namely, through the primordial communion of persons constituted by man and woman together."[146] John Paul refers to "the line of authentic development of

---

142. Martin, "The New Feminism," 146–147.
143. John Paul II, *Man and Woman He Created Them*, 163.
144. Ibid.
145. John Paul II, *The Trinity's Embrace*, 345–346.
146. John Paul II, *Man and Woman He Created Them*, 243; this is also developed in his pre-papal thought: "passage from *Gaudium et Spes* 24 ... emphasizes that the human being's likeness to God occurs *by reason of a relation that unites persons*. The text speaks of 'a certain likeness between the union of the divine persons and the union of the children

the image and likeness of God, in its Trinitarian meaning, that is, in its meaning precisely 'of communion.'"[147] The communion of persons does not blur the distinction of the two, however: "In this communion of persons, the whole depth of the original solitude of man (of the first and of all) is perfectly ensured and, at the same time, this solitude is permeated and enlarged in a marvelous way by the gift of the 'other.'"[148]

Corbon also locates the image of God in man in the mystery of communion: "man is in the image of God because he is a mystery of personal communion … Man's reality therefore is not that of an isolated entity, a solitude that has received form, but of a capacity for communion, and 'openness to.' He becomes himself only when he becomes communion with another."[149]

The first time John Paul mentions the *communio personarum* within the catecheses, he refers to its use by the Second Vatican Council: "But God did not create man a solitary being. From the beginning 'male and female he created them' (Gen 1:27). This partnership of man and woman constitutes the first form of communion between persons."[150] John Paul's theology of the body, as a theology of the communion of persons, is a development of this expression of the Second Vatican Council.

5) Procreation

John Paul immediately connects the original experiences thus far and shows their link with procreation: "On all this, right from the beginning, the blessing of fruitfulness descended, linked with human procreation (cf. Gen 1:28)."[151] The experiences of original solitude include the meaning of one's internal identity, which includes consciousness, self-

---

of God joined in truth and love.' It thus draws attention to the Trinitarian dimension of the fundamental truth about human beings that we find at the very beginning of Sacred Scripture and that characterizes the theological plane of Christian anthropology … Human beings are like unto God not only by reason of their spiritual nature, which accounts for their existence as persons, but also by reason of their *capacity for community with other persons*" (Karol Wojtyla, "The Family as a Community of Persons" in *Person and Community*, 318).

147. John Paul II, *Man and Woman He Created Them*, 427.

148. Ibid., 201.

149. Corbon, *Path to Freedom*, 53–54.

150. Second Vatican Council, *Gaudium et Spes*, 12. See John Paul II, *Man and Woman He Created Them*, 162.

151. John Paul II, *Man and Woman He Created Them*, 164.

knowledge through self-awareness, and self-determination in and through the body. This dynamic is oriented outside the person in a search for another who fulfills. This search is resolved on the basis of original unity, in which man is presented with a being like himself, who fulfills him and who leads him to a new consciousness on the basis of the body. Man's deepest identity is revealed when he enters into the communion of persons in reciprocal relation.

The blessing of fertility is not added in an extrinsic manner to the emerging picture of the identity of the human person. As Balthasar notes, at least two realities present to Adam's (and Eve's) consciousness and knowledge of self at the moment of recognition: First, "Adam recognized the gift presented him by God as being, at the same time, himself, his own flesh: 'Then the man said, "She now is bone of my bone, and flesh of my flesh; she shall be called Woman, for from her man she has been taken"' (Gen 2:23)."[152] Both know the relation one-to-another in unity through the recognition, but in this first reality there is a second simultaneous knowledge, the mystery of procreation:

> Hence God's command to Adam and Eve to be fruitful and multiply was not just a moral command … they were to reflect something of the archetype according to which they had been created … it was, at the same time, the result of the physical fecundity that God effected in Adam while he slept and that became, by the formation of Eve from the one living body of Adam, a direct physical image of the origin of the Father's substance or the eternal Son who shares his nature.[153]

Within the Genesis accounts, fertility is simultaneous and coextensive with the identity as a union of the two. Their fertility is an intrinsic feature of their unity. The procreative and unitive meanings of their union, especially in the conjugal act, are inseparable from their very foundation.

6) The Conjugal Act

In his thorough teaching on the identity of the human person, John Paul has analyzed and brought together the human capacity for con-

---

152. Balthasar, *The Christian State of Life*, 227.
153. Ibid.

sciousness, self-awareness, self-knowledge, and self-determination. All these are expressed in and through the body in the midst of the visible world. His analysis has focused on man's relationship to the other who is like himself—how man and woman experience one another and the essential help each brings to the other. This mutual help completes their identity. John Paul then considers how all this finds fulfillment in the conjugal act: "Adam united himself with Eve his wife, who conceived and gave birth to Cain and said, 'I have acquired a man from the LORD.' Then she gave birth also to his brother Abel" (Gen 4:1–2).

The conjugal act is not something external to the relation of Adam and Eve. Man's identity points immediately to the meaning of the conjugal act. The central act of married love, expressed in and through the bodies of the spouses, is a direct expression of all they are as persons. Human sexuality finds its meaning in "[T]he conjugal relation of man and woman, that is, the fact that through the duality of sex they become 'one flesh.'"[154] The meaning of the conjugal act, therefore, can never be distanced from the person's deepest identity. As such, the conjugal act has two inherent meanings: unitive and procreative. As man and woman unite in the conjugal act and "[t]ogether, they thus become one single subject.... "[155] so too the unitive and procreative meanings are united as a single reality in the marital act.

The sexual act is not simply a culmination, however. It is at the same time a *discovery* and a *revelation*: "[T]he reality of conjugal union in which man and woman become 'one flesh' contains in itself a new and in some way definitive discovery of the meaning of the human body in its masculinity and femininity."[156] In this way, the unity and procreation inherent in the conjugal act as seen in Genesis 4:1 point "to *a further discovery of the meaning of one's own body*."[157] The new plateau brings an immeasurable breakthrough: "Procreation brings it about that 'the man and the woman (his wife) *know each other reciprocally in the 'third,' originated by both.*"[158] This is an intense realization. You and I, in our deepest identity, are born from an act of love. My parents came together in an act

---

154. John Paul II, *Man and Woman He Created Them*, 206.
155. Ibid., 207.
156. Ibid., 208.
157. Ibid., 210.
158. Ibid., 211.

of love some forty years ago. I was born in August 1967. This means that sometime in November or December 1966, my parents engaged in an act of love. In this act they made a total gift of self one to another that involved their entire beings and identity. My mother and father took all they were, being conscious, and having self-knowledge and self-determination, and expressed it in and through their bodies. Through all their masculine and feminine particularity, they made a total gift of self one to another. That act of love they engaged in during late fall 1966 has never ended. It is writing this book right now. I am that act of love, walking around. Their love, no matter what their shortcomings later, lacked nothing. I am their gift of love. My identity is their gift of love. This is who I am—a gift of love. I am a gift; nothing less than being a gift can fulfill my identity. Unless I make a gift of myself, I will fail to fulfill my identity. Their gift was so perfectly united that it is another person, me. The two became one, so that they might become three. Unity and procreation are inseparable in the act of conjugal sexual love.

The identity of the human person is expressed in and through the body with its sexuality. Human sexuality is expressed in a physical way and reveals in itself a twofold meaning. Unity and procreation are inherent and inseparable. All other meanings of the sexual act are related in a tangential, though vital, way. The erotic, the sentimental, the affective—are all intelligible only within the procreative and unitive meanings. The tangential vanishes if the essentials are deliberately excluded. This is why contraception, same-sex marriage, cohabitation, and adultery are immoral. John Paul goes on to consider original nakedness as Genesis presents this theme. Using this category, he will further explain how both meanings of the conjugal act are revealed in and through the body.

c. Original Nakedness

Recall that each original experience focuses on the identity of the human person. Each original experience contributes something essential to delineate the identity of the human person that is emerging.[159] As he explains the identity of the human person, John Paul describes the third original experience, original nakedness. The third experience sums up all

---

159. Ibid., 169–170.

that has been stated regarding original solitude, original unity, and the communion of persons. Original nakedness is based on the text, "Now they were both naked, the man and the wife, but they did not feel shame" (Gen 2:25). The nakedness described in the text does not merely mean that Adam and Eve had no clothes. Nakedness is more about what they do have: it describes the quality and meaning of the body and the reciprocal relations by which man enters into the communion of persons.[160]

Their nakedness is *an awareness of meaning* which fills their consciousness and self-knowledge.[161] Original nakedness represents the state of consciousness that man had before the fall.[162] It is difficult for us, after the fall, to understand the original relationship of man and woman that had no burden of sin. John Paul notes that after original sin the meaning of original nakedness must be reconstructed from the text.[163] The Genesis text roots the meaning of human personhood.[164] Prior to original sin and its effects, which John Paul refers to as "shame," man had a "fullness of consciousness" of that which united him in the communion of persons.[165]

Man and woman found themselves naked and not ashamed. This constitutes an "act of discovery" which consists of "that fullness of consciousness of the meaning of the body."[166] As man encounters the visible world through his senses, he is not inhibited from seeing the authentic meaning of things. One of his first intuitions is that he is different from the rest of the visible world.[167] Within this difference, he sees in the visible world both himself and the other as persons. The nakedness signifies "their reciprocal experience of the body, that is, the man's experience of the femininity that reveals itself in the nakedness of the body, and reciprocally, the analogous experience of masculinity by the woman."[168] They did not feel shame in this experience. Man's "exterior

---

160. Ibid., 174.
161. Ibid., 171.
162. Ibid., 174.
163. Ibid., 173.
164. Ibid., 171.
165. Ibid., 174 (cf. 171).
166. Ibid., 175.
167. Ibid.
168. Ibid., 171.

perception of the visible world" brings him immediately to the interior worth and dignity of the self and other.[169] The body plays an integral role in this perception: "The body manifests man and, in manifesting him, acts as an intermediary that allows man and woman, from the beginning, to 'communicate' with each other according to that *communio personarum*."[170] This fullness of communication is made possible by the transparent nakedness of the reciprocity between them. Their *communio* knows no shame, but only an "original depth."[171] This immediate relay from viewing the "exterior fullness" of the other in nakedness to its correspondence with "the 'interior' fullness of vision" takes place because man is the image of God.[172] As the image of God he shares in the vision of the Creator.

1) To Share the Vision of the Creator

The first creation account relates that God looked at all he made and said it was very good (Gen 1:31). Original nakedness describes the manner in which Adam and Eve share the vision of the Creator.[173] Their nakedness is not an embarrassing threat to them. Instead, they see each other with the original vision of God. In this vision they understand the meaning of their own body and that of the other. They see the dignity of the person in and through the body in a direct, immediate, simple, full, and complete manner. Corbon insists: "[O]ur body is the visible expression of our personal mystery. In the original gift of life nudity reveals not just 'the flesh' but the person (Gen 2:25)."[174]

The nakedness allows the sight to penetrate to the deep identity of the person. As the man stands before the woman and the woman stands before the man, their nakedness reflects a crucial realization: the human person is meant for communion with the other through the openness created in sexual difference. All this reveals the meaning of the body. They are aware of the *total reciprocity* between man and woman as a

---

169. Ibid., 175.
170. Ibid., 176.
171. Ibid.
172. Ibid.
173. Ibid., 177.
174. Corbon, *Path to Freedom*, 49.

reciprocity manifested in the body. Previously, consciousness, self-awareness, self-knowledge, and self-determination made man aware of the visible world through tilling the soil and naming the animals. But now the sight of the body of the other like himself fills his consciousness, self-awareness, self-knowledge, and self-determination. The body of the other, in and through sexual difference, reveals a meaning that fills the internal identity of the human person.

2) Sexual Difference

Of its very nature, the sexual difference between male and female gives the human person the capacity to express self-giving love in a unique way. The original sign of the other is the other who is such through the sexual difference. All of the endowments of man's identity—consciousness, self-awareness, self-knowledge, and self-determination—find their total realization in love.[175] The reciprocity is not mere sentimentalism or a complementary coexistence of male to female. Reciprocity between a man and a woman is based on their sexual difference and seeks the good of the other through relation. Sexual difference opens the way and allows man and woman to be formally united by a complementarity that arises within a true reciprocity. Gerhard Muller describes this as

> not a symmetry of equality, but rather a symmetry of difference. This symmetry does not consist in an equality of the phenomenological or ontological, essential sort, but rather in the personal mutuality of man and woman, which has its foundation in the distinctive value and distinctive reality of masculinity and femininity. The lover can communicate himself to the other only through his being different.[176]

---

175. Andrew Woznicki points this out from his study of Wojtyla's early philosophy: "Referring to the Church's mission, John Paul II calls love the source of 'all humanity's various spheres of existence.' Love, understood in these terms, becomes the ultimate and fundamental principle of 'self-realization' of man as a 'person-act.' Wojtyla reasons as follows: 'It should be stressed here that love is the fullest realization of these potentialities with which man is endowed. This potentiality ... proper to a person is, to the fullest, actualized through love ... A person finds in love the fullness of his being, of his objective existing. Love means that particular action, that particular act, which expands to the fullest the existence of a person'" (*A Christian Humanism*, 30–31).

176. Gerhard Muller, *Priesthood and Diaconate: The Recipient of the Sacrament of Holy Orders from the Perspective of Creation Theology and Christology* (San Francisco: Ignatius Press, 2002), 94.

The sexual difference of male to female is not a surface happenstance but is as essential as the unity itself: "It is precisely masculinity and femininity which allow this unity (love) between human persons to be realized in a bodily way."[177]

Basing himself on the teaching of John Paul, Angelo Scola develops his thought on sexual difference in the wider context of his development of the nuptial mystery. Mary Shivanandan points out that Scola delineates the crucial role of sexual difference in the nature of the unity achieved via reciprocity:

> The reciprocity is asymmetrical. The other always remains "other" for me ... the other always remains other in order to leave space for a third, the child who is also an "other." The reciprocity of the conjugal act signifies love but because it is asymmetrical, it is open to the fruits of love, fecundity and procreation.[178]

The difference between man and woman is an indispensable precondition of their unity. Only two things that are truly different can be united. Two things that are the same form a set, but cannot form a unity. Two things that are the same are aligned extrinsically. But they have no substantial difference in their very nature that can give them a reciprocity. Unity presupposes difference. The difference can never be reduced: It is not a difference in name only, but in the nature of things. The difference leads to a unity that never absorbs or overrides the difference. The sexual difference takes place in and through the body in all its masculine and feminine fullness, and is the matrix for the total gift of self.

Scola describes sexual difference as an "event":

> [S]exual difference forms a privileged path along which the individual is introduced to reality. Sexual difference possesses the character of an event and encounter, since the path of the individual's sexuality can never be reduced to a purely biological fact but is always placed within the various forms of relationship to the other.[179]

Sexual difference always means that man cannot settle or establish his identity within himself. His difference is an opening to the other, as

---

177. Hogan and LeVoir, *Covenant of Love*, 47.

178. Mary Shivanandan, "Body-Soul Unity in Light of the Nuptial Relation," *Dialoghi sul mistero nuziale*, G. Marengo and B. Ognibeni, eds. (Rome: Pontificia Università Lateranense, 2003), 372.

179. cf. Angelo Scola, *The Nuptial Mystery* (Grand Rapids, MI: Wm. B. Eerdmans, 2005), 86.

Shivanandan notes: "Yet he cannot resolve the difference that lies at the heart of the being disclosed. The other always remains a mystery. It is that difference that allows relationship."[180] Thus in marriage husband meets wife, and wife meets husband in such a way that the most recognized institution on the earth and in history emerges. The two come together in an act of unity that is never exhausted, because the gift as it is given and received, by its very nature, establishes a new horizon of love. This new horizon immediately invites me to go deeper, beyond myself, and out to the other. The sexual difference is essential to man's very being as a person:

> Man exists as male and female ... he has always before him the other mode of being human, and this other mode is beyond his reach.... We can characterize the relationship between male and female as a relationship at once of identity and of difference ... this difference ... has to be understood ontologically.[181]

The deepest dimension of all reality is the gift of self.

John Paul II notes in his apostolic exhortation *Familiaris Consortio* that this manifestation through the body is "by no means something purely biological, but concerns the innermost being of the human person as such," and is the "sign and fruit of a total personal self-giving."[182] John Paul's understanding of the body never reduces it to a mere physical mechanism. The body is a fully personal reality truly united with the soul. The body has a spousal meaning realized in and through the gift of self. Sexual difference, for Scola, is part of the nuptial mystery and human identity:

> The expression nuptial mystery indicates firstly the organic unity of sexual difference, love (objective relationship to the other) and fecundity; and secondly [the nuptial mystery] objectively refers, thanks to the principle of analogy, to the diverse forms of love which characterize the relationship man-woman, in all its parts (paternity, maternity, fraternity, etc. and the relationship of God with man in the sacrament, in the Church, and in Jesus Christ, in order to reach the Trinity itself.[183]

---

180. Shivanandan, "Body-Soul Unity in Light of the Nuptial Relation," 373.

181. Angelo Scola, "The Formation of Priests in the Pastoral Care of the Family," *Communio: International Catholic Review* 24:1 (Spring 1997), 64–65.

182. John Paul II, *Familiaris Consortio*, 11.

183. Scola, *The Nuptial Mystery*, 81. (Cf. Balthasar, *Theo-Drama IV*, 472.)

3) Gift

John Paul's extensive teaching on the identity of the human person from original solitude to original nakedness culminates in "the hermeneutics of the gift."[184] John Paul has presented his teaching in slow motion, frame by frame. If it is to be expressed through one idea, it would be the notion of the gift. The gift is not the gift in the sense of politeness or custom, or of doing something extraordinarily nice for a friend. For John Paul the gift is directly related to the creation of the world *ex nihilo* and *bara'*.[185] Man is called from nothingness by the Good which loves. Man does not simply *receive* a gift, he *is* a gift. And man can know this: he finds himself within the gift of creation and "is able to understand the very meaning of the gift in the call from nothing to existence."[186]

For John Paul the gift can never be limited to one dimension. In the "'gift-of-self': giving and accepting the gift interpenetrate in such a way that the very act of giving becomes acceptance, and acceptance transforms itself into giving."[187] The human person is meant to "exist in a relation of reciprocal gift."[188] The gift is the *help* of which God spoke when he said, "It is not good that the man should be alone; I want to make a helper similar to himself" (Gen 2:18). The gift relieves the aloneness, animates the help, and reveals the essence of personhood. The gift, to live "in a reciprocal 'for,' in a relationship of reciprocal gift," is the seal of the communion of persons.[189] The mutual gift creates the communion of persons.[190] For John Paul, nakedness is the "gift [that] allows both the man and the woman to find each other reciprocally...."[191] As man discovers all the steps that John Paul describes from original solitude to original nakedness, he is discovering the spousal meaning of the body in a primordial way. The capacity to express love in and through the body reveals the meaning of the gift.

---

184. John Paul II, *Man and Woman He Created Them*, 179.
185. Ibid., 180.
186. Ibid.
187. Ibid., 196.
188. Ibid., 181.
189. Ibid., 182.
190. Ibid., 195.
191. Ibid., 187.

Much has been said about the identity of each person in terms of self-awareness, self-knowledge, self-determination, the importance of the body, and sexual difference. None of this is lost, submerged, or used as an instrument in the union of man and woman. Rather, the discovery of the human person's spiritual identity is meant to be communicated as a gift of self to another person.[192] Making a gift of one's self does not diminish a person's identify but fulfills it.

The body and sexuality always manifest the person. Due to the dignity and nature of the person as an objective subject, the only appropriate context for sexual acts is found in the spousal meaning of the body in marriage. In *Familiaris Consortio*, John Paul shows that the gift must be total because it always contains the total fullness of the person: "The total physical self-giving would be a lie if it were not the sign and fruit of total personal self-giving, in which the whole person, including the temporal dimension, is present: If the person were to withhold something or reserve the possibility of deciding otherwise in the future, by this very fact he or she would not be giving totally."[193]

A baptized man and a baptized woman culminate their married love in the conjugal act. This act takes place with all they are; it is a total action of unity in which they become something new. They become a source of unconditional love in a most excellent manner. The sexual union of husband and wife is unconditional love because it is a total union. If it were not total, it would not be unconditional. At the same time the ultimate gift from this total and unconditional love can be another person, the child. The identity of that child comes from everything that the mother is, united with everything that the father is. At the same time, the child is neither the mother nor the father. The child is the embodied newness of unconditional love. Couples who because of injury, illness, or age experience the pain of infertility have not deliberately deprived the conjugal act of its procreative potential. They still engage and receive all the blessings of the gift of self in love. Their witness of

---

192. John Crosby has pointed out that Wojtyla's philosophy reveals "that by probing the selfhood of the person we attain to a vastly deeper level ... to the level at which the person has dignity, ontological nobility, and even to the level at which we find that preciousness in the person that can awaken the love of another...." (*The Selfhood of the Human Person* [Washington, DC: Catholic University of America Press, 1996], 71).

193. John Paul II, *Familiaris Consortio*, 11.

love, often lived in the shadow of the cross, is a unique contribution to the meaning of marriage.

4) Contraception

How do we know the conjugal act is total? Because sexual expression is, by its very nature, all encompassing. However, we sometimes deliberately curtail the complete nature of sexual expression. Married couples turn to contraception for what seem like good reasons: financial security, health concerns, spacing of children. They accept the contraceptive lifestyle that our society routinely promotes. They view the decision as practical and often undertake it with no conscious ill will, but the best of intentions. Unfortunately, their intentions cannot prevent the inescapable harm contraception does to marriage and unconditional love.

The decision to contracept, to deliberately deprive the conjugal act of its procreative potential, utters a "no" in the midst of the total, unitive gift of unconditional love between spouses. Even if uttered for practical and well-intentioned reasons, this "no" damages the total gift. It is no longer total because spouses deliberately withhold their procreative potential. The dominoes begin to fall: If the conjugal act ceases to be unconditional, it ceases to be total; if it ceases to be total, it ceases to be a union; if it ceases to be a union, it ceases to be a gift. If I take what can only be a total gift and downgrade it to such an extent, I have placed something else above the gift: I have been selfish, perhaps for seemingly well-intentioned reasons, but selfish nonetheless.

The effects of the decision to contracept are not limited to the married couple's intimate sexual relations. Using contraception introduces an ongoing self-centeredness into what is supposed to be a total self-gift.

This self-centeredness builds and spreads into a couple's daily interactions. Even if done out of good intentions, this influx of self-centeredness begins to erode the spouses' experience of the gift.

Many have given in, unwittingly and even with what they deem as the best of intentions. And they suffer. They suffer the physical side effects of contraception. They suffer the spiritual side effects that prevent love from reaching the heights it is called to, because it is lulled and drugged into selfishness. And from this stupor they do not know what is causing the breakdown of all their plans for their marriage. Is it a lack of problem-solving skills? Is it a need for conflict negotiation? Is it family-of-origin issues we thought we had dealt with? Is it his inability to deal with his anger? Is it her inability to deal with him not dealing with his anger? Where is it all coming from?

Kenneth Schmitz points out, "the reception of a gift points to a deeper flow of energy."[194] The gift is not merely notional, but profoundly intentional. "Something more moves with a gift" than just a relocation or an external exchange of property.[195] The gift "draws the giver as well as the receiver into the relationship," and an "interior bond" is brought about.[196]

> To an uninvolved spectator a gift might seem to detach itself from one possessor to pass over into the possession of another. But that is to observe only the physics of transference that sometimes accompanies a gift; it is not to grasp the metaphysics of the gift itself.... In the act of endowment the giver makes himself present to the receiver.[197]

Because the exchange between man and woman is a gift of self, they may not "use" any aspect of the identity of the other: "To use means to employ some object of action as a means to an end,"[198] Wojtyla asserts, adding that "a person must not be *merely* the means to an end for another person. This is precluded by the very nature of personhood, by what a person is."[199] If one person treats another as a means to an end, he "does violence to the very essence of the other."[200] Wojtyla applies the "personalistic norm": "This norm, in its negative aspect, states that the person is the kind of good which does not admit of use and cannot be treated as an object of use and as such the means to an end."[201] He continues, "In its positive form the personalistic norm confirms this: the person is a good towards which the only proper and adequate attitude is love."[202] Original nakedness reveals the original instance of the personalistic norm.

---

194. Schmitz, *The Gift: Creation*, 58.
195. Ibid.
196. Ibid.
197. Ibid., 59.
198. Wojtyla, *Love and Responsibility*, 25.
199. Ibid., 26.
200. Ibid., 27.
201. Ibid., 41.
202. Ibid.

5) *Gaudium et Spes* 24

Original nakedness means that man and woman are not threatened by their gaze on one another. The gaze summons the gift that leads to fulfillment: "We recall here the text of the most recent Council in which it declares that man is the only creature in the visible world that God willed 'for its own sake,' adding that this man cannot 'fully find himself except through a sincere gift of self' [*Gaudium et Spes*, 24.3]."[203] The gift, because it is a gift *of self*, requires that freedom be the first movement of the gift. Their experience of the body-person of the self and other is such that man and woman know directly and immediately the spousal meaning of the body. In this they also are aware of the moral meaning of the body.[204] They see and interpret sexual difference and attraction in light of the true good of the communion of persons. Thus their freedom is self-mastery ordered to the expression of the gift.[205]

6) The Body as Part of *Imago Dei*

The nature of the gift of self, with its immediate relation to the identity of the human person, excludes selfishness in regard to the body. The body of the other or the self may never be used as an object in a selfish manner. To value the spousal and moral meaning of the body is not to give free reign to all of its inclinations. Rather, natural inclinations must be directed toward the "authentic fulfillment" of the human person, rejecting any "manipulations of human corporeity which alter its human meaning...."[206]

In a secular culture of individualism, utilitarianism, and hedonism, "the body is no longer perceived as a properly personal reality ... It is reduced to pure materiality" rather than a gift.[207] In a culture that appreciates the profound meaning of the identity of the human person, the body is the sign that the other is always and only a gift.[208] Love and life

---

203. John Paul II, *Man and Woman He Created Them*, 186.
204. John Paul II, *Veritatis Splendor*, 77.
205. John Paul II, *Man and Woman He Created Them*, 186.
206. John Paul II, *Veritatis Splendor*, 50.
207. John Paul II, *Evangelium Vitae*, 23.
208. John Paul II, *Man and Woman He Created Them*, 179ff.

always take the form of the gift of self. The meaning of the body for life and love is a spousal meaning. The reciprocity between man and woman is inscribed with the gift of self. The gift includes from the beginning the blessing of fertility.[209] In the communion of persons in marriage, the two become one so that they may become three. This is so profound that, as John Paul notes, the communion of persons is decisive for man as the image of God:[210]

> Man is the image of God not only as male and female, but also because of the reciprocal relation of the two sexes. The reciprocal relation constitutes the soul of the "communion of persons" which is established in marriage and presents a certain likeness with the union of the three Divine Persons.[211]

The body is integral to this relation and communion for John Paul:

> The conviction that man is the "image of God" because of the soul has frequently been expressed. But traditional doctrine does not lack the conviction that the body also participates in the dignity of the "image of God" in its own way, just as it participates in the dignity of the person.[212]

He includes the notion that man in his "bodiliness" is "'similar' to God."[213] Corbon concurs: "[O]ur body makes each one of us a being standing in relation to all other human beings both on the biological and spiritual level."[214] Balthasar notes that "[T]he Church Fathers often ask the explicit question: Cannot the human body—particularly in view of the incarnation of the Son and the resurrection of the flesh—also be part of the image of God?"[215] Corbon has emphasized this point as well: "[W]hen God creates a body, he creates it in his own image and imparts to it his own breath...."[216] He also maintains, "our biological origins are transfigured and become a call to communion with others."[217]

---

209. Ibid., 164.
210. Ibid., 163, 168, 184, 201, 243, 427.
211. John Paul II, *God, Father and Creator*, 232.
212. Ibid., 228.
213. John Paul II, *Man and Woman He Created Them*, 164.
214. Corbon, *Path to Freedom*, 51.
215. Balthasar, *Theo-Drama II*, 322.
216. Corbon, *Path to Freedom*, 46.
217. Ibid., 9.

7) Marriage

Human sexuality and the conjugal act derive their meaning not from the human person as an isolated subject, but from the human person as he or she engages in the gift of self. The gift is irrevocable, permanent, and fruitful. When man and woman see one another for the first time in Genesis, the pattern is set for every encounter between man and woman that will ever occur. The gift of self is the central form of the identity of the human person. This is expressed most profoundly in human sexuality in the conjugal act: "The unity about which Genesis 2:24 speaks ('and the two shall be one flesh') is without doubt the unity that is expressed and realized in the conjugal act."[218] The conjugal act brings to its peak an awareness of the meaning of the body and the person: "Genesis 2:24 is a future-oriented text ... in every conjugal union of man and woman, there is a new discovery of the same original consciousness of the unitive meaning of the body in its masculinity and femininity."[219] Because human sexuality immediately reaches all that the human person is in the deep recesses of identity, it can never be removed from the gift of self. The awareness of man and woman as they look upon one another is an awareness of the union that is possible because of their sexual difference: "[T]his union *carries within itself a particular awareness of the meaning of the body in the reciprocal self-gift of the persons.*"[220] Outside of monogamous marriage, the gift can only take the form of abstinent and chaste dedication to the good.

Marriage reminds us that love can never be reduced to the satisfaction of our own personal needs, erotic or otherwise. Sin has wounded the spousal meaning of the body but has not destroyed it. John Paul shows that when a person chooses to doubt the gift, he "casts God from his heart" by sin.[221] The fourth original experience, original shame, outlines the effects of concupiscence as the flesh wars against the spirit.[222] The theology of the body reasserts the original meaning of the identity of the person as a gift. This is fulfilled in an original way through the gift of self

---

218. John Paul II, *Man and Woman He Created Them*, 167.
219. Ibid., 169.
220. Ibid.
221. Ibid., 237.
222. Ibid., 242.

in marriage. The theology of the body strengthens a person to turn away from acquisition to be a gift, away from materialism to spend himself for the other, away from seeking only pleasure to the beauty of the gift of self.

d. Pope John Paul II's Interpretation of Scripture

Charles Curran has objected that the Wednesday audiences are not authoritative teaching: "… the speeches given at the weekly audiences at the beginning of John Paul II's service as Bishop of Rome … have little or no authoritative character. They are often just greetings to the various people in attendance…."[223] Curran's claim is unfounded. While the audiences included a greeting, they went beyond mere greeting to catechesis. The pope is the universal and primary teacher. Catholics from all over the world attended the Wednesday audiences. The Holy Father thus carried out his teaching mission in a most opportune, regular venue. Michael Waldstein has responded to Curran's claim.[224] More objections came from certain Scripture scholars who claimed that John Paul's teaching failed to take account of modern scholarship. But as other Scripture scholars attest, John Paul "showed himself to be aware of the presence of [underlying] sources in Genesis 1–3."[225] In his encyclical *Dives in Misericordia (Rich in Mercy)*, he uses philology.[226] He is "aware of what the exegetes say about these passages and brings that material into play at various points."[227] In particular, John Paul bases his study of the Scripture on the Second Vatican Council: "Without doubt, the pope employs the criterion from Vatican II's *Dei verbum* of reading individual biblical passages within the interpretive context of 'the unity of Scripture.'"[228] In addition to his knowledge of the findings of exegetes, he employs "phenomenological and philosophical reflection on the

---

223. Charles Curran, *The Moral Theology of Pope John Paul II* (Washington, DC: Georgetown University Press, 2005), 4.

224. Michael Waldstein, introduction, *Man and Woman He Created Them*, 16–17.

225. Terrence Prendergast, SJ, "A Vision of Wholeness: A Reflection on the Use of Scripture in a Cross-Section of Papal Writings" in *The Thought of Pope John Paul II*, 77.

226. Prendergast, "A Vision of Wholeness," 95.

227. Earl C. Muller, SJ, "The Nuptial Meaning of the Body," 90.

228. Kurz, "The Scriptural Foundations of *The Theology of the Body*," 27.

meaning, nature, and action of human persons *qua persons*."[229] He also brings to this a reading of Scripture that is similar to the patristic method.[230] Yet he also brings "traces of personalist phenomenology, historical criticism, and Thomistic ontology" to his reading of the texts.[231] The teaching of John Paul quotes Scripture "frequently and at length" and also appeals to Scripture through "major liturgical, patristic, systematic, conciliar and magisterial documentation ... these traditions are one with the Scriptures which they try to embody and actualize in each new set of circumstances of ecclesial life."[232] Contemporary Scripture scholarship can certainly be contentious, yet John Paul has shown positive regard for the academic study of scriptural texts.

---

229. Ibid., 33.
230. Ibid., 38.
231. Ibid.
232. Prendergast, "A Vision of Wholeness," 91.

CHAPTER FIVE

———⌣———

Sin and the Effects of Sin

Just as the identity of the human person has several dimensions, so too does the complex wound of sin. Sin is not simply crossing a line or violating a rule. Sin is an offense that deeply wounds human nature itself. It disfigures the identity of the human person. As such, an adequate analysis of sin must consider original sin, the remote roots of temptation, man's choice to sin, the seven steps involved in temptation and sin, the effects of sin, Saint Augustine's thought on sin, the seven deadly sins, and other images of sin.

A. John Paul II on Original Sin: Original Shame

The teaching of the Church in general, and the catechesis of John Paul in particular, highlights the profound identity of the human person. How then does one account for pain, suffering, wars, inhumanity—all those ways of refusing the gift that disfigure the identity of the human person? What stands behind all the violence, perfectionism, betrayal, abandonment, trauma, blame, hostility, and perversions that fill history books and therapists' files? John Paul responds:

> However disturbing these divisions [of sin and its effects] may seem at first sight, it is only by a careful examination that one can detect their root: it is to be found in a *wound* in man's inmost self. In the light of faith we call it sin: beginning with *original sin*, which all of us bear

from birth as an inheritance from our first parents, to the sin which each one of us commits when we abuse our own freedom.[1]

John Paul points out that the term "original sin" does not appear in Sacred Scripture.[2] But the third chapter of Genesis makes it evident that Adam's sin of disobedience is the original sin that invades the "whole world … by a kind of universal infection of all humanity."[3]

Original sin is a wound inherent in man's rejection of the gifts that God has bestowed. "… [S]in in its original reality takes place in man's will—and conscience—first of all as 'disobedience,' that is, as opposition of the will of man to the will of God."[4] From the moment it is committed, this sin also causes "an inclination to sin. From that moment, the whole history of humanity will be burdened by this state."[5]

Prior to original sin, man lived in the fullness of sanctifying grace. In the original innocence of this grace, man knew he had come forth as the creation of God. All of his capacities led him to understand he was meant to return to God. Man's choice to sin interrupted the *reditus* of man to God. After sin, the human person is disoriented in his affection for God. With the fall, the human person's consciousness, self-awareness, self-knowledge, and self-determination are clouded and wounded. The human person no longer stands in readiness to trust his identity as a gift. Fear has replaced the gift as man attempts to become his own *exitus-reditus*. After original sin, man suffers a privation of grace through this primordial sin, the effects of which are evident from generation to generation through its hereditary character.[6] Man has fallen, and cannot, of himself, come out of the fall. God must "come down," pour himself out in "a new beginning of goodness" in the Incarnation. This new beginning culminates in the kenosis in which the Son of God pours himself out in his death on the cross.

Original sin strikes directly at the seat of man's identity in his capacity to know and love God and neighbor, and thus fulfill himself through

---

1. John Paul II, *Reconciliatio et Paenitentia*, 2.

2. John Paul II, *Jesus, Son and Savior: A Catechesis on the Creed* (Boston: Pauline Books & Media, 1996), 33.

3. Ibid.

4. John Paul II, *Dominum et Vivificantem*, 33.

5. John Paul II, *Jesus, Son and Savior*, 28.

6. Ibid., 29, 37, 43.

a gift of self. It is only in the context of and at the expense of his identity in the grace of original innocence that the woundedness of the
human person is experienced on such a perplexing and intense level:

> Man was placed on this earth to remain firm in his original state and
> so to advance toward the final state of union with God in heaven. At
> the proper time, God would have extended to him the fruit of the tree
> of life (Rev 2:7) and bestowed upon him that other-heavenly-immor-
> tality from which there would have been no falling away. But because
> he succumbed to temptation, he was obliged to seek by long detours
> the entrance to the final state that would have been near and easily
> accessible to him if he had remained in the state of innocence.[7]

Simply listening to the evening news reveals that the *reditus* is disturbed. The tragic effects of painful choices have far-reaching
ramifications, from personal, to family, to national, to global. Sin continues to interrupt the *reditus* of man to God. Whence does sin emerge?
What causes the wound of sin? The answer is at least twofold: Man is
tempted and he then sins. Man chooses to act against the *reditus* through
assenting to a temptation to sin. Saint Paul explains: "Through one man
sin entered the world and with sin death" (Rom 5:12, 19). Genesis 3
relates the refusal of the gift on the part of man.

B. The Remote Roots of Temptation

Man is created good and can freely choose to love. He ought to place
this love with God. The human hunger for love can only find its full and
complete response when it is fulfilled in God. Sin is not natural to man.
John Paul explains: "as we see from the biblical account, human sin does
not have its primary origin in the heart (and in the conscience) of man.
It does not arise from his spontaneous initiative."[8] Man instead places
his love in created things rather than the Creator. Evil and sin in the
world are the result of man's free choice. But things cannot be the *reditus*
of love. Therefore, man experiences pain. How did the temptation to sin
enter man's horizon? Whence does sin arise?

> It is in a certain sense the reflection and the consequence of the sin
> that had already occurred in the world of invisible beings. The tempter,

---

7. Balthasar, *The Christian State of Life*, 123.
8. John Paul II, *Jesus, Son and Savior*, 30.

"the ancient serpent," belongs to this world. Previously these beings endowed with knowledge and freedom had been "put to the test" so that they could make their choice commensurate with their purely spiritual nature. In them arose the "doubt" which ... the tempter insinuates in our first parents.[9]

Sacred Scripture attributes temptation to the devil. Why does the devil tempt man? Saint Paul asserts that the devil's sin was pride: "[man] may become conceited and fall under the same condemnation as the devil" (1 Tim 3:6). The Book of Wisdom states, "God formed man to be imperishable; the image of his own nature he made him. But by the envy of the devil death entered the world...." " (Wis 2:24). It appears, then, that the sin of Satan is twofold: pride and envy. The order is important. It was through *pride* that Lucifer was cast out of heaven. It was through his *envy* that sin entered the world.

Jean Daniélou explains the teaching of the Fathers on this point. When the world was created, "great creations had been prepared" by God.[10] The archangels were set over various parts of creation. Lucifer, the bearer of light, was set as guardian of the visible world. He was charged with "administering the substance of material natures."[11] In this governance, Lucifer became envious of the human person. In his perfect knowledge Lucifer foresaw the Incarnation. He realized that the Word would assume not the nature of angels, but of man. Lucifer refused to accept that God would deign to take flesh instead of taking the pure spirit of angelic nature. In his pride, Lucifer opposed the plan of God. Lucifer's decision was permanent because by their very nature, angels "determine themselves through one act outside of time."[12] The evil angels made a choice against God which perdures because of their perfect knowledge. Because humans have only imperfect knowledge, human choices are revocable.[13] John Paul teaches:

---

9. Ibid.

10. Jean Daniélou, *The Angels and Their Mission: According to the Fathers of the Church*, trans. David Heimann (Westminster, MD: Newman Press, 1957), 45. See also, Gabriel Bunge, OSB, *Dragon's Wine and Angel's Bread: The Teaching of Evagrius Ponticus on Anger and Meekness* (New York: St. Vladimir's Seminary Press, 2009), 29-31.

11. Jean Daniélou, *The Angels and Their Mission*, 46.

12. Melina, *Sharing in Christ's Virtues*, 48.

13. Ibid.

They [the evil angels] had contested the truth of existence, which demands the total subordination of the creature to the Creator. This truth was supplanted by an original pride, which led them to make their own spirit the principle and rule of freedom ... They had chosen themselves over God, instead of choosing themselves "in God" ... [14]

Lucifer fell in love with his own beauty and could not allow that God would take human nature in the Incarnation. In his pride, Lucifer was cast out from heaven. Satan's sin demonstrates the nature of pride. Pride alienates itself from love because pride cannot admit the love of another without controlling it. By its nature, love cannot be controlled. Instead of relenting to love, pride flees and is cast out. From that low pinnacle of pride, Satan grows envious of man. Envy seeks to destroy the good of the other through sin. The devil would not permit man to have on earth what Lucifer could not have in heaven.

C. The Juncture of Man's Choice

To explain the nature of sin and its effects, John Paul turns again to the book of Genesis, in particular to the account of original sin in the third chapter.

We must meditate, and not just once, on this "archaic" description. I do not know if many other passages can be found in Holy Scripture in which the reality of sin is described not only in its original form, but also in its essence, that is, where the reality of sin is presented in such full and deep dimensions, showing how man used *against* God exactly what in him was *God's*, that is, what should have served to bring him nearer *to God*.[15]

John Paul explains that the "'first sin' ... is described in the book of Genesis so precisely that it shows all the depth of the 'reality of man' contained in it."[16] The account of original sin highlights the profound identity of the human person in the image of God, and the sinister nature of sin, designed to attack precisely this image of God.

The experience of evil in the world is directly related to man's free choice. God created man with a choice. The basic conditions of man's

---

14. John Paul II, *Jesus, Son and Savior*, 31.
15. General audience, December 20, 1978, *Talks of John Paul II*, 507.
16. Ibid., 506.

choice arise from his identity within creation. Man is created in between. He is made from the highest, the breath of God, and the lowest, the mud of the earth. Philosophers articulate this with the traditional understanding of creation *ex nihilo*, or out of nothing. Man is made by God, who is the source and end of all, yet man also bears a relation to nothingness in that he does not ordain or arrange his own creation. Man, as a gift, has the capacity to choose, to accept or reject the gift. When man accepts the gift and lives in the image of God, rationally and relationally, he matures and develops. When man rejects the gift, he turns toward nothingness and mud, and inverts his creation. When man pursues the antilogic such that he tries absurdly to "arrogate divine nature to itself," he sins.[17] Hans Urs von Balthasar explains that sin is predicated upon the creature's choice to "refuse to acknowledge that it owes its freedom to the Creator."[18] Man refuses his contingent relationship to God, and contradiction takes the place of the gift.[19]

1. Seven Steps of Sin: The Ritual of Temptation

Sin is not just crossing a line into an impure state. Sin is turning away from the gift, and turning toward nothingness based upon the illusion of temptation. The third chapter of Genesis presents the sequence of events that characterize temptation and sin. John Paul explains:

> [I]t cannot be denied that one sure element emerges from the detailed account of the sin. It describes a primordial event, that is, a fact, which according to revelation took place at the beginning of human history. For this reason it also presents another certain element, namely, the fundamental and decisive implication of that event for man's relationship with God, and consequently for the interior "situation" of man himself, for reciprocal relations between people, and in general for man's relationship with the world.[20]

The account of original sin from Genesis chronicles a primordial event of the fall of man. It also gives the pattern of every sin to follow. The third chapter of Genesis presents the series of steps found in every

---

17. Balthasar, *Theo-Drama IV*, 328.
18. Ibid.
19. Ibid.
20. John Paul II, *Jesus, Son and Savior*, 27.

temptation and sin. Temptation is never a remote or disinteresting experience. Temptation is based upon a clever illusion that strikes at the heart of our humanity. Nevertheless, temptation, sin, and their immediate effects follow a predictable pattern. John Paul teaches that the first temptation "is echoed in all the other temptations to which man is more easily inclined to yield as a result of the original Fall."[21]

Whether one is a pimp or a saint, temptation always charts the same course. The devil makes the same appeal to surface externals, to pleasure and satisfaction, to narrow vision, and to focusing on one's own immediate need to the exclusion of the good. Despite its best efforts to attempt to pass itself off as illustrious and original, sin is always a dull, banal, routine procedure. Sin can never be new because it is linked to death. The account of the first provides an insight into the pattern of every sin:

> Now the serpent was the most cunning of all the animals that the LORD God had made. The serpent asked the woman, "Did God really tell you not to eat from any of the trees in the garden?" The woman answered the serpent: "We may eat of the fruit of the trees in the garden; it is only about the fruit of the tree in the middle of the garden that God said, 'You shall not eat it or even touch it, lest you die.'" But the serpent said to the woman: "You certainly will not die! No, God knows well that the moment you eat of it your eyes will be opened and you will be like gods who know what is good and what is bad." The woman saw that the tree was good for food, pleasing to the eyes, and desirable for gaining wisdom. So she took some of its fruit and ate it; and she also gave some to her husband, who was with her, and he ate it. Then the eyes of both of them were opened, and they realized that they were naked; so they sewed fig leaves together and made loin cloths for themselves. When they heard the sound of the LORD God moving about in the garden at the breezy time of the day, the man and his wife hid themselves from the LORD God among the trees of the garden. The LORD God then called to the man and asked him, "Where are you?" He answered, "I heard you in the garden; but I was afraid, because I was naked, so I hid myself." Then he asked, "Who told you that you were naked? You have eaten, then, from the tree of which I had forbidden you to eat!" The man replied, "The woman whom you put here with me—she gave me fruit from the tree, so I ate it." The LORD God then asked the woman, "Why did you do

---

21. John Paul II, *Veritatis Splendor*, 102.

such a thing?" The woman answered, "The serpent tricked me into it, so I ate it." (Gen 3:1–13)

Seven strategic steps are hidden within the familiar account of original sin. The seven steps present in original sin are present in every ensuing sin, from the most common fault to the most grave transgression. The steps constitute a type of ritual or liturgy of temptation.

a. The First Step: Bypass the Family Structure

The first step in the strategy of temptation appears as a casual meeting: "Now the serpent was the most cunning of all the animals that the LORD God had made. The serpent asked the woman.... " (Gen 3:1). Satan's first move is the setup, which appears to happen by mere chance: The first step of temptation is to bypass the family structure. Satan approaches Eve alone.

When Satan starts to spread out the trap, it does not yet look like the final product. Much more needs to be added. But everything that follows as the temptation unfolds is built on isolation. As the popular horror writer Stephen King writes, "Alone ... the most awful word in the English tongue. Murder doesn't hold a candle to it and hell is only a poor synonym.... "[22] J. R. Moehringer writes in his memoir that growing up without a father present made him feel so alone, and that aloneness was so painful, that he often "wished there was a bigger, longer word for alone."[23] Satan dares to approach only after he has isolated the man and the woman. When they are together, their bond is so profoundly and immediately rooted in the image of God that the devil cannot bear it. He isolates them from each other so that he may act.

Some of the early theological writers and Fathers of the Church note the absence of Adam. Saint Augustine theorizes that Adam is nearby Eve, but she does not rely upon him and he is not aware of what is going on. Adam should have said something when he saw the puzzled look on Eve's face as she was being pulled away from reality and relationship. Thus, sin involves some sort of isolation or alienation. The isolation, while visible externally, sinks to the depths of the person's consciousness.

---

22. Stephen King, *Salem's Lot* (Garden City, NY: Doubleday, 1975), 214.
23. J. R. Moehringer, *The Tender Bar* (New York: Hyperion, 2006), 61.

"[S]in is understood by the Fathers as the destruction of the unity of the human race, as fragmentation and division."[24] The "bypassing of the family structure" is the remote occasion of sin. It never remains on the surface. Touch the family and you touch man.

This step is repeated in every sin. Satan hates community, and he isolates the person. It takes form again in the tremendous pressures and stress placed on families in America today. The contemporary assault on the family through the dark side of the Industrial Revolution and sexual revolution was the forerunner of the culture of death. The proponents of secularism began to draw spouses apart, and knew that families would also break up. Families follow an incredibly hectic schedule of appointments, practices, games, and other pursuits that continually propel family members in many directions All this activity tends to tear apart the bonds of relationship, leaving all persons vulnerable.

The union of marriage and the family is the structure of unconditional love. In every temptation, Satan bypasses this structure of unconditional love, leaving a wound that makes it harder for family members to draw strength from one another in withstanding temptation and difficulties. The devil weakens believers by distancing them from the basis of love.

b. The Second Step: The Innocent Little Question

The second step of sin in the sequence of temptation is not immediately apparent. The devil does not appear with a bold proclamation of atheism. He does not argue against the existence of God. Satan's prime move is not to try to get us to think God does not exist. Satan would sooner have us believe that *he*, the devil, does not exist. Satan wants the human person to take the existence of God for granted. He knows that despite whatever man may encounter on earth, God can always be found close by. The devil's strategy is beginning to take shape as he continues to set the trap.

The devil's next step is so simple that it is almost unnoticed. It blends right into the background, casually camouflaged. He merely asks an innocent little question. The devil even attempts to have the woman

---

24. Benedict XVI, *Spe Salvi*, 14.

recall God's words, with one twist. He makes an inroad by simply asking for information, just to clarify the facts: "Did God *really* tell you not to eat from any of the trees in the garden?" Notice that the devil takes God's existence for granted. Yet, Satan throws in one spin to confuse Eve: "from any tree of the garden?" Satan knows well that God forbade them to eat from only one tree. But the devil is a liar. The 1970s movie *The Exorcist* was flawed in many respects, but it was accurate about the nature of the devil. The old priest Merrin visits the home of the possessed girl after the young Jesuit priest-psychiatrist had been there. The young priest thinks the girl has multiple personality disorder. An experienced exorcist, Merrin has come to discern whether there is a real case of possession. The young priest suggests that the girl has multiple personalities, but Merrin says no, there is only one. "The demon," he says, "is a liar."

The devil inevitably lies and skews the truth. We see it again with various temptations against the dignity of sexuality and marriage: "Is this pornography really all that bad? ... I'll just look for fifteen minutes ... after all I'm not out with a prostitute, am I? I've never been unfaithful to my wife." Notice the confusion. A spouse is supposed to be faithful. Faithfulness does not earn one the right to sin. The innocent little question skews one's thinking.

The evil one distorts the divine command. Balthasar explains, "Craftily, the serpent spreads the shadow of God's prohibition over all the trees, turning the freedom of man's obedience into the seeming deprivation of his sovereignty over all creatures."[25] The apparently innocent little question gives an insight into the way we experience temptation. This segue is the key to temptation. The seemingly innocent question entices us to sin.

For example, think of a high school student working as a receptionist in the rectory office from afternoon until evening. He has watched TV, listened to music, played computer games, sent text messages to his friends, and even done some homework. Notice that the activities prior to homework all tended to isolate him, to bypass an interactive or family structure. The evening calls have tapered off, he has an hour and a half left, and no one is around. He gets bored, then he gets curious. Stealthily, the innocent little questions come up. He begins to look around and opens the drawers of the secretary's desk. In the first drawer he finds a stapler, tape, pencils,

---

25. Balthasar, *The Christian State of Life*, 90.

and pens. In the second drawer he finds certificates, letterhead, and enve-
lopes. In the third bigger, double-faced drawer he finds a small tin box with
a lock on top. There must be something valuable inside. He flicks the
switch on the box and it opens. He lifts the lid and sees a portrait of
George Washington staring up at him. He flips through and sees Andrew
Jackson, Alexander Hamilton. He has come upon the Mass card account
box. Then an idea arises in his mind in the form of an innocent little question. "Do they really pay me enough for what I do here? I make so little,
and the Church is so rich." Then a second question arises in his mind:
"Would it really be that bad if I just took one of the five dollar bills, one of
the ten dollar bills? After all I deserve it, they have others right there in the
box, and they won't even miss it." He slips a five dollar bill into his pocket.
Two weeks later he is there again. No one had noticed anything. "Would
it really be all that bad if I took more?"

While the above circumstances may seem petty, they are actually a
training exercise for further sin. They are a type of evangelization in
reverse that feeds on concupiscence. Original sin has several effects on us.
While the sin, that is, the wounding or breaking of our relationship with
God, is forgiven in Baptism, the effects of sin remain in us. We experience a fragility and inconsistency that characterize our "mysterious inclination to sin."[26] Concupiscence is the tendency to sin that remains in us
after sin has been forgiven. This tendency or inclination to sin comes
from sin, but is not itself sin. It is the tinder for sin, and as such, leads to
sin. The reception of the sacraments can weaken concupiscence, but it
remains in us.

Consider another example, of a traveling businessman. He has had a
long week away from his family. He has endured tiring flights and long
waits in anonymous airport terminals. Every field office he arrived at was
more confused than the last. This morning he had a cold cup of coffee,
and he stepped deep into a puddle as he emerged from a taxi. He has had
to review long contracts, please the home office, and negotiate with ven-
dors, all on a tight timetable and tighter budget. Finally, he arrives at the
airport hotel and settles into his room, tired, overdrawn, and lonely. He
begins to flip the channels on cable television and comes across the adult
entertainment channel. The question arises in his mind, "Would it really

---

26. Melina, *Sharing in Christ's Virtues*, 15.

be so bad just to look?" He experiences that crucial moment in temptation that always appears so pedestrian and matter-of-fact: the innocent
little question. The question deceives us into thinking that what we are
about to do doesn't matter. But it inevitably leads to a cliff.

Adam and Eve fall over the cliff. Acting on behalf of both, Eve
answers the devil. She dialogues with evil. This is how the devil makes
inroads to our weaknesses. The ancient advice is "give no time to the
devil." He is "a liar from the beginning" (Jn 8:44) and, given his perfect
knowledge, he quickly outwits us. Whatever we say, the devil will lie to
us. We do not want him inside our heads. In temptation the devil urges
us to sin, tricking us into desiring the supposed benefits of sin. When we
fall and sin, the devil then switches gears and reproaches man, saying to
us, "You call yourself a Christian and you just sinned. You are a husband
and father but you give in so easily to sin, you are not a good husband or
father.... " The Desert Fathers tell us that when the devil reproaches us
after we commit the sin that he tempted us into, we are to simply remind
him of his end. Or better yet, we should speak the name of Jesus or Mary,
and then have recourse to a spiritual director to learn to grow in grace
and virtue.

c. The Third Step: The Lie

Once he has isolated the person from the family structure, and dis-
armed him through an apparently innocent little question, Satan then
unleashes a flurry of movement that stuns the person. These next two
steps are the "one-two punch" of sin. Because they come almost simultaneously, it is hard to tell which comes first. This is the Muhammad Ali
of sin, the left hook and the upper cut in flash sequence: the lie and then
the fear.

The third step of sin is the lie the devil tells. In his laziness, the devil
takes the truth and distorts it just a bit. Balthasar says that the lie, "only
exists by courtesy of the truth."[27] Eve tells Satan that they are not to eat
of the tree, and he responds, "You certainly will not die! No, God knows
well that the moment you eat of it your eyes will be opened and you will
be like gods who know what is good and what is bad" (Gen 3:4). John

---

27. Balthasar, *Theo-Drama IV*, 328 (cf. *Theo-Drama V*, 77).

Paul teaches that the history of sin begins "when man no longer acknowledges the Lord as his Creator and himself wishes to be the one who determines, with complete independence, what is good and what is evil."[28] The lie rushes in as Satan releases his onslaught. The lie is "you will be like God." Why is this a lie? Adam and Eve already were like God. They were created in his image and likeness (Gen 1:26–27). The lie is not meant to convince us of what we can be, but to blind us to what we already are. John Paul quotes the Gospel of John, which calls Satan "a murderer from the beginning, because there is no truth in him. When he lies, he speaks according to his own nature, for he is a liar and the father of lies (Jn 8:44)." The Holy Father continues, "This 'lie' is found at the beginning of history as the root of sin in the world of created beings endowed with freedom in the image of the Creator."[29]

The lie tries to convince us that we are not worthy. We are told time and again that we do not fit in, that we have to buy all kinds of products, spend all kinds of money, see all kinds of specialists, simply to be worthy of love. This intensifies the general wound of isolation from the love of others and lures us further into temptation, to do something that will somehow make us important. The lie denies what Adam and Eve already were. They were created in the image and likeness of God. "The content of the temptation strikes what the Creator himself molded in man—for, in fact, he was created 'in the likeness of God,' which means: 'in a way like God.' It also strikes the desire for knowledge that exists in man, and the desire for dignity."[30] The lie, once believed, spawns new insecurity in the person.

The Desert Fathers use a compelling image to present the subtle nature of the lie within every temptation. The Fathers emerged soon after Constantine legalized Christianity in the early fourth century. In the persecutions that preceded Constantine, many martyrs gave their lives for their faith in Christ. The drama of the Christian life was clear: unite yourself to Christ, even if it leads to martyrdom. After Christianity was legalized, however, the ideal of martyrdom receded as Christianity became part of daily life.

---

28. John Paul II, *Veritatis Splendor*, 102.
29. John Paul II, *Jesus, Son and Savior*, 69.
30. General audience, December 20, 1978, *Talks of John Paul II*, 507.

Within this context something new began to emerge. Christians began to take on the style of the marketplace. They were tempted to lie, cheat, and steal to get ahead. A group of Christians recognized this danger, and they began to flee the noise, hurry, and crowds of the world. Their actions became known as the *fuga mundi*, or flight from the world. It is also known as the *contemptus mundi*, or contempt for the world. This contempt is not an inner prison of anger, but a realization that the way of worldly fear impedes the life of grace. These early Christians fled to the desert so they could look deeply at their calling and the motivations of their hearts. The Fathers of the Desert then shared their hard-fought wisdom with those who sought them out, seeking holiness. Saint Antony the hermit was foremost among the Desert Fathers. He sought arid places where he could be alone with Christ and learn the nature of following the Lord. As a result he closely examined the movements of the human heart and the nature of temptation.

One of the devil's tactics, according to Antony, is to tempt us with what is glittering and alluring. This takes the form of an illusion the devil throws in our path. Antony says, "How many times he [the devil] presented the illusion of gold to me in the wilderness, in hopes that I would just touch and gaze on it!"[31] Saint Athanasius says of Antony:

> The enemy, observing his zeal and hoping to thwart it, threw in his path the apparition of a great silver dish. But Antony, knowing the craft of the despiser of goodness, stood looking at the dish and exposed the devil in it, "A dish here in the wilderness? Where did it come from? ... This is the craft of the devil. You will not frustrate my purpose by this, Devil! Take this with you to destruction!" As soon as he said this, it vanished like smoke from a fire. And as he continued, he saw next no illusion, but actual gold thrown in his path. It is not clear whether the enemy pointed it out, or whether some more excellent power was training the athlete [that is, the monk] and demonstrating to the devil that he was not, in fact, concerned about money.[32]

The Christian must stand steadfast with the truth and resist the appearances of evil. This is difficult, because the devil knows the person's

---

31. Athanasius, *The Life of Antony and the Letter to Marcellinus*, trans. Robert C. Gregg (New York: Paulist Press, 1980), 61.

32. Ibid., 40.

desires and weaknesses. He sets up an array of appearances and rational-izations to lure us with what seems familiar and innocent. But each one—a slight deviation, a compromise, a concession—opens a doorway that leads to sin. Once the person walks through it, the illusion draws him into a fantasy world based on ego. He then becomes the unfortunate prisoner of his own needs.

d. The Fourth Step: Fear

The lie can be effective only because it is followed immediately by the fourth step, fear. While the first two steps of temptation may take min-utes, days, or hours, the third and fourth are closely connected, almost simultaneous. The lie cannot persist long without fear, nor fear without the lie. They depend on each other. Fear is the essential ingredient of every sin. The lie ignites Eve's fear, and fear is the marrow of temptation. After the woman responds that she may not eat from the tree in the center of the garden, the devil introduces fear. He says: "You certainly will not die! No, God knows well that the moment you eat of it your eyes will be opened and you will be like gods who know what is good and what is bad." Notice the feeder implicit in the devil's statement. "You certainly will not die." What is the devil saying?

The devil is twisting the words of God and introducing the fear of death. Saint Augustine and other Fathers of the Church note that Adam should have stepped in at this point and defended God's words. He should have conquered the fear, stood up against the fear that the devil was introducing. Fear is a central step for us when we face sin and temp-tation. What is he suggesting? The devil's words imply that *unless* they eat of it, they will die. The two sentences mix. "It is Satan who suggests that they should *do* something to become like God, that they should take their likeness to God into their own hands. The gesture of taking the fruit and eating it is an obvious symbol of a man taking something into his own hand and then storing it away safely inside himself. It is a symbol of possession which has become such an obsessive concern of fallen man."[33]

---

33. Tugwell, *The Beatitudes*, 22.

Advertisers try to make us believe that unless we have the perfect hairline, waistline, portfolio, and retirement property, we will never be loved. The devil did the same thing in the garden. He suggests that without this five or ten dollars that I steal, without viewing this adult "entertainment," I will die the death of not having what I want: I will not advance ... I will not have pleasure ... I will not enjoy the kind of life I truly deserve. Temptation pivots on our fears. The fear implies that if we do not upgrade to the newest version of whatever is offered, that we will not matter ... will fall behind ... be unattractive, unloved, overlooked, be a loser. The fear at the root of all our other fears is that we are not enough. This immediately offends God, who created us in his image. Temptation induces us to believe that God did not create us good, that we must look for something else.

Listening to temptation always drags us down. Its illogic plays on our weaknesses and overwhelms us, so that we seek our dignity in something other than God. The more time we dally with temptation, the more it feeds. Time spent fueling temptation would be better spent in contemplating Christ. Temptation lures us to forgo the truth God has proclaimed and to fail to see what is truly good. Temptation leads man to surrender and disregard God's words. All this constitutes "the genuinely demonic situation into which the serpent tried to lure Adam: the situation that would have him choose with indifference between good and bad."[34]

e. The Fifth Step: The Choice and the Act

The fifth step in the sequence of temptation is the choice and action of sin. Adam and Eve take the fruit and they eat it. They break the law of God. Breaking the law is not a mere external crossing of a line. It is a rupture in man's innermost being. John Paul teaches that man is the "subject and agent of this choice ... made with a misuse of these faculties."[35] In a certain sense man's action consolidated the whole process of the separation from the family structure, the deception, the fear, and lying. This is the climax of the sin. The act of sin has an effect on a

---

34. Balthasar, *The Christian State of Life*, 38.
35. John Paul II, *Jesus, Son and Savior*, 22–23.

human person's very being. In choosing sin a person chooses to embrace
and to love something that is evil. When we love something "[it] con-
forms us to itself," and "our moral judgment can become distorted and
our tastes can become disordered."[36] By his choice to act on these initia-
tives of the devil, at the same time man internalized the horror of each
step in his disobedient action. Man has brought into himself the separation, alienation of family structure, the divisive question, the fear and the
lie. All that preceded this crucial step of choice and action was the devil's
influence and inspiration, the tendency to provoke iniquity.[37] But with
choice and action, man inhales, breathes in the evil influence. The sin
inheres in the conscience. Adam and Eve perceived disobedience toward
God as a good, made a choice, and acted upon this understanding. This
action caused a reaction in the depths of their being:

> Our acts not only concern the realization of [perceived] goods external
> to us—they not only change the external state of affairs by effecting
> advantages or disadvantages—but they give us our very own identity.
> The choices made by the acting person can be worthy or unworthy
> of him. In free action the author of the action puts his own identity
> into play.[38]

The notion that the person internalizes and externalizes sin is very
important. Sin actually *brings a lack into being* in the form of a break, a
hindrance, a misalignment in a person's relationship with God, with self,
with other people, and with the world. Sin wounds the human person in
the depths of his being and nature. This wound is constituted above all
by the loss of sanctifying grace and the preternatural gifts, the deprivation of which distorts man's harmony with God and alters the interior
equilibrium in man.[39]

We have seen what motivated Satan to tempt man to original sin and
every sin thereafter: Satan's prideful fury that man, body and soul, was
created in the image and likeness of God. Satan always tries to corrupt
that which is good. He attempts to turn man to use wrongly the freedom

---

36. Servais Pinckaers, *Morality: The Catholic View* (South Bend, IN: St. Augustine's
Press, 2003), 99.

37. Ignace de La Potterie, SJ, and Stanislaus Lyonnet, SJ, *The Christian Lives by the
Spirit* (New York: Alba House, 1971), 43.

38. Melina, *Sharing in Christ's Virtues*, 42.

39. John Paul II, *Jesus, Son and Savior*, 24.

that comes to him with being an image of God. Satan suggests that man use his freedom for something that is not true: "For this likeness to God brings a danger with it: it has the power to create something that even God cannot create: evil. Evil only attains reality in our will."[40] Original sin introduces human evil into the visible world. Satan plants this anti-seed of evil near to man's being the image of God and attempts to destroy the image: "Saint Augustine, with extraordinary perceptiveness, described the nature of this sin as follows: *amor sui usque ad contemptum Dei*—self-love to the point of contempt for God."[41]

Original sin can often seem remote to us. Unfortunately, original sin "is not an isolated event at the dawn of history."[42] It remains as if it were some distant crime for which parole is repeatedly denied. Saint Augustine approximates the nature of this sin. Original sin takes the character of a wound in man, a wound in his very nature. In his *On Genesis Against the Manichees*, Saint Augustine describes the very nature of the disobedience at the heart of this wound: man *took* when he was only meant to *give* and *receive*. As the image and likeness of God, man's nature is made up of the motion to give and to receive love. This is enough for man. In the deepest places of his existence man is called to give and receive love. Sin introduces a foreign movement, alien to the nature of the human person. Adam and Eve chose to take rather than to give or receive. Saint Augustine explains:

> [T]hey used wrongly that middle rank by which they were subject to God and held their bodies in subjection. This middle rank was like the fruit of the tree placed in the middle of paradise. *Thus they lost what they had received in wanting to seize what they had not received. For the nature of man did not receive the capability of being happy by its own power* without God ruling it. Only God can be happy by his own power with no one ruling.[43]

Saint Augustine's description of original sin is one of the best. The Pontifical Biblical Commission described it in a similar way: "... Adam, despite the prohibition, tried with his own strength, to seize the fruit by his own powers without waiting for God to give it to him in due time."[44]

---

40. Balthasar, *Theo-Drama II*, 220–221.
41. John Paul II, *Memory and Identity* (New York: Rizzoli, 2005), 6.
42. John Paul II, *Jesus, Son and Savior*, 31.
43. Augustine, *On Genesis*, bk. 2, ch. 15, 118.
44. Pontifical Biblical Commission, *The Bible and Morality*, 11.

This was the disobedience of original sin. Adam and Eve had not been given the faculty *to take*. They had been given the only two movements possible for the human person, to give and to receive: the *exitus* and *reditus* as the dynamic of communal love. The devil tempted them to go a third way that was not open to them. The devil tempted them to deny that they were the image of God by loving their own power to excess in an attempt to be God. When this takes place it ruptures something in the nature of man:

> Lust replaces self-giving love with grasping or appropriation of the other (as in the grasping [at equality with God] in Genesis 3 that Jesus' self-emptying of his divine prerogatives in Phil 2 reversed). Lust loses sensitivity to the gift of the person and to communion of persons that sexual union should embody.[45]

That first sin has a "legacy" that continues.[46]

Adam and Eve used the "middle rank of their subjection to God" wrongly. That is to say, they misused their *relationship* to God. The "middle" is a "relationship" that is the avenue for union. If distinct parts are united, they can only be united by having a *relationship* between, or *in the middle of*, them. Man and woman used, made an object of, *and instrumentalized*, their relationship to God and to each other. They consented to do this by an act of the will: they consented to *receive by seizing*. The attempt to *seize* wounded their capacity to *receive* and give.

The union that ought to exist between their reason and will has also been wounded. Once they tried to *receive* by *seizing* they had already repudiated what it means to *receive*, and they fell. "Man depends on the Creator and is subject to the laws by which the Creator has established the order of the created world, the essential order of existence (*ordo rerum*)."[47] The created order is an order of gift and reception. An act of *taking* or *seizing* violates gift and reception. We could say that such an act damages the very ontology of reception, and therefore the nuptial structure at the heart of man's identity. Reception's proper mode is not seizing, but patient acceptance of reason. Far less is God ever to be an object, let alone an object to be seized. We can only approach God with reception. This touches upon a profound disorder: the attempt to "fill" *reception* by

---

45. Kurz, "The Scriptural Foundations of *The Theology of the Body*," 43.
46. John Paul II, *Jesus, Son and Savior*, 31.
47. Ibid., 25.

violent seizing of what can only be received. By consenting to such an act, the first human persons committed original sin. This caused a wound within the relational structure of the human person. Balthasar notes:

> The natural powers of man's soul were, so to speak, enveloped and polarized by the all-embracing act of obedience to God in faith. It was only with the destruction of obedience that these powers appeared in their nakedness as "critical intellect" and "freedom of will." They had originally been intended to function as internal organs within faith, which is the form of obedient love.[48]

When man sins, evil is introduced, and it causes a wound deep in human nature and in the order of the world:

> According to revelation, sin is the principal and fundamental evil. It contains the rejection of God's will, of the truth and holiness of God, and of his fatherly goodness, as they are already revealed in the work of creation, and above all in the creation of the rational and free beings who are made "in the image and likeness" of the Creator. It is precisely this "image and likeness" that is used against God, when the rational being of his own free will rejects the finality which God has established for the existence and life of the creature. Sin therefore contains a particularly deep deformation of the created good, especially in a being that, like man, is the image and likeness of God.[49]

John Paul says the mystery of sin is introduced at the moment of original sin, when "the covenant was broken in man's heart."[50] In that primal instant "in man's heart, doubt is cast on the Gift."[51] How often this moment is repeated in temptation. At the same time the doubt is cast, man makes "a fundamental choice and carries it through against the will of the Creator."[52] Because of this choice and action, man casts God from the human heart. John Paul points to the Genesis account: "Then the eyes of both were opened, and they realized that they were naked; they sewed fig leaves together and made themselves loincloths" (Gen 3:6). He notes that the very first word of the verse, "Then ... " signifies "man's 'situation' after sin, and it shows the new state of human nature."[53]

---

48. Balthasar, *The Christian State of Life*, 93.
49. John Paul II, *Jesus, Son and Savior*, 19.
50. John Paul II, *Man and Woman He Created Them*, 235.
51. Ibid., 236.
52. Ibid., 237.
53. Ibid., 238.

In contrast to Genesis 2:25, "they were naked ... but did not feel shame," Genesis 3:6 points to "the birth of shame in connection with sin."[54]

Shame touches man in his deepest level, shakes the very foundations of his existence, and deforms his heart.[55] Prior to sin, nakedness was man's sign of participation in the gift. After sin, nakedness conveys the opposite: man is deprived of participation in the gift.[56] He suffers resistance in the way in which he engages the world. The "'man of concupiscence' took the place of the 'man of innocence.'"[57] Instead of walking in harmony with God, self, the other, and the created world, man now walks with fear and suspicion. The taking at the center of his action has spread out and infected his very nature. Man and woman feel shame before each other and before God. Now man experiences a "fundamental disquiet in the whole of human existence," and this manifests itself in fear.[58] Man now approaches God, self, the other, and the world through an "interior imbalance."[59] Sin has an impact on every aspect of his nature and his relatedness. His consciousness is no longer filled with an immediate, direct, spontaneous knowledge of the meaning of the world and of the other. After sin, his consciousness is preoccupied with fear and alienation. In particular, man experiences "a specific *fracture of the personal integrity of his own body.*"[60] Man's heart has become hardened.

The knee of the human leg provides an analogy. The joint is made to move the leg in two directions: back and forth, or up and down. When I walk, run, swim, kick, play soccer, dance, or jump, my knee is doing what it was made to do. If my knee were to have a will and intellect and decide to go laterally, that is, to move to the side at a ninety-degree angle, my knee would break and I would experience immense pain. If it goes in a direction it was not created for, it thwarts the direction it was created for. Once broken, it can no longer perform the acts for which it was made, to go up and down.

---

54. Ibid.
55. Ibid., 238, 251.
56. Ibid., 239.
57. Ibid., 242.
58. Ibid., 244.
59. Ibid.
60. Ibid., 245.

You and I were never meant to take. This disobedience of choosing to take thwarts our ability to give and receive. Once we step out of giving and receiving and take, we move the joint in a way it was not meant to go. We wound ourselves.

f. The Sixth Step: Hiding

The sixth step in the cycle of temptation and sin is characterized in the verse, "When they heard the sound of the LORD God moving about in the garden at the breezy time of the day, the man and his wife hid themselves from the LORD God among the trees of the garden" (Gen 3:8). John Paul teaches that after sin there is "the necessity of hiding oneself before the 'other' with one's body, with what determines one's own femininity or masculinity."[61] They are aware of the wound. They feel its effects in their nature. God is still present, but in their freedom they move from God, they break the covenant of creation. The "breezy time of the day" in Palestine is the end of day, when darkness descends. The spiritual meaning of the text is that darkness of another sort is descending and impinging—a spiritual darkness caused by man's choice and action to commit the sin of disobedience.

Their hiding, likewise, has a spiritual meaning. In sin, man hides from the truth. Instead of witnessing to the truth, "Adam was forced to learn how to make excuses. These excuses were words of untruth, of distance and alienation...."[62] Man refuses to acknowledge the gift. This is the fourfold alienation of sin: from God, from self, from the other, and from the created world. The hiding of Adam and Eve shows the consequence of original sin. The first human persons hide before God amidst the trees. They hide before themselves with excuses and blame. They hide before each other with fig leaves. They hide from their own bodies and the body of the other. Sin always reduces the meaning of the body in the mind of the sinner. The mind chooses to form a union with something other than the body for personal identity. Instead of the body, the mind

---

61. Ibid., 249.
62. Adrienne von Speyr, *Light and Images: Elements of Contemplation* (San Francisco: Ignatius Press, 2004), 31.

wishes the soul to be united to fashion, sensation, pleasure, power, or some other illusion.

Adam and Eve hide from creation by misusing it to disguise themselves. They have hindered and distorted their ability to engage God, self, the other, and the world. They use these as objects. They fear their inadequacy will leak out. Each of us knows our inadequacy very well— whether it concerns our height, body image, or abilities. We magnify the thing we do not like about ourselves. Hiding is a strategy that never works. We must have a place where we can reveal the absolute truth and abandon the game of hiding. People hide for forty and fifty years, but eventually the inadequacy comes out. Some people hide in a bottle or on the Internet. Some hide behind a fashion designer, or before a television screen. Some hide in an affair, in grades, politics, or money. We have to reveal our hiding places in a safe place.

God calls out, "Where are you?" (Gen 3:9). Do we really think the all-powerful, all-knowing, all-good God does not know they are scrunched down behind the fourth bush on the left? He calls out for them. He sees them, as he has all along. His question is a redemptive question. God is seeking them. They are not where they should be, next to him. They are using each other. God immediately starts the cycle of redemption in *exitus-reditus*. He goes outside himself to draw them in. His question prompts their conscience. They are not where they ought to be. They heard God moving. Notice the indirect discernment. They hear God but they don't see him.

In the midst of the hiding, however, man remains the image of God: "man's 'image' ... —even after he has fallen from God—cannot be lost."[63] An odd, inverted scene emerges. Man, the image of God, is now in a situation fraught with contradiction: The world that was set to reveal the beauty of God now hides the one made in his image and likeness. Man's action reverses the dispensation of Genesis. Instead of exercising dominion over the visible world, and thus revealing the beauty of one made in the image and likeness of God, man sees his dominion upended to hide the image and likeness of God. Man cannot recognize himself or the world. He "has become entrapped."[64]

---

63. Balthasar, *Theo-Drama II*, 320.
64. Ibid., 292.

g. *The Seventh Step: Blame*

An extension of the hiding continues in the seventh step of temptation and sin: blaming. As man is hiding, God calls out: "Where are you?"
(Gen 3:9). Man responds that he was afraid because he was naked, and
therefore hid himself. The Lord inquires as to who told him he was
naked, and asks whether man had eaten from the tree he was barred
from. Immediately man responds, "The woman whom you put here with
me—she gave me fruit from the tree and so I ate it" (Gen 3:12). Notice
that man blames the woman and God: "the woman whom *you* put here
with me." The woman then blames the serpent (Gen 3:13). Blaming is a
false way of "externalizing our problems. In other words, we give the
responsibility of whatever we are saddled with away to some outside
agent."[65]

Man sins not only because he fails the natural moral law, infringes the
rights of another, or is delinquent in his own duties. Man sins because he
betrays the very form of his creation and identity; he turns away from
relationality. By sin man chooses to invert the order of his being and to
turn against the inherent wisdom of relationality. In its most common
denominator, sin is hostility to the Trinity.

2. The Effects of Original Sin

The experience of sin does not end with the final step of blame. Sin
has effects. Sin initiates a cycle by which man continually attempts to
achieve an illusory plateau of meaning. John Paul emphasizes: "As a
consequence of original sin the whole man, body and soul, has been
thrown into confusion.... "[66] It was God's intention, prior to sin, that
man continue to live in creation in the state of original innocence. In the
decision to sin, however, man, of his own free choice, refuses the
Creator's design: "The unity that existed in the state of innocence and
was intended to continue into the heavenly state was ruptured by man's
fall into sin. For the solidarity of those who share human nature is so
great that the defection of even one individual cannot be without

---

65. Henry Cloud and John Townsend, *Safe People: How to Find Relationships That Are
Good for You*, (Grand Rapids, MI: Zondervan, 1995), 36–137.

66. John Paul II, *Jesus, Son and Savior*, 51.

consequence for all."[67] John Paul teaches that "Original sin is an inherited condition. As such, it signifies the innate sinfulness of man, his radical inclination toward evil instead of good. There is in man a congenital moral weakness which goes hand in hand with the frailty of his being, with his psycho-physical fragility."[68] The human person is tempted time and again to find fulfillment in his own nature. By the wound of sin, man refused affection for God, and delivered himself to affection for his own methods and endeavors. This changed his very experience of the world. For man, the earth that had been a sign of plenty prior to sin now becomes a place of scarcity, restlessness, uncertainty, loneliness, exile, and violence.[69] Distrust, indifference, hostility, and even hatred become inbred attitudes.[70] "As regards spiritual faculties this deterioration consists in a darkening of the intellect's capacity to know the truth, and in a weakening of the free will."[71]

Saint Thomas Aquinas details the specific kinds of concupiscence that afflict man. Concupiscence may be attributed to four forms: weakness, ignorance, malice, and concupiscence in the appetites.[72] Aquinas notes that the powers of our soul are no longer naturally directed to virtue and are therefore wounded. In the depths of our person we are easily deprived of pursuing the truth (the wound of ignorance); we are deprived of strength in choosing the good (the wound of malice); we are often deprived of the discernment needed to do what is arduous (the wound of weakness); and we have a difficult time moderating that which is pleasurable (the wound of concupiscence). These wounds result from original sin in the man, and are reinforced by every sin man commits. Concupiscence weakens our inclination to the good of virtue. Reason is obscured; the will is weakened.

In the earlier example of the businessman we see concupiscence in the form of ignorance as the man is wounded in regard to seeing the truth of the meaning of marriage and of his own body. The truth of these

67. Balthasar, *The Christian State of Life*, 133.
68. John Paul II, *Memory and Identity* (New York: Rizzoli, 2005), 18.
69. John Paul II, *Evangelium Vitae*, 9.
70. Ibid., 36.
71. John Paul II, *Jesus, Son and Savior*, 51.
72. Aquinas, *Summa Theologiae*, Ia IIae q. 85, a. 3.

things, so palpable as he kissed his wife goodbye, now seems like obscure voices in a distant room when the heat of temptation entices him. Malice is the wound because of which he cannot see the good in passing the cable station and letting it go, forgotten. "Goodness" now boils down to his impending satisfaction of his personal and immediate erotic needs and cravings. Weakness is the concupiscence through which he refuses to fight for the true and the good. He knows he should change the channel, call his wife, leave the room, but instead of fighting for what is true and good, he begins to rationalize and relativize the lie and the evil. He thinks, "At least I am not out with a prostitute.... After all, it has been a long day ... I am not hurting anyone.... Just this one time.... I'll only watch for fifteen minutes." Fourth, concupiscence in the specific sense is the inflaming of the sensible appetites that seek comfort and erotic sensation.

John Paul inherits the understanding of the effects of sin which Saint Thomas presents. The pontiff expresses the effects of sin in the language of experience, and describes the effects that ongoing, unrepented sexual sins and carnal passion have on a person. If given habitually to sins of the flesh, without having regular recourse to the sacrament of Penance, a person experiences a series of effects that are like the grandchildren of concupiscence. First, the deepest voice of conscience is silenced within the person. He or she is out of touch with true and authentic knowledge of self and the world. The person begins to make excuses that substitute for knowledge. Second, restlessness results. The person cannot sit still. Third, the inner man is reduced to silence. His reason is excluded as fantasy. He does not consider the entire picture and the long-range impact of his actions. Fourth, with the inner man silent, the senses begin to stand out and dominate his acts. If he has a craving, he must have a fix. He wants to be first in every category. Impatience rules the day, as he always needs the last word and the fat bottom line. Fifth, he is consumed by the appetites. Sixth, reflective activity is blunted within him. His life becomes a chore. His mind and his body are not united. This is, in one sense, a major goal of the devil. He hates unity wherever he finds it. The unity of the Person of the Word with flesh was his initial occasion of sin. Ever since that proposition, Satan has sought to disturb every manifestation of unity within the world and within man. Seventh, because the person seeks satisfaction at the expense of life and has little or no reflective activity, he becomes worn out. Eighth, he reaches a point where, in his exhaustion, he can only use things, including his body, as objects. His sin covertly reverberates between his soul and his body, and then echoes out through many personal acts that affect his vocation, his family, his community, and the world.

After original sin, when man encounters the visible world, he approaches through the filter of his ignorance, malice, concupiscence, and weakness. Man is under the strong and insistent impulse to attempt one more time to be happy on his own without God. Balthasar notes that this repeated delusion is an effect of original sin:

> For man in his fallen state, the fullness of paradise was turned into the scarcity of earth. As a result, the search for the necessities of life and for private possessions became inevitable; man's drives became the determining factor for the propagation of the race; and the choice between good and evil by an intellect schooled in worldly wisdom became the norm of moral behavior.[73]

3. Saint Augustine's Notion of Sin: The Wound and the Fever

The nature of sin is often treated in a legalistic and superficial manner in contemporary thought. A more legalistic approach understands sin as a mark that is to be taken away. After the mark is removed, the person is as good as new, and therefore must avoid any further taint through sin. This view of sin has an all-or-nothing quality that does not adequately correspond to the way sin wounds us. The focus shifts to the person's efforts, rather than the sin itself and its devastating effect on the person.

Saint Augustine teaches that even though burdened by sin, the person is still called toward that which fulfills him: his triune origin is the only authentic fulfillment for man in his deepest identity.[74] The person is created in the image of God, and therefore carries a seed of returning to God. For Augustine, sin takes on the character of a wound and a fever.[75] Original sin is similar to a weapon thrust into the body. It is one thing to be free from the wound of the sin itself, but quite another to be free

---

73. Balthasar, *The Christian State of Life*, 158.
74. Augustine, *De Trinitate*, bk. 14, ch. 12.
75. Ibid., bk. 14, ch. 17.

"from the infirmity which the fever produced." The body must not only be free of the weapon that invaded the flesh, but also the person must gradually recover and heal from the effects of the wound. While Baptism frees the person from the wound of original sin, it does not completely do away with the weakness that follows the fever—that is, concupiscence. A long convalescence is required. A constructive process of renewal must take place as the person moves closer to salvation each day. For Augustine, the essential sign of the Christian life is the journey of the traveler or the pilgrimage of the stranger who dwells in the earthly city toward the city of God.

4. The Desert Fathers

A fourth description of sin emerges from the teaching of the Desert Fathers. Through their long-fought experience with temptation, the Fathers alert us to the granular manner in which sin works in the life of the person. Sin, in its proper dimension, is not merely crossing a line. Rather, sin weaves a network of experiences that lead deeper into foreign territory. Sin begins with a *logismoi*, which "is essentially a train of thought which engages the mind, so that bit by bit one drifts away from what one is supposed to be doing into a world of fantasy."[76] The *logismoi* is the whole series of the seven steps described above as it occurs in the mind of the one being tempted. A practical description of a *logismoi* is easily observable in driving. As I cruise down the highway in the left lane, the speedometer arcs past sixty to sixty-five miles per hour. My sedan gradually overcomes the lumbering SUV in the right lane. A feeling of surpassing power washes over me. I speed along to seventy-five as the other vehicle disappears into the rearview mirror. Then I recall the speeding ticket and the points it cost me last summer. But I am ahead of everybody else. The open highway lies before me. Besides, today is Sunday. What police officer would give a ticket on Sunday? I start to play the odds. Then a red sports car gains on me, and I feel diminished. Thoughts of safety fade, and thoughts that I must win predominate.

---

76. Tugwell, *Ways of Imperfection*, 25.

a. The Sin of David

The Fathers use the sin of King David to illustrate how the network of sin becomes the overarching matrix in a person's inner life and decisions. The Lord takes David from the fields of the shepherd to the throne of Israel. David inherits the promises and protection of God. Despite this, he falls into serious sin, as the second book of Samuel recounts.

One evening David rises from a nap, walks on the roof of his palace and catches sight of a beautiful woman, Bathsheba. He inquires about her, invites the woman to his house, and commits adultery with her. Bathsheba soon informs David that she is pregnant. He learns that the woman is the wife of a soldier, Uriah, who is fighting the battles of Israel. David has Uriah sent home so the soldier might spend time with his wife, and in natural course engage in the marital act. Through this subterfuge, Uriah will think the child is his own. But David, in his unfaithfulness, had not counted on the faithfulness of Uriah. The soldier will not engage in the marital act with his wife because it is forbidden during times of battle. David, frustrated with Uriah's faithfulness, makes plans for Uriah to die in battle (2 Sam 11:1–27).

The Fathers examine the complicated situation of David's actions. They ask, "What is the sin of David?" Most often, we think that the sin of David is the adultery he committed with Bathsheba or the ensuing murder of Uriah, or both. Certainly, both actions are gravely sinful. But the Desert Fathers moved beyond simply designating an act as sinful. They sought, through discernment, the whole matrix of sin: what leads to sin, what underlies it, and what flows from it. Thus, the true nature of the evil of sin is revealed.

If we look at the actions of David, we find a sequence. Adultery leads to murder. If we look further, we see a more extensive network. What was David doing that led him to the adultery? Certainly he lusted, but what occasioned the lust? David had risen from a siesta, or a nap. In fact, the entire account of David's sin begins with the phrase, "At the turn of the year when kings go forth with their armies, David ... remained in Jerusalem." David was supposed to be out with the army. Instead, remaining at home, he is not where he is supposed to be. Thus, the initial sin of David is not lust, adultery, or murder, but sloth. David's laziness, or acedia, is the initial sin in the network of sin that leads to lust, adultery, and murder. Instead of doing the work he was supposed to be doing, David becomes bored. Being bored, he goes up on his roof and begins to look around. He sees something he likes. As the Fathers analyze sin, it is never simply an isolated act, but follows upon a network of isolation, appearances, lies, fear, and neediness.

b. The Network: Seven Deadly Sins

The foregoing analysis of sin can be extended to every sin. The Fathers discerned several predominant strains of sinful thoughts. Writing in the fourth century, John Cassian was the first to treat "the connection between the vices in a recognizably systematic manner."[77] Cassian taught, "There are eight principal vices that attack humankind ... the first is gluttony ... fornication ... avarice ... anger ... sadness ... acedia ... vainglory ... pride."[78] With the acumen that comes with being a student of human nature and experience, Cassian asserts that this list of sins is not a selective catalog. Rather, the sins are progressive, one leading to another. There is an "interlinking ... the overflow of the previous ones serves as the start of the next one."[79] The struggle with sin is not simply the battle of a person's will versus a particular action. The combat also involves discerning what leads a person to sin, the factors that facilitate the sin, and the network of elements that builds up against the sinner. The tradition in the East delineates eight deadly sins, but in the West writers and theologians have settled on seven ways in which sin confronts the person.

c. Vanity and Pride

East and West both consider the fundamental evils to be vanity and pride. In the East, the two are treated as separate sins, while in the West they are treated together. Vanity or vainglory is a sin by which the person

---

77. John Cassian, *The Conferences*, trans. Boniface Ramsey, OP (Mahwah, NJ: Paulist Press, 1997), 178.

78. Ibid., 183.

79. Ibid., 189.

daydreams about his own magnificence.[80] "The term 'vanity' literally means vapour or breath, and refers to all that is ephemeral, transient, incomprehensible, enigmatic."[81] This reaches its fullest manifestation in pride. The person beset by vanity and pride projects an aura of superiority and unrealistic self-sufficiency, pervaded by a denial of any need for community.[82] Pride is a practical refusal of community that may actually engage others, but does so with aggressive self-centeredness and manipulation that excludes the value of the other.[83] The basis of this egoism is self-love, indulged to such an extent that the person does not show much love of others. Prideful persons are aloof and inaccessible. While they may interact with others, they do not have a real interest in other people.[84] Their projects always come first, and their main project is themselves.

Pride and vanity connect all the other sins: "The sins are interwoven" and pride "runs through almost everything that we do."[85] Even those who have advanced far along the spiritual life are susceptible to pride: "The devilish strategy of pride is that it attacks us, not in our weakest points, but in our strongest. It is preeminently the sin of the noble mind."[86] Pride has a rare passport into the most refined of spiritual consciences: "even the perfect and those who have conquered all the vices could be struck."[87] Pride seeks out the inner emptiness and illusion of self-sufficiency that can often lurk behind our greatest accomplishments.[88] Pride can subvert good deeds, even the most charitable ones. As we gaze upon all our accomplishments, the emptiness that can so quickly boil up within us can interfere. The merits of the noble deeds, instead of retaining their quality as gift, are diverted inside in an attempt to fill the emptiness: "Self-pleasing is the vanity of pride."[89]

---

80. Tugwell, *Ways of Imperfection*, 27.

81. Pontifical Biblical Commission, *The Bible and Morality*, 58.

82. Henry Fairlie, *The Seven Deadly Sins Today* (Indiana: University of Notre Dame Press, 1995), 40.

83. Ibid.

84. Ibid., 41.

85. Ibid., 43.

86. Ibid.

87. Cassian, *The Conferences*, 187.

88. Fairlie, *The Seven Deadly Sins Today*, 53.

89. Ibid., 53.

Pride easily mixes with honest and noble achievements. The prideful person pretends that he has gained sufficiency based on his efforts alone. Pride isolates us. Vanity and pride were enthroned on a cultural level a few years ago when "you" were chosen as the person of the year—*Time Magazine's* person of the year was a mirror: Behold YOU. Yourself. You can do it. You did it. Be all you can be. YouTube. You are the star. It is a proclamation of pure, absolute narcissism."[90] The entitlement of pride leads to the idea that there is no rule higher than ourselves, and no source other than the self to consult.

Pride then spreads out in a web of other sins to which we can fall victim all the more easily if we do not understand them correctly. Gluttony, for example, goes beyond the idea of merely eating too much. Such a narrow view can prevent us from seeing gluttony in its more pervasive sense, which is excessive anxiety about one's health. Gluttony can make us think we will never have enough to sustain our health and life. It is the "gnawing sense that there will never be enough for oneself."[91] Before refrigeration became common and food would quickly spoil, people tended to hoard provisions. This hoarding reflects the fear that we will be left without. Essentially, gluttony is the fear that we will not be sustained, and that our health will fail. We begin to fault the spiritual life as not providing or as siphoning off the necessary material resources that could provide for an otherwise bleak future. Gluttony leads us to sin against a faith-filled trust that God will provide for our health and well-being. We can see gluttony at work in Adam's sin. He took the food the devil suggested because Adam feared that God would not provide.

Pride can disrupt the sensible appetites in another way. Lust arises from inordinate preoccupation with the self. When we regard ourselves as having lofty importance, we begin to fear the future. From this fear the need arises to satisfy the appetites and soothe the alarm. As it arises from fear, lust is never to be confused with healthy sexual attraction. Lust transforms sexual attraction into sexual fantasy. The "slide into fantasy" paints "real life as intolerably stalked by scarcity," and the person turns to

---

90. John F. Kavanaugh, "Autonomous Individualism," *America*, January 15–22, 2007, 8.

91. Mark A. McIntosh, *Discernment and Truth: The Spirituality and Theology of Knowledge* (New York: Crossroad, 2004), 100.

illusion for comfort.[92] In lust we corrupt the perennial summons of our sexual nature and use it to fuel an unreal world with no future. The alchemy of lust turns attraction into fantasy, and fantasy into frustration. If we are preoccupied with the self to the extent that we repeatedly attempt to fill the self with external goods or internal delights, we will never find fulfillment. In the face of ongoing defeat, we float aimlessly in the sea of the "compulsive neediness" fomented by greed or avarice.[93] Such greed is not the miser's Scroogelike pinching of every cent. Greed is the "resentment of others" to the extent that we can never accept anything as a gift, but only as a good to be taken and grasped.[94] Greed leads us away from the real world to an unreal world where we think that everything will go wrong and that no one else will ever care for us. Greed prompts us to continued planning for financial security against the worst-case scenario. Augustine refers to this sin as a particular ambition of the clergy.

These sins have a common element: looking at the created world from the perspective of fear. Instead of discerning the goodness that lies at the heart of everything, these sins lead us to catastrophize our situation and rely on our own efforts to subsist. When, self-preoccupied, we experience the scarcity of gluttony, lust, and greed, we give up—or don't try at all. This is the evil of sloth or acedia. When, having given in to gluttony, lust, and greed, we see the honest efforts of others to live in the world, we refuse to be inspired and to turn in a new direction. Instead, we find sadness at the good fortune of others. This sadness is envy, a self-inflicted pain at seeing the happiness of those who know the meaning of the gift.

The efforts to feel important and fill the inner emptiness from without always leave human persons frustrated. And frustration easily turns us to the next line of sinful thought, anger. Anger spreads from the thoughts into the body. It can erupt when we are inconvenienced and we seethe with anger at other people. What do we do when we discover an "out-of-order" sign taped across elevator doors, forcing us to climb three

---

92. Ibid.
93. Ibid.
94. Ibid.

flights of stairs? How do we feel when we must fill out three extra forms to mail a package at the post office during the Christmas rush, as the line snakes out the front door? How do we feel when we are out of cash and running late, only to find the ATM machine closed? Between our disappointing experience and the flash of anger, a moment of choice passes quickly. Our pride tag-teams with our anger, and we begin to grow impatient. All our anger goes back to one crucial fact: we are not God. If we were God we could fix the inconvenience and be treated as we feel we deserve. Anger sinks its roots into resentment over being a creature.

When we constantly indulge the appetites, we feel the cumulative effects of uncontrolled passions. The passions exercise such undue influence on our decisions and goals that an unreal world is created. This world fails to satisfy, compounding our original pain to a type of ongoing inner despair. Anger serves only to tighten the bonds of frustration. Anger wears us out, and we then can find little or no meaning in life. We grow disaffected, especially toward the things of God. Our sloth drives us further into preoccupation with the self, which creates a hunger from which we seek solace, venturing out again into gluttony—and the cycle repeats itself.

As the sins build upon one another, pride is the ridge between each of them. The prideful person secures things for himself to the exclusion of others. He values his own imagined importance while devaluing others. He acquires goods, both tangible and intangible. He is greedy for praise, affection, grades, recognition—hoping to fill an inner emptiness that pride and vanity have hollowed out within him. Vanity or vainglory is the "habit of living in unreality" in which our entire existence is measured on the illusory greatness of the self despite the emptiness within.[95] Pride denies the beauty of creation, of others, of the authentic self, and ultimately of God.

The sins are not necessarily experienced in the linear sequence described here. They also circle back upon one another and reinforce empty and vapid beliefs about self, God, and the world. A prime example of this is the sin of envy, which proceeds from pride and feeds on anger. Envy differs from jealousy, which can be a healing type of poison, because envy is always noxious. Jealousy can be the feeling of motivation we have

---

95. Ibid., 102.

when we see the good of another. If I am jealous of someone's athletic ability or academic prowess, I then attempt to imitate that goodness and strive for a form of excellence I see before me. Envy, however, does not motivate us to reach a goal. Instead, envy seeks only to destroy the good of the other. Envy is sorrow at another's good, which delights in hidden gratification when the other's good is blighted or lost. Envy is grieving the good of others, not simply because others have it, but because by their having it, we are somehow brought low.[96] This sin "crosses our faces in a split second" when we glance across the driveway and see that the neighbor's children are wearing jackets from the high-priced, prestigious academy in the next town.[97] Envy is often the sin of intellectuals, of university faculties where the envious seek signs of prestige and interpret any praise that is not directed to the self as some type of "imaginary disadvantage."[98] Envy thus breeds gossip, which seeks to tear down the good reputation of the other. Envy also stands at the center of the fascination with celebrity that dominates contemporary culture.[99] This enchantment with a famous person captivates us in a way that is ironically more about escape than independence. Consumerism dominates an economic system centered on envy.[100] In the final analysis, envy stands revealed as the most bitter of sins. Other sins "provide at least some gratification in their early stages. But there is no gratification for Envy...."[101]

Each of the sins reveals how we try to compensate for love not received. Love alone fulfills us. The deadly sins offer plastic imitations of love which, instead of fulfilling our identity, drain it. They do not bring what they promise. Instead, they hollow out and increase the emptiness in the heart. But we cannot identify or trace the pain. The roots of sin grow deeper when we continue to return to and rely upon the failed schemes. We turn again and again to the false fullness of greed, envy, pride, and vanity that give an illusion of fullness, but erode it instead.

---

96. Fairlie, *The Seven Deadly Sins Today*, 64.
97. Ibid., 61.
98. Ibid., 65.
99. Ibid., 81.
100. Ibid., 69.
101. Ibid., 61.

5. An Image of Sin: *Needful Things*

A work by the contemporary horror author Stephen King master-fully depicts the nature of sin. King's bestseller *Needful Things* is set in a sleepy New England town where the residents know one another all too well. As the story begins, the folks are abuzz with curiosity about a visitor who is opening an antiques shop, Needful Things, in a long vacant store-front. The proprietor, an urbane, aristocratic old gentleman, fills the shop with exquisite antique pieces and hard-to-find collectibles.

The storefront features a large central window easily seen from the sidewalk of the main street. As people pass by, each catches sight of a treasured item, long desired. Then begins a feverish chase to obtain it.

But none of the items for sale has a price tag.[102] This only fuels the buyer's pursuit. As each person bargains for the desired object, he or she becomes obsessed and desperate to have it. It is the one thing that person has always wanted, but never found. It is the one thing that will make their life perfect and complete. One man sees an antique fishing rod. Another sees a faded school letter jacket, the one like the quarterback wore. If he had only had that, he would not have been picked on in high school and would have succeeded in life. A woman sees a picture of Elvis Presley, which transports her into the dreamlike presence of the star, and brings her satisfaction and companionship long since lost at home. An older man sees an antique pipe he absolutely must have to complete his collection. Each person is willing to spend or do anything to have the perfect object. The dynamic of the pursuit is "defining [their personal] worth by need."[103] They begin to lose themselves to their obsession:

> Times changed; methods changed; faces, too. But when the faces were needful they were always the same, the faces of sheep who have lost their shepherd, and it was with this sort of commerce that he felt most at home, most like that wandering peddler of old, standing not behind a fancy counter with a Sweda cash register nearby but behind a plain wooden table, making change out of a cigar-box and selling them the same item over and over and over again.[104]

---

102. Stephen King, *Needful Things* (New York: Signet, 1992), 6, 47.
103. Ibid., 51.
104. Ibid., 584.

The sale is really about the soul: "People always thought in terms of souls, and of course he would take as many of those as he could when he closed up shop; they were ... what trophies were to the hunter ... "[105] Strangely, no one ever sees a truck making deliveries, but the store grows more full.[106]

The gentleman owner, Leland Gaunt, waits for special sales when only one customer is in the store,[107] having been lured in by curiosity.[108] The thought of pride follows quickly. The first temptation ensnares a young man who believes his family will finally listen to him as he has gossip and news about the newcomer: The "thought" of having "an in" with the object of everyone's curiosity is what allows the temptation to be "turned easily."[109] When customers first see the "quite old" aristo-cratic proprietor they feel a "cramp of fear."[110] The old man engages the customers and lures them into temptation with "interest and pleasure." He encourages those who approach his store to "enter freely" as the door shuts behind them.[111] As the man talks, a certain "hissing sound" can be heard.[112] But the customers don't notice it, nor do they see that his manicured hands are really talons.[113] Each customer begins to feel "the certainty that he was living the best hour of the best day of his life."[114] Stunned and excited, the customers can see a future for themselves in which they escape from the drudgery of their daily life.[115] They are "like a kid looking into a toyshop window."[116] As they leave with their treas-ured object, they feel as if they are drifting and floating.[117]

Inevitably the customers do not have enough cash to buy their special object. So, the owner accepts the performance of some deed as payment.

---

105. Ibid., 340.
106. Ibid., 165.
107. Ibid., 166.
108. Ibid., 18.
109. Ibid., 20.
110. Ibid., 23.
111. Ibid., 23, 450.
112. Ibid., 25.
113. Ibid., 635.
114. Ibid., 77.
115. Ibid., 78.
116. Ibid., 79.
117. Ibid., 95.

To have their desired trinket, they each must play a "joke" on another person. One person must sling mud at another's newly washed sheets as they dry in the sun. Another must throw a rock with a threatening note through a neighbor's window. Each of these deeds inflames the town's long-held grudges. As with any small town, the lines have been drawn for a long time between persons and groups. Prejudices, slights, irreconcilable differences, and feuds abound. The tricks are designed to be attributed to the most likely cause: the one who held the grievance, when in fact someone else, who knew nothing of the grudge, carried out the deed. When people discover the dreadful pranks, they think that the person who had a grudge against them did it. The labels pave the way to destruction. The third-party prank drives enemies against one another in the final chapter of a long feud. So the Catholics war against the Protestants, the bartender against the regular drunk, the police officer against the notorious town speeder, the energy folks and the environmental activist, and so on, until it all blows up and the people begin to kill one another. The devil aligns himself with the hidden hatreds simmering in the town and provokes them. And it all began with people willing to do anything to get what they always wanted, the one thing that would fix their life: the "one thing in all the world, the one useless thing, that you want so badly that you get it mixed up with needing it."[118] Their obsession is later revealed as "a disease that looks like a cure."[119] The folly of temptation is evident when the devil character says to himself: "Perhaps all the really special things I sell aren't what they appear to be. Perhaps they are actually gray things with only one remarkable property—the ability to take the shapes of those things which haunt the dreams of men and women."[120]

Only one character remains unaffected by the window: the town sheriff. As he passes by the shop, he experiences something that no one else in the novel does. He forgets about the shop the moment he passes it: "The place [Needful Things] slipped from his mind as soon as he passed it."[121] All the others "had to go back" after they passed by, drawn

---

118. Ibid., 711.
119. Ibid., 685.
120. Ibid., 370.
121. Ibid., 58.

by some article under the glass.[122] The sheriff begins to connect the awakening of all the ancient hatreds in the town with the arrival of the new shop, and he says, "I have to see this guy for myself."[123] In contrast, the devil character thinks that the sheriff is someone "a man would do well to steer clear of,"[124] because, as he says, "Men like Pangborn saw too much."[125] Thus the sheriff does not come face to face with the owner while everyone else in the town has. The sheriff says, "He seems to have something for everyone else in town, so why not something for me?"[126]

At one point, the sheriff, still suspecting that the murderous events in the town can be traced back to the store, approaches the window while the shop is closed. As he gazes in, the devil character, Leland Gaunt, is on the opposite side of the glass, looking out. Whereas others saw their needs in the window, the sheriff sees nothing. The store appears empty to him. He does not even see the proprietor standing there. In fact, the sheriff is startled when he sees his own reflection in the glass.[127] Others see their need, but he sees his own image.

At the end of the novel the sheriff finally enters the store during his investigation, and he finds a bare floor, bare walls, and a number of glass cases. The cases were empty, the stock was gone. Everything was blanketed by a thick fall of dust, and the dust was undisturbed by any mark. [He thinks:] "No one's been here for a long, long time."[128] The only furnishings that matter are the ones that can be seen from the street.[129] The sheriff pieces together all that has happened while he thinks about the devilish nature of the store and its owner. He says, "His power is over need, not will."[130]

Toward the end of the novel, as the true nature of their deeds becomes visible, the people realize that the thing they thought they always wanted has been their downfall. They have murdered one another, killed spouses,

---

122. Ibid., 77.
123. Ibid., 69.
124. Ibid., 171.
125. Ibid., 225.
126. Ibid., 321.
127. Ibid., 223.
128. Ibid., 686.
129. Ibid., 339.
130. Ibid., 599.

lost their homes and lives. In their final despair, each person looks at the object that began the downward spiral, and its true nature is revealed. The autographed baseball card was really an old piece of trash; the photo of Elvis Presley was really rotten cardboard; the faded school letter jacket was actually a moth-eaten rag; the antique pipe was in reality a straight razor. Wrapped up in their need, they looked at these things with blinders on.[131] Thus they were prevented from seeing the true nature of the things. Their need came from their emptiness and gave form to illusions upon which they staked their lives. The temptation was the central move that precipitated their downfall.

6. The Temptation of Christ

The Gospel accounts about the temptation of Our Lord teach us to what an extent Jesus emptied himself.[132] The devil hears there is a son of God in the world. This is nothing new to Satan. He has a long history of dealing with the sons of God. He dealt with Adam, causing him to fall from paradise. Satan brought Moses to anger, and David to sloth, lust, and anger. He duped Samson and tried the prophets to no end. Now he hears a new voice, one that had been heard over the Jordan. Now Jesus is led by the Spirit of God into the desert. Scripture notes, "those who are led by the Spirit of God are sons of God" (Rom 8:14). So the devil warms up with the first temptation: gluttony. Although we reduce gluttony to overeating, it has very little to do with food and everything to do with fear. Gluttony is the fear that we will never have enough, so it leads us to hoard. Gluttony has many objects. We can be gluttonous for knowledge, from the fear that unless we are regarded as an expert we may not be heard. We can be gluttonous for attention.

Satan tells Jesus, "If you are the Son of God command this stone to become bread" (Lk 4:3). The devil directs his attack at the identity of Jesus, "If you are the Son of God," in an attempt to discern his status. This temptation is to betray the Creator by changing the nature of things to serve one's needs. Change the stone to bread. Change minerals into plants. You need to eat, so change the laws of existence as God has set

---

131. Ibid., 667.
132. Mt 4:1–11; Mk 1:12–15; Lk 4:1–13.

them: Make that stone be something it can never be—bread. The other food miracles, the changing of water into wine at Cana and the multiplication of loaves, are natural progressions. Water becomes wine in the natural world on a regular basis—the rain feeds the vine that produces the grapes that become wine. But this action does not anticipate or speed up nature; it betrays nature as the Creator intended it.

So many temptations come in this form. Command that arguing and fighting become family life. Command that violence becomes peace. Command that cheating becomes a way to succeed. Command that the Internet becomes relationship, that pleasure becomes beauty, that the child in the womb becomes simply an inconvenience that a woman can dispose of to avoid discomfort. Command that marriage is not about the beauty of a love that reaches across sexual difference, but that it is about personal sentiment, so that two men or two women may marry. Betray the order of nature that the Creator intended. Make this stone bread. Jesus answers this temptation with Scripture, "One does not live by bread alone" (Lk 4:4 [Dt 8:3]). Jesus answers again at the Last Supper. He commands not that stone become bread, but that the bread become his body to nourish and refresh hearts that can turn easily to stone. Any old god can turn a stone into bread. But only the Christian God turns bread into his flesh to nourish the world. Pleasure had worked before as a temptation, but not this time.

The devil turns to his second temptation. He takes Jesus "up" and shows him all the kingdoms of the world in a single instant (Lk 4:5). Imagine every regime, every celebrity, every government—whether dictatorship, democracy, or monarchy—every economic power and financial empire. Just browse the pages of *People* magazine to view this temptation up close. Every kingdom that had ever been conquered was compressed and condensed into a single moment. Why did the devil not prolong the show and let Jesus muse on it? Why did he show this to Jesus only for a single instant? Because the kingdoms of this world last only for a moment. Even the devil cannot make them last longer. They are made of plastic; they are hollow and empty. If these kingdoms of the world are so spectacular, why does the devil even want to give them away? This temptation will return at the passion as well. What Jesus refuses from the devil, Pilate accepts. And it crumbles. Jesus responds again with Scripture: "You shall worship the LORD your God, him alone shall you serve" (Lk 4:8 [Dt 6:13]). Jesus offers a kingdom far more enduring than Satan's instant variety. Jesus' kingdom lasts for eternity.

The third temptation follows, with Satan taking Jesus up to the parapet of the Temple of Jerusalem. Satan again questions the identity of Jesus, "If you are the Son of God, throw yourself down from here ... " (Lk 4:9). Satan has caught on by now. He even quotes Scripture to Jesus, noting that angels will protect the Son of God. This temptation is to pride, the very one by which Satan fell—and notice that pride always falls downward. Satan urges Jesus to do exactly what Satan did—fall downward. Satan urges Christ to view his sonship pridefully as entitlement, and to reformulate his basic message: to be served rather than to serve. Christ does not throw himself down, but ascends. He ascends to the cross where the devil who departed as a serpent returns as a lion and repeats this temptation in the words of the passersby: "'If you are the Messiah ... come down from the cross" (Mk 15:29–32). Jesus does not descend, but ascends in filial trust to the Father and breathes forth the Spirit (Jn 19:30). Then, he rises from the dead and later ascends into heaven.

Part III

The Theology of the Body, Life According to the Spirit

~

CHAPTER SIX

Renewing the Image

As we have seen, John Paul appeals to the teaching of Jesus regarding "the beginning" to explain the identity of the human person (cf. Mt 19). The Pope uses the categories of original solitude, original unity, and original nakedness to outline the capacities inherent in human nature. These concepts convey the inviolable dignity of the human person created body and soul in God's image. "Before sin, man possessed sanctifying grace with all the supernatural gifts that make him righteous before God"[1] and man "maintained in himself an interior equilibrium."[2]

John Paul refers to original shame to describe the wound of sin that man experiences, disfiguring his identity as the image of God. Christ appeals to the beginning a second time: he instructs the apostles that the devil is "a liar from the beginning" (Jn 8:44). The devil's attack leaves a wound of sin in man, which distorts the meaning of the gift in him. Man is tempted toward sin and wounded by its effects. The attack takes place at the level of man's identity, in an attempt to corrupt his body and soul, intellect and will, choice and freedom.

But God is faithful to his love. God does not leave man to his own devices. God does not grow angry when man sins. God does not say, "I told you so." Instead, the first thing God says when man sins is, "I have a plan." John Paul notes that even Cain's punishment does not destroy

---

1. John Paul II, *Jesus, Son and Savior*, 24.
2. Ibid.

his dignity: "Not even a murderer loses his personal dignity."[3] The punishment is healing, not vindictive. It is not some arbitrary temperamental act of a frustrated God. Rather, "the punishment of sin ... principally occurs in the process of the righting of the imbalance within the creature."[4] The punishment/plan is not a deprivation, but a restoration.

God's first question to man is a redemptive question: "Where are you?" (Gen 3:9). God knows well where Adam and Eve are hiding. He poses the question as an examination of conscience for man. From there, the Lord proclaims the *protoevangelium*, or first proclamation of the Good News of man's salvation. God says to the devil: "I will put enmity between you and the woman, between your offspring and hers; he will strike at your head, while you strike at his heel" (Gen 3:15). John Paul comments: "The divine oracle promises to the man, dragged down the path of evil, the coming of another man, descended from the woman, who will bruise the serpent's head."[5]

The creation of man was intricate and profound. The fall of man was tortuous and convoluted. The effects of sin upon man are tragically dramatic. John Paul teaches, however, that despite all that, "reconciliation cannot be less profound than the division itself. The longing for reconciliation itself will be complete and effective only to the extent that they reach—in order to heal it—the original wound which is the root of all other wounds: namely, sin."[6] God's response to sin is not so much wiping a mark off the soul as it is a plan of salvation that astounds all creation. Sin is not a series of unrelated transgressions. As John Cassian had noted, the sins bleed and overflow into one another: the effects of one sin prepare the ground for the next one. Sins can choke a person's life like weeds in a garden choking out flowers. For Cassian, this insidious overflow "must be fought against in a similar way and by the same method, and we must always attack the ones that follow by beginning with those that come before."[7]

---

3. John Paul II, *Evangelium Vitae*, 9.

4. Romanus Cessario, http://www.ewtn.com/library/CHRIST/FR91101.TXT Web article.

5. John Paul II, *The Trinity's Embrace*, 11–12.

6. *Reconciliatio et Paenitentia*, 3.

7. Cassian, *The Conferences*, 189.

As humans look upon the world they see generation after generation of pain and hardship. However, John Paul indicates God's plan has already overcome the damage that sin wreaks on man's identity, on the family, and on the world:

> Nevertheless, that same enquiring gaze, if it is discerning enough, detects in the very midst of division an unmistakable desire among people of good will and Christians to mend the divisions, to heal the wounds and to reestablish, at all levels, an essential unity.[8]

Yet, man cannot achieve reconciliation with God on his own, but must rely on God's plan. Balthasar notes, "The reality of sin could not be transformed into unreality by a purely external decree of God. The Son of God had to take its guilt upon himself and atone for it in the abandonment of the Cross."[9]

A. Seven Steps of Grace

As we saw in the previous chapter, man fell into sin through disobedience when he consented to the devil's temptation. The seven steps of sin trace the path behind temptation and the choice to sin. God responds to the evil of temptation and sin with a plan of salvation, which likewise takes place in seven steps—the seven steps of grace. These steps correspond in a medicinal manner to the seven-step program of temptation and sin. The plan begins with the coming of Jesus Christ into the world. Jesus is the Savior who leads us into the kingdom of God by his complete gift of self, his kenosis, his outpouring by his death on the cross. The death of Jesus is a gift of self, and in this he reveals the mercy of the Father and forgives sin.

1. The First Step: Enter Family Structure

The Gospel of Saint Luke records the steps of God's saving plan with particular detail: "In the sixth month the angel Gabriel was sent from God to a town of Galilee called Nazareth, to a virgin betrothed to a man named Joseph, of the house of David, and the virgin's name was Mary"

---

8. *Reconciliatio et Paenitentia*, 3.
9. Balthasar, *The Christian State of Life*, 133.

(Lk 1:26–27). The passage is particular and specific, but is not a simple recitation of facts. God sent an angel not just to any town, but to one in Galilee called Nazareth; not just to anyone there, but to a virgin; not to any virgin, but to one named Mary, betrothed to Joseph: God is aiming, focusing, sharpening the kingdom. As grand and as wide as it is, the kingdom has an address. God draws near in a particular way and in a particular place.

The annunciation of the birth of Jesus begins the culmination of God's saving plan. Ever since the *protoevangelium* of the Book of Genesis, God's people have been living in hope and expectation. God has been preparing a wounded world through the entire Old Testament. Finally, in Mary, the plan crests. The annunciation to Mary is the great reversal. Gabriel announces that the plan of God is taking place not in a distant temple or military maneuver, but in the very family structure proper to the identity of the human person. The fallen angel Lucifer whispered a temptation to the virgin Eve and wounded the family structure. Now the archangel Gabriel announces the plan of God to the Virgin Mary in the very midst of the family structure. God offers a remedy to the evil of sin. Whereas Satan bypasses the family, the occasion of grace always paves its way with unity. The angel is sent "to a Virgin betrothed" (Lk 1:27). To conquer sin, God uses a way opposed to the pattern of evil. The true manifestation of love and mercy enters the family cycle. As Pope Benedict XVI teaches, "'[R]edemption appears as the re-establishment of unity....'"[10]

2. The Second Step: Announcement of the Saving Plan

Gabriel confidently announces God's saving plan: "Behold you will conceive in your womb and bear a son, and you will name him Jesus." The name Jesus means "Yahweh saves." Gabriel is unabashed as he proclaims Mary's holiness and the salvation from God in Jesus. How different this is from Satan's approach. The evil one slithers next to Eve and whispers a deceptive request for information, just a small subtle question

---

10. Benedict XVI, *Spe Salvi*, 14.

about the rules. Gabriel does not hint or suggest. He comes with no disguised questions. He makes a clear, direct statement: He proclaims salvation in Jesus.

The second step of temptation was to ask an "innocent little question." Satan led Eve with a sly solicitation: "Did God really say not to … ?" (Gen 3:1). The angel Gabriel does not approach Mary with an innocent little question. Instead, he makes a bold proclamation: "Hail, favored one! The LORD is with you!" (Lk 1:28). The Greek word used for "favored one" is κεχαριτωμένη (*kecharitomenē*). This is difficult to translate into English. It means overflowing with grace to such an extent that it is like a fountain within a fountain. The abundant water flowing from the fountain is completely pure and radiant. *Kecharitomenē* is like a superlative placed upon a superlative.

3. The Third Step: Truth

Jesus said Satan was a "liar from the beginning." After Satan had induced Eve to doubt what God really said, he then went for the flash fire, a two-step program of a lie and fear. Whereas Satan lied, Gabriel tells the truth. The Son whom Mary shall bear will save the world through an unending kingdom of unity: "He will be great and will be called Son of the Most High, and the Lord God will give him the throne of David his father, and he will rule over the house of Jacob forever, and of his Kingdom there will be no end" (Lk 1:32–33). Gabriel speaks on earth that which he has beheld in heaven since his own creation: The Son receives everything from the Father from all eternity. The lie must eventually fall before the gift of self.

The falsehood of "you will be like gods" (Gen 3:5) contradicts the truth that Adam and Eve already were like God, created in his image and likeness (Gen 1:26–27). Each lie must eventually be revealed as false. The lie that they "would not die" when they ate of it (Gen 3:4) is disproven by the thousand deaths we die in learning that the true shape of self-giving love is always cruciform.

We must continually use discernment to find the truth. Whatever enters our mind must pass through the lie detector of good judgment. This is a type of purification. Pope Benedict XVI emphasizes: "We must free ourselves from the hidden lies with which we deceive ourselves. God sees through them, and when we come to stand before God, we too are forced to recognize them."[11] Cassian concurs: Man must "examine all the thoughts that emerge in our heart, first tracing their origins and causes and their authors."[12]

The life of grace and virtue requires discernment of thoughts. Conscience must sift each thought to determine if it is truly good or only apparently good. The Desert Fathers practiced discernment frequently. They spoke of the need to routinely judge the nature of one's course of action. The devil disguises things that are bad for us, making them look good and appealing. The Fathers compared Satan to a counterfeiter who sought to make evil thoughts appear good. The spiritual director has to assist the Christian to discern the true nature of such false goodness hidden in our thoughts:

> The very high skill and training of such persons [spiritual directors] exists for the sake of determining whether something is gold of the purest sort ... or whether it has been less purified by fire[,] ... not being deceived by common brass ... under the guise of shining gold.... [They] [s]hrewdly recognize coins displaying the heads of usurpers but also define with a still finer skill those which are stamped with the image of the true king but are counterfeits. Finally, they submit them to careful weighing in case they are lighter than they should be.[13]

The Christian soul must "be able to turn down those [thoughts] which ... portray in the precious gold of Scripture the face not of the true king but of a usurper" and must "refuse as too light and condemnable and insufficiently heavy those coins whose weight and value have been eaten away by the rust of vanity...."[14] The danger is that the Christian attempts to "pursue counterfeit loves while imagining that one loves God...."[15]

The truth finds a home in Mary because she is humble. The Desert Fathers knew that "true discretion is not obtained except by true humility."[16]

---

11. Ibid., 34.
12. Cassian, *The Conferences*, 59.
13. Ibid.
14. Ibid., 62.
15. Cessario, *Introduction to Moral Theology*, 49.
16. Cassian, *The Conferences*, 90.

4. The Fourth Step: Do Not Be Afraid—Entrust

The plan of God continues as a point-for-point response to the evil of temptation and sin. Eve was perplexed and duped by the words of the fallen angel. Mary is troubled at the words of the archangel (Lk 1:29). Whereas Satan relied on Eve's self-centered fear, Gabriel addresses the humility of Mary: "Do not be afraid, Mary, for you have found favor with God" (Lk 1:30). The fallen angel implicitly induced fear; Gabriel immediately and explicitly calls for trust. The trust is not a mere summons of confidence by which Mary resolves to press forward. The trust is an *entrusting* as well. The rejection of fear takes the form of the further decision to love. Mary entrusts herself to the Trinity: "The Holy Spirit will come upon you, and the power of the most High will overshadow you. Therefore the child to be born will be called holy, the Son of God" (Lk 1:35).

5. The Fifth Step: The Choice / Act—*Fiat*

Recall that in the steps of temptation and sin as found in the third chapter of Genesis, the choice and the action internalize the previous steps: the isolation, alienation, question, doubt, lie, and fear. The effects of original sin leave these wounds in the person, and when internalized, they take the form of John Paul's category of original shame. Adam and Eve made a choice and acted to internalize the fear. People continually play this out in every subsequent sin.

God seeks to heal this internalized wound through the plan of salvation. The healing, however, cannot be the mere abstract waving of a wand. Magic does not heal, it merely masquerades for a time. Christ offers us an integral salvation, which responds immediately and directly to the wound of sin in the human heart.

In his wisdom, God plans that all of salvation history waits for the yes of a woman, the Blessed Virgin Mary. Her yes, her *fiat*: "Let it be done to me as you say." Her *fiat* is her *reception* of the word of the angel. She first conceives in the humility of her heart. She receives God's plan into her soul so abundantly that she conceives the Son of God in her womb through the Holy Spirit. At this moment, all the riches of heaven enter her womb. Recall Saint Augustine's words: Our first parents lost what they had received by trying to seize what they had not received. In the plan of God, Mary receives, rather than seizes, and she carries the seed to restore all of man's self-taking. She has received the greatest revelation of the Father and his love.

Mary's *fiat* is not an autonomous enterprise. In her humility she is actively receptive to the word of God. This active receptivity is docility in the classic sense. Saint John says, "They shall all be taught by God" (Jn 6:45). The word for "taught" in the Vulgate is *docibiles*, from *docēre*, meaning to teach, from which derives the English word *docile*. Docility is not some fragile demeanor of passive compliance. Docility is the defined stance of open resiliency. Ignace de La Potterie and Stanislaus Lyonnet explain, "The mystical attitude in the life of grace will, therefore, consist of directing one's attention less on the human effort than on the divine action and our openness to it: here docility is primarily important."[17] A docile person waits for God and stands ready to receive all God has to offer, without condition or compromise. The charity of Christ makes a Christian always ready to give first place to the teaching of the Church. This docility allows the human person to be receptive to the impulse of the Holy Spirit and to act on it.[18] Mary's action unites with the previous action of God. His act always precedes our own. This is made clear in the dogma of the Immaculate Conception. By a singular privilege, God keeps Mary free from all sin from the first moment of her conception, in view of the merits of Jesus. The grace of her Son preserved Mary from sin. She does not merit special treatment on her own. Rather, God, by his action, bestows this privilege on her as her own. She is thus humble and docile in the classic sense.

The Son of God is conceived in humility. The Incarnation, his taking on of human nature, is the action by which the Son of God, a divine Person, unites himself to a true human nature. Balthasar emphasizes that Mary's *fiat* is always united and in fact preceded by that of the Son: "Mary's *fiat* too, uttered vicariously for all and founding the Church as the bride of Christ, is empowered to institute this only by this kenotic

---

17. La Potterie and Lyonnet, *The Christian Lives by the Spirit*, 191.

18. Servais Pinckaers, OP, *The Pinckaers Reader: Renewing Thomistic Moral Theology*, eds. John Berkman and Craig Stevens Titus (Washington, DC: The Catholic University of America Press, 2005), 59, 63, 68.

fiat of the Son.... "[19] The Son, from all eternity, has been handing himself over to the Father in the Holy Spirit. In the plan of salvation, the Son carries out this movement in time in a unique way.

God created the world out of love. Recall the *ex nihilo, bara', dabar* sequence that reveals God's loving plan of creation. That same love goes to an even deeper measure in the redemption wrought on the cross. He who created the world, and ultimately man, out of nothingness, now redeems out of the void of alienated emptiness. "Here lies the 'unfathomable' (Eph 3:8) mystery of the Cross, in the momentum of the collision of the entire burden of sin with the total powerlessness of the kenotic existence."[20]

The Son is always *going forth*: He is eternally proceeding from the Father and eternally giving himself back to the Father in the *ad intra*, immanent life of the Trinity. Out of this same love for the Father, and proceeding from within this same circulation of love, he reaches out for humanity in the Incarnation. The Son's taking flesh is for the love of the Father and for the love of the human race.

Balthasar emphasizes that the Son, in his love for the Father, shows man how to love: "... the authority that comes from God was to take effect strictly in the sphere of powerlessness, and more radically still in the handing-over of entire existence, including its death, into the disposition of God who was to give it form."[21] Love takes the form of a sacrificial gift of self. Sacrifice is always the raw material God uses to convert man to love. In the plan of salvation, the Son's sacrifice is the acceptance of death. "The Son has taken death's purely punitive character upon himself and thereby released the character of grace for his brothers, whereby he unveils and fulfills the purpose of finitude."[22]

6. The Sixth Step: The Visitation

The sixth step of grace responds definitively to the sixth step of sin. Recall that Adam and Eve hid after they sinned. This was because fear filled the place that was meant for the gift. Instead of reaching out to

---

19. Hans Urs von Balthasar, *The Glory of the Lord VII*, 218.
20. Ibid., 208–209.
21. Ibid., 202.
22. Adrienne von Speyr, *The Boundless God* (San Francisco: Ignatius Press, 2004), 23.

each other and to God, they hid their relationality to the other and God. In grace, the gift is *recreated* by the self-giving love of Jesus on the cross, and communicated by the Holy Spirit into the depths of the redeemed man as humility. The gift of the Son on the cross is already discernable in his Mother in the home. It is from there that Mary, instead of hiding, moves outward as a gift of self: an act of charity for all to see. After the annunciation, she immediately proceeds into the hill country on a mission of charity: "And behold, Elizabeth, your relative is now in her sixth month…" (Lk 1:36).

Mary is the first of the redeemed, preserved from all stain of sin by a singular action of God, in view of the merits of her Son. The presence of the perfect gift of self in her womb, and the effects of that gift in her heart, propel her outward in an act of charity. With Christ in her womb she goes into the hill country of Judea. Some thirty-three years later she will again journey into the hill country of Judea with Jesus on another mission of charity. Already the form of the cross is taking shape in Mary's life.

The cross is the perfect expression in time of the eternal love of the Triune God. This self-gift of love takes the form of charity: "Charity is the essence of God's own inner life, for 'God is love'" (1 Jn 4:8, 16).[23] Saint Augustine said, "but thou dost see the Trinity if thou seest love."[24] When charity enters our life it "gives shape without ever simply becoming a shape, [it is] the way in which God discloses himself without ever losing his mysteriousness."[25] This charity is not meant to be a helium-filled, mannerly existence that politely drifts among those we like. Rather, it is a gift of self that we make through the grace of God. Charity is the form of the Christian life: "It is only by the love that is charity that God's life is in ours."[26]

7. The Seventh Step: The Magnificat

Charity is literally alive in Mary, and her actions reflect it. Charity is the counterbalance that tips the scales of sin and evil. Recall that Adam

---

23. Paul M. Quay, *The Mystery Hidden for Ages in God* (New York: Peter Lang, 2002), 16.
24. Augustine, *De Trinitate*, VIII, 8, 12.
25. Tugwell, *The Beatitudes*, 51.
26. Quay, *The Mystery Hidden for Ages in God*, 16.

and Eve, when they had sinned against charity, began to blame. Instead of blame, Mary's self-giving love overflows in praise. She sings the Magnificat: "My soul proclaims the greatness of the Lord; my spirit rejoices in God my Savior" (Lk 1:46ff.). Mary proclaims her joy because it is the natural overflow of the love that is within her:

> The heritage of the eternal Father passed through Mary's heart and was thus enriched by all that the extraordinary feminine genius of the mother could bring to Christ's patrimony. In its universal dimension, Christianity is this patrimony, in which the mother's contribution is highly significant.[27]

B. The Efficacious Nature of the Self-gift of Jesus

The seven steps of grace provide an outline as to how the gift of grace in Christ conquers sin. Sin brings fear. Christ's sacrifice brings the self-gift of his grace, which saves humanity. The cross is the self-gift of love that bestows grace on the person. John Paul points out the ongoing need for the person "to penetrate deeply into the *mysterium Crucis.*"[28]

Love takes center place in the mystery of the cross. The cross is not a mere example of love; rather, "the mystery leaves its efficacious mark."[29] How is man to access effectively the power of the cross? First, we can understand the mystery of the cross as the obedient, sacrificial gift of self that Jesus, the Son of God, makes for us. The gift of the Son brings humanity back into communion with God. The Holy Spirit makes it possible for man to reach into the self-gift of Jesus on the cross. Through grace and virtue, the Holy Spirit transforms the identity of the human person wounded by sin. The new evangelization is a gift of self before all else. The new evangelization takes up all that Catholics are familiar with and allows them to discover the gift of self Jesus makes upon the cross as a kenosis of love. We can do this from several vantage points, four in particular: Jesus' cry of abandonment on the cross, his opened side on the cross, the parable of the Prodigal Son, and the parable of the Good Samaritan.

---

27. John Paul II, *Memory and Identity*, 62.
28. Ibid., 7.
29. Ibid., 20.

1. The Cry of Abandonment

Balthasar notes how two contradictions converge: human sin and the guiltless Son.[30] The result is "the loneliness of the Son."[31] The self-giving love of the Son collides with the self-taking sin of man. All God's self-giving love, pouring forth from eternity, collides with the self-absorbed antilove of the world that Satan induced through sin. Balthasar focuses upon Jesus' cry of abandonment from the cross. It expresses the outpouring of love that moves to the greater depths of divine love:

> The momentum of the collision lies beyond the sound barrier: just as the love of God in creation and election is unfathomable, so is sin, the hate of the world (Jn 15:25). But the abyss of the unfathomable love has entered the abyss of the meaningless hatred and hidden itself there.[32]

The cry of the cross is the follow-through of all charity. Yves Congar explains:

> Christ's charity is a charity of the cross, a charity whose conclusion is the cross: *majorem dilectionem*. Christ's kingship gains its full reality on the cross; on the cross he declared his kingship (Jn 18:37); on the cross he was declared to be king (Mt 27:37; Mk 15:26; Lk 23:38; Jn 19:19); on the cross he drew mankind to himself (*cum elevans fuero*). It was when he was naked and dying on the cross that he heaped wealth on us and gave us life.[33]

As Adam stood in his aloneness in Eden, so Christ is crucified into the aloneness of sin on the cross. Just as Adam cried out in his aloneness in search of the other, the "helper," so Christ, the new Adam, cries out toward the Holy Spirit and the Church. Adam, in his original nakedness, called out, "This one, at last, is bone of my bone and flesh of my flesh!" So too Christ cries out in his nakedness on the cross, and thus redeems the relationality of Adam that has been covered in shame since sin. The cry of Jesus does not simply describe a gift, it *is* a gift.

---

30. Hans Urs von Balthasar, *Explorations in Theology IV: Spirit and Institution, The Word Made Flesh* (San Francisco: Ignatius Press, 1995), 269.

31. Ibid., 269.

32. Balthasar, *The Glory of the Lord VII*, 210.

33. Yves Congar, *Faith and Spiritual Life* (New York: Herder and Herder, 1968), 48.

Balthasar says, "The crucified is beyond such words; in Mark and Matthew, he forces out only the cry of abandonment and expires with a loud shout (Mk 15:34, 37)."[34] Jesus' cry is "... the cry to the lost God ... the spring of living water that wells up to eternal life, who wills to give all drink from himself (Jn 4:10, 13ff.; 7:37ff.), is poured out to such an extent that he himself is dying of thirst."[35] The world falls into darkness before the divine drama: "Only God himself can go right to the end of the abandonment by God."[36] The action of the Son on the cross is the perfect revelation of the Trinity in time: "The selflessness of the divine persons, as of pure relations in the love within the Godhead, as the basis of everything: this selflessness is the basis of a first form of kenosis...."[37] The cry expresses the obedient kenosis of the sacrificial self-gift of the Son. This gift is completely efficacious because it is made by a divine Person perfectly united to human nature. Congar can thus say, in light of the Son's obedience on the cross, that "The cross of Jesus Christ is the centre of the whole spiritual history of the world."[38]

2. The Opened Side

John Paul notes that Jesus "gives the Holy Spirit through the wounds of his crucifixion: 'He showed them his hands and his side.' It is in the power of this crucifixion that he says to them: 'Receive the Holy Spirit.'"[39] John Paul notes specifically that Jesus "pours out" the gift of the Holy Spirit from "his pierced side on the Cross."[40] Saint John gives particular attention to the wound in Christ's side: "The one who saw this has given testimony, and his testimony is true. And that one knows that he has spoken the truth that you too may believe" (Jn 19:35). Ordinarily "that one" is understood to refer to the evangelist himself or his eyewit-

---

34. Balthasar, *The Glory of the Lord VII*, 210.

35. Ibid., 226.

36. Ibid., 211.

37. Ibid., 213–214.

38. Yves Congar, *A Gospel Priesthood* (New York: Herder and Herder, 1967), 91–92.

39. John Paul II, *Dominum et Vivificantem*, 24, cf. 40; and *The Trinity's Embrace*, 71, 103.

40. John Paul II, *The Trinity's Embrace*, 103.

ness source. Balthasar says that the "one" mentioned is Christ himself: "in Greek *ekeinos[,]* probably referring to Jesus and not to the witness himself; compare the same word in 1 John 2:6; 3:5; 7:16; 4:17."[41]

Saint John the Evangelist notes that a soldier pierced the side of Jesus with a spear. By its construction, a spear embodies the notion of a point, an edge, a straight line. It marks a point beyond which there is no more admittance, no more intactness, no more life. Unlike a curved blade, the edge and point of a spear pierce, invade, and repel. They could not have existed in paradise, for they evoke fear and refusal. The spear introduces hate and traces the line of violence beyond which man's life may not pass. In contrast, a curve evokes invitation, inclusivity, protection, and bonding. Curves attract. The eternal actions of the Trinity are a turning toward one another, and are easily represented by an arching or inclining toward in a bond of fruitful, eternal love. All love is predicated on a curve.

Man in sin forges the spear that pierces the curve of the heart of God. And man pours into the spear all of the pain, abuse, hatred, ultimatums, rejections, abandonments, and divisions that he has ever known. All of the wars, lusts, scandals, lies, thefts, and betrayals of history are melded into the point of the spear. The worst that man can do, all the hatred of hell and the sins of humanity, are forged into the spear's point. And after all the harm it has wreaked through time and history, it now advances upon the body of Christ. But God's response to all this is to love.

Pope Pius XII maintains that the spear that opened the side of Christ also opened the heart of Christ.[42] Jean Laffitte finds similar reference in *Deus Caritas Est*, the first encyclical letter of Pope Benedict XVI: "[The encyclical] speaks of the 'opened' side, while the verb *nussō* (*enuxen* in the aorist) used by the evangelist means 'struck' or 'pierced.' Here, too, the choice of the tradition, inspired by the translation of the Vulgate, is particularly felicitous: 'he opened' translates '*ēnoixen*.' In 'opening' the side of Christ, the lance traces a path to his heart."[43] This passage speaks not just of the side, but of the heart of Jesus: "… from the opened heart, out of which flows what is uttermost.…"[44]

---

41. Balthasar, *Explorations in Theology IV: Spirit and Institution*, 271.

42. Pope Pius XII, *Haurietis Aquas in Gaudio*, May 15, 1956, 78.

43. Jean Laffitte, "Love and Forgiveness," *The Way of Love: Reflections on Pope Benedict XVI's Encyclical* Deus Caritas Est (San Francisco: Ignatius Press, 2006), 171.

44. Balthasar, *The Glory of the Lord VII*, 197.

The wound in the side represents the ultimate self-giving, in which the sacraments are given to the Church. Balthasar continues, "John is nowhere more solemn than in his testimony to this event at the extremity ... the sacraments have their source here...."[45] The Swiss theologian says elsewhere that the mystery of the opening of the side of Jesus is

> ... the giving forth of all that still lies most deeply within Jesus, the central point of this Eucharist of the Cross: the giving forth of the Spirit on the one hand, and of the open and liquefied heart on the other.... The place of his heart is open, empty for all to enter; in this self-emptying, the kenosis has reached its fulfillment.[46]

Just as Adam's side was opened as he slept in paradise, the body of Christ is opened as he sleeps in death upon the cross. Whereas Adam's body gave forth woman, Christ's body gives forth the Church. The spear pierces into the curve of eternal love, and the curve yields, giving itself up to include even all the sins of man. And in this yielding of love, the wound transforms the spear into a gift. The spear is baptized and converted, changed forever. The words of the ancient Easter hymn sound clearly: *Felix culpa*! Man's worst place, farthest from God, is changed forever to a life-giving gift by Christ.

God gives an even more superabundant gift: access to the open heart of Christ. The heart of God, the innermost core of love itself, pours forth in a never-ending cascade of mercy upon man, heals man's sin, and restores his dignity. Simon Tugwell notes, "For God is himself only in pouring himself out. We cannot fathom the whole of the mystery of God, plainly, but whatever we can know is characterized by this total giving of self."[47] In the face of all human sin, the heart of God loved. "The opening of the heart is the gift of what is most interior and personal for public use: the open, emptied out space is accessible to all."[48]

John Paul's reference to the way Jesus gives the Holy Spirit through his wounds, especially his pierced side, is particularly significant.[49] The wounds are central to the glorified body of Jesus. For Balthasar, the

---

45. Ibid.

46. Ibid., 226.

47. Tugwell, *The Beatitudes*, 24.

48. Hans Urs von Balthasar, *Mysterium Paschale* (Grand Rapids, MI: Wm. B. Eerdmans, 1993), 131.

49. John Paul II, *Dominum et Vivificantem*, 24; cf. 40.

wounds prove the identity of Jesus, and are the means through which the world is saved, "because it is through his opened body (a hand can be reached inside his body through the wound: Jn 20:27) and the infinite distribution of his flesh and shedding of his blood that men can henceforth share in the substantial infinitude of his Divine Person."[50] Jesus gives the Holy Spirit from his heart, through the wound in his side. And the Holy Spirit gives the believer a new heart: "This 'new heart' will make it possible to appreciate and achieve the deepest and most authentic meaning of life: namely, that of being a gift which is fully realized in the giving of self. This is the splendid message about the value of life...."[51] The power of the cross of Jesus actually communicates strength through the sacraments to the believer to live the moral life: "It is in the saving Cross of Jesus, in the gift of the Holy Spirit, in the sacraments which flow forth from the pierced side of the Redeemer[,] that believers find the grace and the strength always to keep God's holy law, even amid the gravest of hardships."[52]

3. The Prodigal Son

John Paul emphasizes that the parable of the Prodigal Son (Lk 15:11-32) is the "high point" of "how great and profound is the Father's mercy toward all his children."[53] The parable demonstrates the mystery of the kenosis of grace in the form of a gift of self. The usual interpretation of the parable is that man, through the mercy of God, can always return to God in this life. This is not inaccurate, but we can find a richer understanding in light of the original Greek terms used in the parable.

The younger son approaches the father and asks for his share of the inheritance (or the estate or property, depending on the translation). We might think that the son is asking the father to make an advance on his

---

50. Balthasar, *Theo-Drama IV*, 363.

51. John Paul II, *Evangelium Vitae*, 49.

52. John Paul II, *Veritatis Splendor*, 103. ("It is the very life of God which is now shared with man. It is the life through which the sacraments of the Church—symbolized by the blood and water coming from Christ's side—is continually given to God's children...." *Evangelium Vitae*, 51.)

53. John Paul II, *The Trinity's Embrace*, 254.

last will and testament. In other words, it seems as if the son wants the father dead so he can pocket some money.

The original Greek word for what the younger son rudely requests from the father is *ousias*. Persons familiar with the early Christological controversies will recognize this term as referring not to the monetary inheritance but to the "substance" of the father. The younger son comes to the father and requests that the father bestow *some of his own substance* on the younger son. The younger son has mistakenly equated the tremendous holdings the father has with who the father is. The son thinks the father's substance is in the money, in what the father *does*. This wealthy father has robes, calves, fields, and rings. The son demands not only money, but the father's substance. He asks, "Give me your ability to make something from nothing. Give me your Midas touch."

The father does give the younger son his share of the estate. But according to the Greek text, the father hands over not the *ousias* but the *biov*. This word refers to "the ability to sustain life." The son has asked for the *substance* of the father, and has received what he *thought* was the father's identity and substance. The father hands over the ability to sustain life. The son does not know the difference. So the son gathers his belongings—the ability to sustain life. Notice that the belongings are so vast that it takes the younger son "a few days" to gather them and leave.

The son then goes off and tries to be the father. The son spends and spends, thinking that this is the substance, the *ousias*, of the father. We find out later in the parable that the son was going through the father's property with "loose women." As he continues to spend money, thinking that this makes him the father, the son is only paying his way into slavery. That big wad of cash is not the substance of the father, but only the *biov*, the ability to sustain life. The son soon exhausts the money. He looks around and is empty. He would gladly eat the food of the pigs. He has lost dominion. Then he comes to his senses. He recalls the image of God within him: the capacity to know and to love. But he uses it only for survival through manipulation: Driven by his hunger and need, he asks, "How many hired hands at my father's house have more than enough to eat? I know what I shall do. I will get up and go to my father and say, 'Father, I have sinned against heaven and against you. I no longer deserve to be called your son. Treat me as you would one of your hired hands.'"

The son gets up and begins his return, rehearsing his selfish mono-logue. But the father "caught sight of his son while he was still a long way off." The sense of the Greek is that the father saw the son as he was in the distant land. This seeing is not a casual glance as the father looks up from the paper while sitting on the porch. Rather, the father has been gazing into the distant land and sees the son. The father's look gratu-itously enables the son to "come to his senses." For the son, this is the *compunctio cordis*, the sorrow of heart that follows upon sin. It is the *animi cruciatus*, the crucifixion of spirit that sets in when the grace of the Holy Spirit makes us realize that we are far from God in sin. This *compunctio cordis* is more than guilt and is different from shame. Guilt can be healthy because it is about what I do. Shame is never healthy because it is about who I am. Guilt can become the raw material that makes me aware of the grace of God calling me back to himself by means of his mercy. The *compunctio cordis* flows from the Holy Spirit's action in the sinner's heart. The Holy Spirit begins to move the sinner's heart even while the sinner is still alienated.

The father's gaze wakes up the son created in his image and likeness. The son remembers the father, and he remembers his own capacity to know and to love. He is meant for more. He has wounded his dignity. He gets up, under the father's gaze, and begins to move toward him. At first, the son feels more sorry for himself than sorry on account of the father. But this attrition, this self-interested sorrow, is sufficient for for-giveness all the way to heaven. The father's tears will turn the attrition of the son into contrition: sorrow because of his sin before the love of the father.

As the son trudges home, the father runs to meet him. The texts says the father was "filled with compassion." The Greek is more earthy and relates that what is literally going on in the father is more than mood, emotion, or sentiment. The Greek σπλαγχνα (*splagchna*) is onomato-poeic. The root word for what the father experiences on seeing the son, *splagchna*, means more than he was "filled with compassion." It carries the meaning of his innermost bowels trembling with compassion.[54]

---

54. Laffitte, "Love and Forgiveness," 177 (cf. Erasmo Leiva-Merikakis, *Fire of Mercy, Heart of the Word: Meditations on the Gospel According to St. Matthew*, vol. 1 [San Francisco: Ignatius Press, 1996], 197).

"The Hebrews allocated different emotions to different parts of the body ... compassion was situated in the bowels."[55] The word *splagchna* "has a considerable importance both from the perspective of Christian anthropology and the relation with Christ through faith that grounds it."[56] The heart is the center of the person, from which flows the unitive love of *splagchna*, which is in fact ecclesial love.[57] Oliver Davies notes, "In σπλάγχνα [*splagchna*] natural human affection is refigured by divine self-giving and becomes the foundation of the new life that is the spirit of the Church. Compassion in this sense then represents the transformation of humanity by the supremely compassionate act of God...."[58] The father's innermost places began to tremble in that they were getting ready to pour forth and burst upon the son. Like Jesus' cry on the cross and the opening of the side, the father is expressing a kenosis of love beyond words in and through his body. "The father embraces the son and kisses him." The Greek phrase (ἐπέπεσεν ἐπὶ τὸν τράχηλον αὐτοῦ) indicates that the father *fell upon the neck of the son*—this profound embrace and the kiss engulf the son. The father is pouring himself out in the kenosis of the gift of self. This meeting between the younger son and the father, with the look of the father, the trembling of the father's innermost places, and the outpouring of the profound embrace and the kiss, expresses a tremendous moment. The father is not just receiving the son back, but is *giving* something to the son. The son is receiving something from the innermost places of the father through the embrace and kiss. The son is being given the *ousias*, the substance of the father that he had demanded at the beginning of the parable. The father knew all along that when the son asked for the substance, the father had to give it, but the son in his egoism and sin had to learn who the father *was not* before he learned who the father *was*. And the father's substance is not in his things or possessions, it is in his embrace of his whole person sealed in the fatherly kiss.

After the filial embrace there is the nuptial giving of the ring and the banquet (Lk 15:22–23). This represents the passage from death to life:

55. Tugwell, *The Beatitudes*, 94.
56. Oliver Davies, *A Theology of Compassion: Metaphysics of Difference and the Renewal of Tradition* (Grand Rapids, MI: Wm. B. Eerdmans, 2001), 247.
57. Ibid., 247–248.
58. Ibid., 248.

"...this son of mine was dead and is alive again; he was lost, and is found" (Lk 15:24). Our culture, too, must be found; it must *come back to life*. We might even imagine that the father wept at this moment. The wounds of Christ in the passion, are, in one sense, the tears of God the Father. There are some things that only the tears of a father can give us. I saw my father cry at least once in his life: at the death of my mother. Those tears communicated something of my father to me; they were in a sense *for me*, with my father seeing me crying over the body of my mother when I was twelve. He gave me something in those tears. If we have never seen our father cry, something of our father's substance escapes and eludes us. Fathers alone teach us how to pour our substance out as a gift. Tears are the milk of the father. In the ancient world the craftsmen used to say that when the apprentice is wounded, when he is cut or burned in learning the job, the craft is entering his body. Something similar occurs with the lesson of the parable of the Prodigal Son and the lessons of life.

In the form of the cry of abandonment and the opening of the side, the father shares the *ousias* with the son. When the son says that he no longer deserves to be called the son, the father speaks. He says, "Quickly...." The father will not allow the son to proceed to question his sonship. The son receives a ring to show his union with the love of the father. The son receives a robe, which restores his dignity. Then, the father calls for the fatted calf to be killed. The animals ate better than the son when he was in sin. He had sunk lower than the animal world. That fatted calf is now killed and the son eats it to demonstrate that his dominion (Gen 1:28) is restored. They celebrate with music and dancing. As the older son nears the house, he is disturbed by the sound of music and dancing. Both sons were looking for the same thing. The younger son thought he could receive the substance of the father by outright demanding it. The older son thought he could get it from the father by pleasing the father and manipulatively doing everything he was told. He was the pleaser. He has tried to please so hard that he never took a day off: He has to ask a servant what music and dancing mean! He made the same mistake that the younger son did at first. The older son thinks the father's substance is in the father's material wealth. What the younger son wanted to get by direct seizure, the older son tried to get by attrition. The older son now has to take the same journey that the younger son did, to realize that the substance can only be given. The father hints at this when he says, "My son, you are here with me always, and everything I have is yours." The father seems to say that the younger son will get nothing of the property, or *biov*, because the younger son does not need it anymore; the father has poured himself into the younger son.

This outpouring is receiving the kenosis of the cross, the grace of which the Holy Spirit brings to us in the sacraments. In this way we are brought into the passage of Christ: "His exodus must correspond to our own."[59] As we understand ourselves united to Christ, the Scriptures become in some sense autobiographical for us.[60]

The parable effectively conveys the action of grace in the life of the human person. The younger son represents the human person. The son, in the state of sin, is animated by an initial movement that emerges from the father's gaze. The son remembers the father and moves from being self-centered to self-focused. While slight, the difference is important. The son is animated by something new that is not initially his own. It comes from beyond him, from the father. This something new is not merely an as-yet-untried option that the son's own cunning has devised. This is something new in the sense of the new evangelization: *feliciora*. Something happy, abundant begins to grow within the disposition of the son.

This something new is from the kenosis of the father. The father has poured himself out, to the extent that he still gazes upon the son even through the distance of sin. The son has emptied himself out in sin, the father has emptied himself out in love, and the two emptinesses meet. The son, emptied by sin, can be filled in an unprecedented way by the father's emptying out in love. The new, *feliciora*, shares the same Latin root for the happy, *felix*, fault of Adam. The father's kenosis, or self-emptying love, has moved upon the son's readiness: "I no longer deserve to be called your son." It is only with these words that the newness of identity can emerge, because these words show a readiness on the part of the son. At the opening of the parable, he claimed what he thought he deserved: all the father was. Now the son, in a humility generated from the gaze of the father, sees that he deserves nothing. He is contingent.

---

59. Forte, *To Follow You, Light of Life*, 86.

60. "Even as Jesus was the perfect Jew, who relived all the stages of the life of Israel … so each Christian who lives by the grace of Christ is able to relive Israel's life in and with Jesus." Quay, *The Mystery Hidden for Ages in God*, 9.

The son, who always belonged to the father by creation, has now been adopted by the father in a new and wonderful way in salvation that brings a closeness surpassing the genetic closeness of creation.

The father's gratuitous love, by which he emptied himself out to create the son, is now repeated, and a new assimilation takes place. The intimate union of the father's embrace transforms the son, and at the initiative of the father's love, something was created in the son that penetrated his very substance.

4. The Good Samaritan

The parable of the Good Samaritan presents another perspective on the identity of the human person as related to the kenosis of Jesus on the cross. Popular interpretations of this parable slip easily into the manualist mode of duty and obligation. Hearers are told that the parable means that they are to go out of their way to look for and heal the wounded. This is the second message of the parable. Unless one hears the first message, the second becomes a disconnected chore, a duty, a social service venture.

A lawyer stands up to question Jesus. As is typical, the question is a setup. The lawyer knows the twists and turns of the law. So he asks Jesus about the law. Jesus responds and takes the lawyer a step further. The lawyer asks, "and who is my neighbor?" This is another way of asking, "Where is the line?" and "How far do I have to go?" The parable is routinely interpreted to mean that Jesus is saying that all are your neighbor, even those you may dislike. But perhaps more is at work.

The parable begins with a man going from Jerusalem to Jericho. These places are important. Jerusalem is the city of the temple, the place where God and man interact. It stands for paradise, where God and man are in unity and abide in proper accord. A man goes forth from Jerusalem to Jericho, the city of the world. Jericho is the marketplace, the scene of backroom deals and wink-nod politics, where partners stab you in the back while smiling from ear to ear. A man goes from Jerusalem to the city of the world. A man goes from paradise to the city of sin. Who is this man? This is Adam cast out from paradise. This is everyman.

As he goes he falls victim to robbers. These are the vices. They strip him of his dignity, beat him, wound the image of God in him, and leave him half-dead. How many people are only half-alive in vice? We only see half their lives. This is the mystique behind fashion magazines and gossip, where we see only half the life of a celebrity. At this point in the parable, perhaps the lawyer who asked Jesus the question has been taken a bit farther than he would have liked to go. Maybe he shifts his stance, draws his chin to the side as he squints at Jesus and wonders. Maybe moisture begins to form on his brow. Maybe someone knows. Someone saw.

Jesus continues: A priest and a Levite happen by. In some interpretations these stand for the old law and its rituals. The popular interpretation points out that even those who are supposed to do good sometimes do not. Even though the priest may be ritually forbidden to touch blood, a deeper law abides: Care for those who are suffering. A more interesting question arises: Why is a priest leaving the temple area, and more specifically, why is he on his way to the city of sin and backroom deals? What is he doing in this part of town in the first place?

By now the lawyer is fidgeting, his mind racing, the original question a million miles away. This Jesus knows something. Someone must have told him, which means someone saw. Who else knows? No one is supposed to know. How did he see? Whom will he tell?

Jesus continues his tale: A Samaritan traveler comes along and sees the victim. The Samaritan, without losing his dignity, steps down from the noble position of riding the beast. The kenosis of the Samaritan is beginning. His action, like the cry of dereliction, the opening of the side, and the tears of the father, is a bodily action of re-creative kenosis. He sees the one in sin and vice on the border of Jericho and descends. He pours himself out. Who is this Samaritan? Jesus is the Samaritan traveler who sees us in sin and, without ceasing to be God, empties himself and descends to take the nature of man.

The Samaritan then pours in wine and oil. Like the tears of the father in the Prodigal Son, these are the sacraments. The kenosis of the Samaritan is coming to a culmination. The traveler then wraps the wounds with bandages. These are the virtues that hold in the wine and the oil. The virtues hold the grace of the sacraments in our wounds. Virtues are not in the first mode an exercise we keep trying to do our best at until we get it right and it transmutes to repeated unreflective, robot-like activity. If we then fail to get it right, we blame ourselves, thinking we are doing something wrong: "I keep trying and I am not getting it right. I must try harder to be acceptable. If only I hit upon the right sequence." This is pre-Christian thinking. "In fact, virtue is not a mechanical predisposition for a standardized and uniform behavior. It is totally different from a habit. Virtue does not diminish freedom but rather potency."[61] Saint Thomas Aquinas understood virtue as a *habitus*, in the sense of a dwelling. It is a disposition within the person, formed by the Holy Spirit's action on the person's receptivity. When man then acts for the good in concrete actions "the virtues develop in our inclination toward the good," and he "become[s] sensitive to our inclination to the good when we are confronted with evil and suffering...."[62]

By now the lawyer's eyes have been staring at the dirt road for some time. He wishes he could become like that pebble and roll away. Jesus has traced out the entire story. The lawyer is finally bested; if only he had stayed quiet and not challenged Jesus.

Then the Samaritan hoists the victim onto his own beast. He shares his dignity with the victim, as Jesus shares the dignity of his divinity with us. What Jesus is by nature, man becomes by adoption in grace. The Samaritan takes the victim to an inn, leaves him in the care of the innkeeper, and deposits two coins for his care, with a promise to make good the rest. We can see the inn as the Church, the innkeeper as the magisterium, and the two coins as Sacred Scripture and tradition. The return is the Second Coming. But at the center of it all stands Jesus and his "demand that no limit be set on love of one's neighbor and that one stand by the sufferer with immediate practical help even when he is a national enemy ... it presupposes the universality of love...."[63]

The lawyer looks up into the "universality of love." A crowd has gathered. Jesus has done more than give a lesson on how far we must go to care for one another. He has drawn an example from daily life, perhaps from the tragic daily life of one of his listeners, perhaps from the life of this lawyer: an event buried long ago when the young lawyer was just starting out, not even sure he knew what he wanted to do, and even

---

61. Melina, *Sharing in Christ's Virtues*, 54.

62. Pinckaers, *Morality: The Catholic View*, 102.

63. Rudolph Schnackenburg, *The Moral Teaching of the New Testament* (New York: Herder and Herder, 1971), 97.

before he had studied the law. One day he set out to see what was on the other side of the line, over in Jericho. At first he felt the thrill. He was riding high, going to have a good time. And then they closed in. They stripped him, beat him, and left him only half alive. He was shamed and humiliated. He had violated his tradition and left the holy place. He had been ganged up on, made fun of, beaten, left naked on the road. All his inexperience and naïveté were laid bare. Jesus knew every detail. Was someone watching from the rocks? Had the gossip finally leaked out? Who else knew?

Then along came a traveler whom the young man thought was a Samaritan. The traveler poured in the soothing wine and oil and saved the young man from further shame. The healer bandaged him and took him to a place of care and safety. He then left. Jesus knew every detail. How? And it then dawns on the young lawyer. His eyes widen and he sees Jesus in a new light. That face, those hands, that voice. The Samaritan who rescued the lawyer was, in effect, Jesus. He alone rescues us. The same man the lawyer saw in the Good Samaritan, he is now seeing in Jesus: Effectively and through grace, it was Jesus who rescued the lawyer that day: This man speaking to him was effectively the one who came along, saw him, climbed down, poured the wine and oil, wrapped the bandages, and saved him. Jesus knew every detail because he was the one who saved him all those years ago. And Jesus calls him back now with the question, "Which one, in your opinion, was neighbor to the man who fell in with the robbers?" The lawyer looks up. He feels somehow younger than when this conversation started. And he speaks, slowly, with the dawning realization of one who has had the answer right next to him all along. He answers with slow birth, with more reality than any of his crisp and precise answers he gave his teachers: "The … one … who treated him … with mercy." His eyes fix on Jesus, and the commission is now given: "Then go and do the same."

C. Saint Augustine

Saint Augustine's analysis further explains how the kenosis of grace operates in the transformation of the believer. The transformation from sin is not reduced to grim, automatic efforts of rigid determination to somehow remake ourselves on our own designs and attitudes. The plan of God is much more profound and internal to the identity of the human person. The teaching of Saint Augustine emphasizes that the grace received from contact with the kenosis of Jesus brings forgiveness of sin and also gradually heals the afflicted:

> But as it is one thing to be free from fever, and another to grow strong again from the infirmity which the fever produced; and one thing again to pluck out of the body a weapon thrust into it, and another to heal the wound thereby made by a prosperous cure; so the first cure is to remove the cause of infirmity, and this is wrought by the forgiving of all sins; but the second cure is to heal the infirmity itself, and this takes place gradually by making progress in the renewal of that image.[64]

The kenosis of the Son, which stands at the center of the Father's plan, pours forth upon the human person a new measure of the gift of the Holy Spirit. In the struggle with temptation, sin, and the effects of sin, the human person continually turns toward the grace of Christ for healing. The Christian way of life is no mere exterior allegiance; it is rather a healing adhesion to the Savior. As Pope Benedict XVI quotes from the *Confessions* of Saint Augustine: "My weaknesses are many and grave, many and grave indeed, but more abundant still is your medicine."[65]

D. The Sacraments

The sacraments are God's medicine. The kenosis of the cry from the cross, the opening of the side, the prodigious tears of the father, and the Samaritan's wine and oil represent the outpouring of Christ's grace into the wounds that mar the identity of the human person. Through these wounds, the human person receives a new share in the abundance of Christ. The wounds must receive the sacraments that bestow a *substance* on the human person in and through the passion of Christ. The person who lies wounded within the sequence of temptation, sin, and concupiscence needs to be transformed. This transformation can only come from grace and the life of virtue wrought by the Holy Spirit's action through his seven gifts. The common temptation is that we can work it out on

---

64. Augustine, *On the Trinity*, bk. 14, ch. 17.
65. Augustine, *Confessions*, X:43, 69, as in *Spe Salvi*, 29.

our own, and that what the Church offers is a do-it-yourself plan to make us more effective in life. This semi-Pelagian focus on our own effort or cooperation with God that makes God's plan effective in our lives is an opaque, yet common, form of pride. True transformation is found when the Christian remains docile before God.

Congar explains that the spiritual life benefits from a shift in emphasis "from personal ascetic effort and from salvation considered exclusively as an achievement due to our own hard-won struggle, to God's regal initiative, to the really universal significance and the full extent of the salvation brought about by God in Christ."[66] The sacraments, in particular the sacrament of Penance, halt the cycle of sin. Regular recourse to the grace of Christ restores the gift and casts out fear. From this transformation, the person undergoes far deeper effects: He no longer lives to satisfy the senses, to consume the self, through the blunting of reflection.

Redemption is not an obstacle course that the sinner needs to run through and be rated on at the end of his or her life. Salvation is not fulfilling an extensive legal contract with meticulous obligations that depend on the whim of an absentee landlord. Rather, the ethos of redemption brought about by life in the spirit focuses on the life that grace brings to man through the sacraments. John Paul teaches that human persons are called with effectiveness to turn toward redemption in Christ. This is a beautiful call because at its center is the compelling kenosis of Christ, who literally pours himself out for us. The Holy Spirit works in the mystery of Christ's cross and brings the bond of Trinitarian love to our worst place. The Holy Spirit takes the self-gift of Jesus, made on the cross, and reveals it as a nuptial act—"My body given for you"—to his bride the Church. The spousal meaning at the center of the cross is meant to be rediscovered by every person caught in the dead end of sin. Every sinner is called from outside himself in love to this Other, united in a love that is always fruitful. Redemption restores to man a deeper and mature spontaneity because man has been re-formed by the gift of self which Christ made on the cross. Man accesses this gift through the sacraments and in the life of virtue. Aquinas notes that the sacraments are

---

66. Congar, *Faith and Spiritual Life* (New York: Herder and Herder, 1969), 12.

necessary for man's salvation.[67] They receive their power from Christ's passion. The self-gift of Jesus in his suffering, death, and resurrection is the cause of man's sanctification. The passion of Christ is applied to man in and through grace and the virtues (what Aquinas calls the form of man's sanctification).[68] Congar writes that

> the decisive agent of this application can only be God, and by "appropriation" of the Holy Spirit. Faith and sacraments are therefore the means by which every person is united to the reality of salvation and life which is, for every one, Christ. The role of faith and the sacraments is to establish a contact with him, and thus to enable him, the universal cause of salvation ... to communicate this salvation to us.[69]

The Holy Spirit operates in the heart of the believer so that even when wounded by sin, the Christian has an interior help that begins his transformation. This transformation comes by union with Christ. The Christian can be moral because he has met Jesus, who alone responds to the human quest for happiness.[70] The encounter with Jesus is not a meeting with an abstract concept, but with a Person. We can be transformed only by "turning to the face of Christ" so that we are "conquered and charmed by his beauty."[71] "The Holy Spirit furnishes a distinctive kind of assistance for the moral life."[72] The Holy Spirit is not a remote scorekeeper giving us points for good actions and deducting them if we fail. The Holy Spirit works within us to inspire and form us to do good and avoid evil. Jesus "demanded that action should be the fruit of disposition (cf. Lk 6:43ff.)."[73] The Spirit at work in us enables the Christian to practice virtue in such an innate manner that the good actions are not external divine mandates, but are truly ours: "It is plainly to be seen that Jesus was not concerned only with interior dispositions, but wanted his demands to be interpreted as real commandments that are to be converted into action."[74]

---

67. Aquinas, *Summa Theologiae*, IIIa q. 61, a. 1.
68. Ibid., IIIa q. 60, a. 3.
69. Congar, *A Gospel Priesthood*, 107.
70. Melina, *Sharing in Christ's Virtues*, 27.
71. Ibid., 33.
72. Cessario, *Introduction to Moral Theology*, 21–22.
73. Schnackenburg, *The Moral Teaching of the New Testament*, 70.
74. Ibid., 83.

Chapter Seven

The Gifts of the Holy Spirit, the Beatitudes, and the Virtues

A. The Gifts of the Holy Spirit

The heart of the kenosis that comes via the sacraments is the self-gift of Jesus on the cross and takes the form of the seven gifts of the Holy Spirit. The sevenfold Spirit supports the transformation of the Christian.[1] In speaking of his passion, Jesus tells his disciples, "If I do not go away, the Counselor will not come to you" (Jn 16:7). Then, in the midst of his passion, Jesus utters a loud cry and hands over his spirit. For John Paul the self-gift of Jesus on the cross is

> ... the revelation of the most profound "logic" of the saving mystery contained in God's eternal plan, as an extension of the ineffable communion of the Father, Son and Holy Spirit. This is the divine "logic" which from the mystery of the Trinity leads to the mystery of the redemption of the world in Jesus Christ. The *Redemption accomplished by the Son* in the dimensions of the earthly history of humanity— accomplished in his "departure" through the Cross and Resurrection— is at the same time, in its entire salvific power, *transmitted to the Holy Spirit*: the one who "will take what is mine."[2]

---

1. John Paul II, *God, Father and Creator*, 53.
2. John Paul II, *Dominum et Vivificantem*, 11.

The Son has not answered the mystery of evil and sin with a remote waving of his hand that dismisses man's guilt. The Son does not offer man a suspended sentence or parole. The integrity of the freedom of God and of man, as well as that of love, requires an authentic, total, and completely sufficient answer to the scandal of evil and sin. In sin, man commits an offense against God. The severity of the offense is measured by the one offended. God is infinite; therefore man's offense against God is infinite. Only an infinite response can satisfy the infinite offense. But because man committed the offense, he must offer the response. The Son, a divine Person, without ceasing to be God, assumes a true human nature from the womb of the Virgin Mary. On the cross, as true God and true man, the Son can offer in man's place an infinite response of self-giving love, thereby freeing man from the bonds of sin. Congar notes that the sacrifice of Jesus does not consist primarily

> ... in his tortures—the impenitent thief suffered exactly the same—but in the obedience of love through which Jesus returns to his Father, by accomplishing his will. By this obedience he renders, once for all, the perfect adoration, the perfect sacrifice. The Cross of Jesus is the centre of the whole spiritual history of the world.[3]

On the cross, the Son bears the awful weight of all the sins of the world: "... *every sin* wherever and whenever committed has a reference to the Cross of Christ...."[4] As sin yawns open on the heart of Christ, his love triumphs: "For the greatest sin on man's part is matched, in the heart of the Redeemer, *by the oblation of supreme love* that conquers the evil of all the sins of men."[5] In this victory

> ... the Holy Spirit is the *"fire from heaven" which works in the depth of the mystery of the Cross.* Proceeding from the Father, he directs toward the Father the sacrifice of the Son, bringing it into the *divine reality of the Trinitarian communion....* [T]he Spirit *draws a new measure of the gift made to man and to creation* from the beginning. In the depth of the mystery of the Cross love is at work, that love which brings man back again to share the life that is God himself. The Holy Spirit as Love and Gift *comes down, in a certain sense, into the very heart of the sacrifice* which is offered on the Cross.[6]

---

3. Congar, *A Gospel Priesthood*, 91–92.
4. John Paul II, *Dominum et Vivificantem*, 29.
5. Ibid., 31.
6. Ibid., 41.

Because the one offered on the cross is a divine Person, his sacrifice extends throughout all time and space. His self-gift brings the grace of redemption to all through the sacraments. We see this especially in the cry of abandonment, the opening of Jesus' side, the father's embrace of the younger son, and the Samaritan's care for the wounded traveler. Each moment demonstrates an influx of grace that vivifies the believer. This inflow of grace influences the person: intellect, will, and body, including the "instinct, emotions, sensibilities, passions. All these components cannot be repressed and suffocated, but must be integrated into a harmonious whole, which finds its point of reference in reason, which, in the light of the truth about the Good, orders everything in view of the end."[7] John Paul emphasizes, "Contemplation of Jesus crucified is thus the highroad which the Church must tread everyday if she wishes to understand the full meaning of freedom: the gift of self in service to God and one's brethren. Communion with the crucified Lord is the never-ending source from which the Church draws unceasingly...."[8]

Through the sacraments, the Holy Spirit pours forth grace into the heart of the human person to bring freedom from sin: "Thanks to the multiplicity of the Spirit's gifts, by reason of which he is invoked as the 'sevenfold one,' every kind of human sin can be reached by God's saving power."[9] The seven gifts of the Holy Spirit, therefore, bring the Christian the love of Jesus which flows from the wounds of Jesus. "*The power of Christ* himself" works "*in man's innermost [being] through the Holy Spirit.*"[10] The power of love conveyed in the death and resurrection of Jesus never remains remote. Rather, the love the Christian needs to navigate the world is available through Jesus. The Holy Spirit brings it to the heart of the Christian at every moment through the seven gifts. Love flows forth from the wounds of Christ, and through the Holy Spirit it flows into the human heart through our wounds.

The Son loves infinitely. His action on the cross signifies the new creation: "... what begins now is *the new salvific self-giving of God, in the Holy Spirit. It is a new beginning* in relation to *the first, original* beginning

---

7. Melina, *Sharing in Christ's Virtues*, 53.
8. John Paul II, *Veritatis Splendor*, 87.
9. John Paul II, *Dominum et Vivificantem*, 42.
10. John Paul II, *Man and Woman He Created Them*, 332.

of God's salvific self-giving, which is identified with the mystery of creation itself."[11] In response to the sin of the world, the Son brings the
infinite love of the Trinity and reveals the splendor of love as a self-gift:

> The gift *made by the Son* completes the revelation and giving of the
> eternal love: *the Holy Spirit,* who in the inscrutable depths of the divin-
> ity is a Person-gift, through the work of the Son, that is to say by
> means of the Paschal mystery, is given to the Apostles and to the
> Church in a new way, and through them is given to humanity and the
> whole world.[12]

Through his gifts, the Holy Spirit moves in the soul, disposing a
person to cooperate with the divine action; the gifts perfect man for acts
of virtue.[13]

1. Saint Gregory the Great

The action of the Son on the cross enables the human person to turn
away from sin and become a new creation. Through the gifts of the Holy
Spirit, God gives us special aid so that our human capacities may do their
utmost to practice virtue.[14] The Holy Spirit makes us like Christ, trans-
forming our appetites, our intellect, and our will from the inside out.
Saint Gregory the Great bases his moral theology on the story of Job in
the Old Testament. God blessed Job, who prospered in life. Job had three
daughters and seven sons. One day Satan came before God, and the
Lord touted the uprightness of Job. Satan challenged God that Job
would fall away if sorrow befell him. So the Lord allowed Satan to put
Job to the test. When the initial trials did not sway Job, Satan requested
further rights to afflict Job. So God allowed further distress to come
upon Job. One day his daughters were feasting in the home the brothers
had built. A severe storm blew up and made the house collapse, killing
all Job's sons and daughters.

Saint Gregory teaches that Job's family is like the soul. The brothers'
house is the edifice or dwelling that God builds on the soul of the

---

11. John Paul II, *Dominum et Vivificantem,* 11–12.

12. Ibid., 23.

13. Aquinas, *Summa Theologiae,* IIa IIe q. 68, a. 1.

14. Romanus Cessario, OP, *The Moral Virtues and Theological Ethics* (Indiana: University of Notre Dame Press, 1995), 52.

believer. Gregory points out that Job's seven sons built the house. The sons represent the seven gifts of the Holy Spirit.[15] They serve the three daughters, their sisters within the house, who represent the three theological virtues—faith, hope, and charity. Each of the four corners of the house represents one of the four cardinal virtues, which are connected to one another. When Satan wants to tempt us to sin, he pulls at one of the four corners. Satan tempts us to violate prudence, justice, fortitude, or temperance. Once one begins to sway, the others begin to cave in as well because they are so closely connected.

The seven sons, that is the gifts of the Holy Spirit, build the house and prepare the meal to nourish the three daughters, the three theological virtues. While all the gifts work to build up the virtues, particular gifts correspond to particular virtues. Livio Melina explains, "In the life of charity the virtuous man becomes ever more dependent on God, ever more capable of being docile to the suggestions of the Holy Spirit, mediated through his gifts, which adapt the virtues to the movements of the Holy Spirit."[16]

The sacrament of Baptism first imparts the gifts of the Holy Spirit to the believer, and the sacrament of Confirmation strengthens them. Throughout our lives, the gifts are built up by reception of the other sacraments, in particular the Eucharist and Penance. Prayer, meditation on the mysteries of Christ in the Rosary, good works, spiritual reading, and spiritual direction enhance the operation of the gifts in us.

The writings of Saint Augustine, Saint Gregory the Great, and Saint Thomas Aquinas clarify the relationship between the gifts and the virtues. The gifts build and nourish the virtues, which then enable a person to live the Beatitudes.[17] The threefold relation between the gifts of the Holy Spirit, the virtues, and the Beatitudes is central to John Paul II's theology of the body. We reach purity and temperance not through some steel-willed determination to root out temptation. Rather, we reach purity of heart through the virtue of temperance. This virtue develops through our receptivity to the gifts of the Holy Spirit, in particular

---

15. Aquinas, *Summa Theologiae*, IIa IIe q. 68, a. 1.

16. Melina, *Sharing in Christ's Virtues*, 55.

17. Cf. Hans Urs von Balthasar, *The Glory of the Lord: A Theological Aesthetics II: Clerical Styles* (San Francisco: Ignatius Press, 1984), 320.

through the gift of piety, as John Paul notes. Saint Bonaventure notes this as well: "Those who have suffered the perils of the flesh have at times been liberated through the gift of piety...."[18] Saint Thomas Aquinas attributes temperance to the gift of fear of the Lord. John Paul repeatedly refers to Saint Paul's phrase regarding "life in the spirit": grace and virtue are the result of "a prolonged action of the Spirit, [which] consists essentially of developing in us the life of faith .... *The life of the believer is a life according to the Spirit.*"[19] John Paul emphasizes the importance of life according to the Spirit for internalizing purity: "purity—purity of heart, about which Christ speaks in the Sermon on the Mount—is realized precisely in life 'according to the Spirit.'"[20] The Holy Spirit works in the depths of our conscience and allows us to participate in the love and action of Christ. Thus the law is inscribed on the human heart.[21]

To adequately understand what the theology of the body means for the believer, we must understand this important truth: Jesus is the source of the grace given to man through life according to the Spirit.[22] A "life according to the Spirit" is "the practice of the Christian virtues."[23] The Spirit's life in us is his seven gifts, which fashion temperance in the appetites. In this way, God's plan is further understood not simply as an automatic change of external behavior, but "communion in the life of the three Persons of the Trinity. That good, which is obviously supreme perfection and supreme fullness of life, is not found by human co-operation ... it is communicated from above by faith, hope and charity...."[24]

2. *Habitus*

The cry of Jesus, the opening of his side, the father's tears for the Prodigal Son, and the Good Samaritan's compassion all show forth a sharing in the Father's love. That love has become a principle in the

---

18. Bonaventure, *Collations on the Seven Gifts of the Holy Spirit*, trans. Zachary Hayes, OFM. Vol. 14 of *Works of St. Bonaventure* (New York: Franciscan Institute, 2008), 80.

19. La Potterie and Lyonnet, *The Christian Lives by the Spirit*, 35–36.

20. John Paul II, *Man and Woman He Created Them*, 329.

21. Pinckaers, *Morality: The Catholic View*, 16–17, 82, 109.

22. Ibid., 16–17.

23. La Potterie and Lyonnet, *The Christian Lives by the Spirit*, 6.

24. Congar, *A Gospel Priesthood*, 156.

believer and evokes a new *habitus* in the deepest places of the heart. Grace builds a dwelling, or *habitus*, within us. Romanus Cessario points out that "*Habitus* provides a way for the theologian to explain that grace really transforms the principal psychological capacities of human nature, and at the same time allows the person to use these capacities in ways that are creative and easily adapted to new situations."[25] When Aquinas defined virtue as a good quality of mind, he was speaking of a habit or *habitus*.[26] This is not habit in the sense of a repeated automatic action done with little or no forethought. Rather, *habitus* refers to a dwelling within human nature, a form, a capacity, a disposition to act, and the acting itself. God, through his grace, builds a *habitus* in the person. "*Habitus* signifies the perfection or adaptation of a human capacity so that it functions well."[27] Thus the theological virtues of faith, hope, and love, and the cardinal virtues of prudence, justice, fortitude, and temperance are each a distinct *habitus*. They effect an "internal shaping" in the person so that the person acts well.[28] The virtues "really alter" the intellect, will, and appetites of the person.[29] As the *habitus* or virtue is developed within us, it leaves us ready to choose well and to carry out that choice with ease and facility. We then experience joy and satisfaction when the good action is carried out.[30] As the virtues develop in us, the intellect, will, and appetites are transformed toward good ends.[31] The intellect, will, and appetites are enabled to do good with ease and joy. We find fulfillment in doing the good, for this corresponds to God's image in us and advances our journey toward him.[32] "The virtues are the means whereby the Christian believer is transformed and made into an active image of God."[33] Virtue disposes the Christian for right conduct, but it

---

25. Romanus Cessario, *The Virtues, or the Examined Life* (New York: Continuum, 2002), 10; cf. Cessario, *The Moral Virtues and Theological Ethics*, 42–44.

26. Aquinas, *Summa Theologiae*, Ia IIae q. 55 a. 3: "Human virtue therefore which is an operative *habitus*, is a good *habitus* and productive of good."

27. Cessario, *Introduction to Moral Theology*, 196.

28. Ibid., 34.

29. Cessario, *The Virtues, or the Examined Life*, 100; cf. Cessario, *The Moral Virtues and Theological Ethics*, 57.

30. Cessario, *Introduction to Moral Theology*, 34.

31. Ibid., 131.

32. Cf. Ibid., 32–33.

33. Ibid., 194.

does not automatically make it easy. We can still struggle with habits of sin. But the relevant virtues come to our aid, through the help of Christian faith and spiritual exercises. Our good actions can develop prudence, justice, fortitude, and temperance only so far. To some extent we can acquire virtues and live for true human goods through learning, training, practical experience, and good counsel from others. This path leads us in one direction: to seek fulfillment through the ultimate good made visible in Jesus.[34]

The infused virtues, however, are the unique and exclusive gift of God through the seven gifts of the Holy Spirit, "who alone serves as the efficient cause of their coming to be and remaining in us."[35] We cannot manipulate the infused virtues, for they are God's gifts. Through a life of docile receptive readiness we dispose ourselves for the life of virtue. We can do this by listening to God's word in Scripture, receiving the sacraments, praying, contemplating the Christian mysteries, being faithful to our state in life. The theological virtues of faith, hope, and love are infused in the believer and join the person to God himself. At this juncture, the infused cardinal virtues begin to grow in the Christian.[36] The virtues are not automatic, however. We still need to resist temptation and practice humility. Christian growth ordinarily entails a gradual release from disordered *habitus* (from the effects of original sin), and a gradual growth of well-ordered *habitus*.

In the parable of the Prodigal Son, the *habitus* emerges when the son's emptiness in sin is filled with the father's emptiness in love. The *habitus* infected with sin is purified and nourished by the emptiness of humility. Humility transforms the person, establishing a new *habitus* that becomes a fountainhead of grace. The son moves from self-centered pride to self-focused fear to other-centered love. These same lines can be traced in the life of every person. The humility of Christ shines forth in his self-emptying (see Phil 2:8) on the cross and in the resurrection. His humility constitutes the fullness of grace and virtue that calls and transforms the most hardened sinner.

---

34. Cf. Cessario, *The Moral Virtues and Theological Ethics*, 100.

35. Cessario, *The Virtues, or the Examined Life*, 101; cf. Cessario, *The Moral Virtues and Theological Ethics*, 95.

36. Cessario, *The Moral Virtues and Theological Ethics*, 48–49.

For John Paul, grace enters into our very soul, into our person, the deepest recesses of our identity: "Precisely with regard to these 'unfathomable depths' of man, of the human conscience, the mission of the Son and the Holy Spirit is accomplished."[37] The mission is the creation of a new heart: "I will give you a new heart and place a new spirit within you, taking from your bodies your stony hearts and giving you natural hearts" (Ex 36:26). La Potterie and Lyonnet explain how God operates within the soul through the Holy Spirit: The revelation that comes forth from the Father and is communicated through the Son "attains its fullness when it enters into the most intimate part of our being through the action of the Holy Spirit."[38]

The Holy Spirit takes everything that Jesus taught and makes it interior to the believer. The action of the Holy Spirit can only be received by faith. Once received, the revelation is kept alive and active through the Spirit's work. The Holy Spirit teaches our hearts. His teaching makes love effective in the human heart via his gifts. They strengthen the heart against sin and make us capable of living new lives. The Spirit's sanctifying action makes the human person a child of God.[39] The Spirit's action is not a remote, external coercion. Instead, "pointing out the guilt of the world, the Paraclete will act in a completely interior way, in the secret confines of the disciple's conscience."[40] The Holy Spirit strengthens believers in times of crisis and draws them closer to Jesus, assuring them that the world is in error.[41] We cannot hoard grace as a private possession. Receiving the grace of Christ which transforms us is not "boring routine and uncreative predictability."[42]

To understand the nature of grace, Henri de Lubac writes, we need to appreciate what longing for God means, a longing "which is basic to man."[43] It is more than a psychological longing. Educational and social trends have focused human advancement simply on "experimental

---

37. John Paul II, *Dominum et Vivificantem*, 45.

38. La Potterie and Lyonnet, *The Christian Lives by the Spirit*, 64.

39. Ibid., 182.

40. Ibid., 74.

41. Ibid.

42. Cessario, *Introduction to Moral Theology*, 196.

43. Henri de Lubac, *A Brief Catechesis on Nature and Grace* (San Francisco: Ignatius Press, 1984), 27.

research" and "empirical" considerations.[44] Such a focus limits us to what can merely be observed and detected. Self-help literature and New Age trends are simply a response to the persistent tendency to limit the human to the measurable. New Age techniques are caught up in subjective experiences that are measured by a person's self, not by any others. Grace, instead, frees us from trying to measure spiritual things and introduces us to the unconditional and the infinite. If we try to measure grace and love, we only focus on our own efforts in the sacraments and prayer. Such a focus is a semi-Pelagian concern that continually examines how our personal efforts at prayer bring God's grace into our lives. We then attempt to wrest grace from God in response to spiritual practices. Just as harmful is the idea that any type of religious practice is superfluous because God is "everywhere" and "everything" is spiritual. Either approach is a misunderstanding of the true nature of grace.

Grace is not something added to make human nature somehow acceptable. Grace, the love of God, "unites itself to man, 'elevating' him ... penetrating him in order to divinize him, and thus becoming as it were an attribute of the 'new man....'"[45] A region exists in man that is deeper than the *psyche*; no created methods are capable of plumbing the "profound recesses" of the soul and the *pneuma*.[46] The distinction between the *psyche* and the *pneuma* in the person—between the inner intellectual processes and the soul itself—does not mean we should dismiss the science of psychology. Rather it conditions psychology to attune itself to an authentic anthropology that respects what is deeper in man. Psychology cannot plumb these recesses. God acts in the depths of the human spirit so as to inscribe the eternity of the divine presence on the human heart.[47] Grace received through the sacraments and in prayer "profoundly penetrates the depths of man's being."[48] God's Spirit enters the very substance of man and becomes a "principle of life."[49] We live in a new way, on the basis of a profound union that God is always ready to infuse and renew. We share in

---

44. Ibid., 31–32.
45. Ibid., 41.
46. Ibid., 145.
47. Ibid., 159.
48. Ibid., 41.
49. Ibid., 42.

God's being through grace because God, as Creator and Father, makes this possible.[50]

Grace is not a remote or extra reality in our life, nor is it something that we can control at whim. God bestows it as a gift, pouring it into us through a dynamic relationship of adoption and incorporation. Man thus receives grace through a bondedness that God has initiated and which the Holy Spirit seeks to maintain. Life according to the Spirit is based upon an intimate union that transforms man's innermost being. This union cannot be reduced to what we can estimate, observe, and measure, but it is still effective.

If we try to measure grace, our attempt is always somehow counterfeit. Humility alone can welcome the truly infinite. This is because humility is an outpouring of self, a kenosis that anticipates the kenosis of grace. Grace transforms man's nature by deepening it and fulfilling it at the same time. Only emptiness can receive the fullness. Grace is an invitation to surrender to salvation by emptying ourselves. Then we may be fulfilled in sharing God's life, through the union which he initiates.

Grace and the offer of salvation form us in Christ. This is why a new way of life in a sense is conferred upon us.[51] In the words of Benedict XVI: "[M]y encounter with God awakens my conscience in such a way that it no longer aims at self-justification, and is no longer a mere reflection of me and those of my contemporaries who shape my thinking, but it becomes a capacity for listening to the Good itself."[52]

B. The Sermon on the Mount and the Beatitudes

The Sermon on the Mount is so central that it is understood as "a summary of the entire Gospel." The Beatitudes, which form the first part of the Sermon on the Mount, are so vital that they are considered "a summary of the Sermon."[53] For John Paul, the Beatitudes, "in their originality and profundity" are "a self-portrait of Christ, and for this very

---

50. Ibid., 43.

51. Cessario, *Introduction to Moral Theology*, 192.

52. Benedict XVI, *Spe Salvi*, 33.

53. Servais Pinckaers, OP, *The Pursuit of Happiness: God's Way* (New York: Alba House, 1988), 25.

reason are invitations to discipleship and to communion of life with Christ."[54] Until the seventeenth century, the Sermon on the Mount and the Beatitudes formed the central axis of Catholic moral theology. They were one of the chief sources for the renewal of the Christian way of life.[55] The age of the manualists, that is, those who studied moral theology through tedious analysis of situations and acts, tended to relegate the Beatitudes away from moral theology to the realm of spiritual theology. Cut off from the moral theology and the virtues, the Beatitudes quickly descended to a kind of unreachable idealism meant for a rare few who could reach such high summits. As such, the Beatitudes, along with the Sermon, have received only superficial treatment in moral theology in recent centuries.[56] Often sketched in fine calligraphy on parchment, neatly framed on the wall, the Beatitudes become unreachable. But they are, in fact, the center of the Christian life. They possess a "qualifying character" and "show the Disciples the way to follow Jesus in every action."[57]

The retrieval of the Beatitudes is central to the Christian life. The morality that emerges from the Sermon on the Mount is not simply a duty to do certain actions and avoid others. If understood that way, the Sermon becomes a lofty code reserved for an elite few. Rather, in the Sermon Jesus addresses the very capacities of man that underlie his actions. The ways of the kingdom must penetrate, transform, and emerge from the deepest parts of man. The New Law is thus inscribed in the human heart through the direct action of the Holy Spirit.[58] The Holy Spirit does something concrete in the lives of believers. The chaste life is not an ideal, but a close land, open to all who find the path in Christ through the Holy Spirit's action. Understood in this sense, the Sermon calls man to a concrete transformation. This change concerns not only his actions, but also his attitude, disposition, and very being. It gives birth to a comprehensive morality that goes from the heart to the actions. In this way, the very notion of being a Christian takes on renewed meaning: "Christianity is first of all a concrete way of living, a praxis that is born

---

54. John Paul II, *Veritatis Splendor*, 16.
55. Pinckaers, *The Pursuit of Happiness*, 3.
56. Ibid., 5.
57. Melina, *Sharing in Christ's Virtues*, 85.
58. Pinckaers, *The Pursuit of Happiness*, 15.

of faith: it is not a vague gathering of ideals that can be interpreted in different and contrary ways, according to subjective tastes, but is rather a precise and recognizable form of life."[59]

For the Sermon on the Mount, Jesus goes up the mountain and sits down to teach the crowds. Just as Moses went up Mount Sinai, so Jesus, the new Moses, ascends the Mount of the Beatitudes. Sitting, he assumes the position of the teacher so that he might inscribe his teaching not on stone tablets, but on the hearts of the people.[60] He uses the word "blessed" nine times. The Greek word is μακαριος, which is difficult to translate. It does not correspond to "happy" or "a state of psychological euphoria," but a sense that God looks with approval upon our lives. Yet we are not blessed simply because of this knowledge, but because of the state of our souls themselves.[61] The modern concept of happiness is the subjective "satisfaction of one's own life understood as a whole."[62] The classical concept of happiness sees it "as the perfection of life" according to what corresponds to the natural good of the human person.[63] For the ancient Greeks, only the gods themselves were μακαριος in that they were privileged to be immortal and therefore free from the world's concerns.[64] Jesus proclaims that those who least resemble the Greek gods, the weak and the suffering, are μακαριος.[65] Jesus leads not the entitled, but the poor, hungry, afflicted, and marginalized along the path to the kingdom which he alone knows.[66] The Beatitudes, Servais Pinckaers writes, "overturn many of our ideas about happiness" and show central aspects of the kingdom.[67]

John Paul's theology of the body directs the believer to the "purity of heart" of the Sermon on the Mount. John Paul's reference to the Sermon

---

59. Melina, *Sharing in Christ's Virtues*, 29.

60. Erasmo Leiva-Merikakis, *Fire of Mercy, Heart of the Word: Meditations on the Gospel According to Saint Matthew*, vol. 1 (San Francisco: Ignatius Press, 1996), 181.

61. Ibid., 183.

62. Melina, *Sharing in Christ's Virtues*, 45.

63. Ibid., 46.

64. Leiva-Merikakis, *Fire of Mercy, Heart of the Word*, vol. 1, 184.

65. Ibid.

66. Pinckaers, *The Pursuit of Happiness*, 28. For a reflection on the meaning of authentic happiness see Jean Daniélou, SJ, *The Scandal of Truth* (London: Burns and Oates, 1962), 44–47.

67. Ibid., 29–30.

and to the Beatitudes, especially regarding purity of heart, is an implicit summons. It echoes the Second Vatican Council's call for the renewal of moral theology found in the Decree for the Training of Priests, *Optatam Totius*, 16. In the theology of the body John Paul has given the Church a compelling teaching. The theology of the body moves its hearers to bridge the gap from the manualist style of moral theology to methods and sources as called for by the council. The Holy Father's teaching helps us to find the key that unlocks the treasures of the teaching. John Paul's appeal to the Sermon on the Mount shows how the theology of the body connects with the entire tradition of moral theology.

Morality is often thought of in terms of duties centered around actions that are commanded to be done or avoided. The manuals of moral theology, popular in seminaries from the seventeenth to the twentieth centuries, tended to present moral action as a series of norms to be observed through disconnected acts, which were still external to the person.[68] In the latter half of the twentieth century, the manualist mentality still affected catechesis, preaching, and sacramental practice. Many people think of living a moral life in terms of imposed duties and not crossing certain lines, with penalties for failure. In such a schema, the gifts of the Holy Spirit and the theological and moral virtues are little more than terms to memorize. Obligation and duty are important methods at times in the moral life, but they are not the major ground or foundation.[69]

John Paul's teaching on the identity of the human person can only be unlocked by a renewal of moral theology that receives the teaching of the Sermon on the Mount in highest measure: "What Christ demands from all his actual and potential listeners in the Sermon on the Mount clearly belongs to that interior space in which *man*—precisely the one who listens—*must rediscover the lost fullness of his humanity and want to regain it*."[70] The recovery of the Sermon on the Mount is central to understanding the theology of the body.

The Gospel presents a concept of the moral life far different from that of manualist duty and obligation. The kingdom that Jesus proclaimed

---

68. Pinckaers, *Morality: The Catholic View*, 45, 73, 96.

69. Ibid., 20, 24, 32–34, 40, 91, 109–110.

70. John Paul II, *Man and Woman He Created Them*, 301.

focuses primarily on the human heart as the root of human action. The ways of the kingdom extend beyond mere obligation and duty. The kingdom responds to man's natural desire for happiness *(desiderium naturale)*. Man experiences "an inner power that 'attracts' man to the true, the good, and the beautiful" and by the discovery of this attraction "we see a road opening up ... toward what Christ wanted to express in the Sermon on the Mount."[71]

The Gospels reveal the Kingdom of God proclaimed in Jesus and present in his person. The promise is fulfilled in the words and deeds of Jesus. A common misunderstanding is that the Church is to "build the kingdom." If the focus is on what we build—as we teach, visit the sick, care for the poor—we are easily led to measure how well we built the kingdom today. If we build it, we can then set the terms. We can weigh our deeds and see what we earned or somehow conclude that we let God down. The proper work for the kingdom is not to *build*, but to *inherit*. "Jesus lays down the conditions for 'entering the kingdom of God,' not thereby implying that we can earn it [it is given to us only by the decision of God, and we can only pray for it (Mt 6:10)]...."[72] The kingdom is a gift: we inherit it and pray for it. We do not earn it or construct it. We do not set the terms.

God is the source of the Christian's moral life. The grace of Jesus is infused into the heart of the believer through the gifts of the Holy Spirit. The seven gifts then develop the life of virtue in the believer. The virtues enable us to act according to the Beatitudes.[73] John Paul's theology of the body emphasizes the call to purity of heart in the sixth beatitude. The virtues alone can lead us to purity of heart, and the virtues, in turn, can only be formed by the gifts of the Holy Spirit.

John Paul teaches that the action of the Holy Spirit in the soul is also crucial to the human body:

> What is decisive for the dignity of the human body ... is not only the human spirit, thanks to which man is constituted as a personal subject, but much more so the supernatural reality of the indwelling and con-

---

71. Ibid., 318.

72. Schnackenburg, *The Moral Teaching of the New Testament*, 20; brackets in original.

73. Pinckaers, *Morality: The Catholic View*, 21, 22, 71; cf. Cessario, *The Virtues, or the Examined Life*, 103. Cf. Benedict XVI, *Spe Salvi*, 35.

tinuous presence of the Holy Spirit in man—in his soul and body—as
the fruit of the redemption accomplished by Christ.[74]

The liturgy, prayer, and reading of Sacred Scripture all direct the
believer to Christ. Purity is a movement within the human person: "The
analysis of purity is an indispensable completion of the words Christ
spoke in the Sermon on the Mount ... Christ sees in the heart, in man's
innermost [being], the wellspring of purity...."[75]

After sin, the Holy Spirit brings the grace of Christ into our conscience to strengthen us and direct us toward repentance. We respond to
the inspiration of the Spirit, and thus grow in our personal initiative.[76]
The inspirations of the Holy Spirit become truly our own as we act upon
them.[77] In this way, when human persons choose to act according to the
moral virtues through "an effort of the will," this effort is "a *fruit of the
human spirit* permeated by the Spirit of God, which manifests itself in
choosing the good."[78] It is in this sense that John Paul teaches, "Moral
purity has its wellspring exclusively in man's interior; it comes from the
heart."[79] The believer is exhorted to remain close to Christ through the
Holy Spirit so that the Christian moral life may truly be a form of worship.[80] The Spirit forms our capacities through his gifts, and the virtues
then enable us to practice the Beatitudes. The person "must learn to be a
space within which God can be known to act."[81]

1. The Ladder

The early Fathers and monastics used the image of the ladder for the
Christian life. John Climacus and Guigo II are two who understood the
spiritual life as an ascent. They realized that purity of heart is not automatic.[82] To reach purity of heart, the sixth beatitude, one has to climb

---

74. John Paul II, *Man and Woman He Created Them*, 350.
75. Ibid., 326.
76. Pinckaers, *Morality: The Catholic View*, 70.
77. Ibid., 82.
78. John Paul II, *Man and Woman He Created Them*, 335.
79. Ibid., 328.
80. Pinckaers, *Morality: The Catholic View*, 12, 16.
81. Tugwell, *The Beatitudes*, 50.
82. John Climacus, *The Ladder of Divine Ascent*, trans. Colm Luibheid and Norma
Russell (Mahwah, NJ: Paulist Press, 1982); Guigo II, *The Ladder of Monks: A Letter on*

the ladder beginning from the first beatitude, the poor in spirit. But the image of the ladder should not be taken to mean that success depends only on our own efforts. God provides the ladder. As the human person begins to ascend the ladder, the Holy Spirit provides strength to climb. To ascend to purity, one must receive strength from the Holy Spirit to cultivate the dispositions that lead to purity.

John Paul II teaches that purity is like a wellspring in the believer.[83] While corresponding in some sense to the image of the ladder, the wellspring perhaps better expresses the divine initiative in the spiritual life. It also expresses the mature spontaneity of the upward ascent that marks transformation in Christ. John Paul II is not saying that the wellspring implies that God has predetermined our purity. The wellspring is a *hidden* spring over which the watchman must keep *guard*.[84] Saint Bonaventure, again, has a kinship with the teaching of John Paul: "Just as a fountain of water will not last unless it has a continuous connection with its source ... the grace of the Holy Spirit will not thrive in the soul unless it is referred back to its original source."[85] The images of the ladder and the wellspring help us to understand the fine distinctions that attend the subtle working of grace in the human heart.

Saint Augustine comments on the Beatitudes in *Our Lord's Sermon on the Mount*. The Doctor of Grace writes, "[T]he sevenfold operation of the Holy Ghost, of which Isaiah speaks [Is 11:2], seems to me to correspond to the [stages and sentences of the Beatitudes]."[86] Augustine proposes ordering the gifts this way: "we reckon as it were a gradually ascending series, where the fear of God is first, piety second, knowledge third, fortitude fourth, counsel fifth, understanding sixth, wisdom seventh."[87] In this schema the gifts correspond to particular Beatitudes in the same ascending order. Thus, the Beatitudes form a kind of ladder that the human person ascends through the operation of the gifts and the virtues, leading up the Mount of the Beatitudes.

---

the Contemplative Life and Twelve Meditations, trans. Edmund Colledge and James Walsh (Kalamazoo, MI: Cistercian Publications, 1981).

83. John Paul II, *Man and Woman He Created Them*, 320, 326, 328.

84. Ibid., 320.

85. Bonaventure, *Collations on the Seven Gifts of the Holy Spirit*, 35.

86. Augustine, *Our Lord's Sermon on the Mount*, bk. 1, ch. 4, 11.

87. Ibid.; cf. Aquinas, *Summa Theologiae*, IIa IIe q. 69, a. 1, ad. 1.

To reach purity of heart, we must climb the ladder from the starting point of the first beatitude, the poor in spirit. With strength from the Holy Spirit, we ascend from poverty of spirit to meekness, to mourning, and onward. At each level the gifts form the virtues that give us the strength to live poverty, meekness, and mourning in the image of Jesus. At times, through sin, faults, and bad habits, we may fall down the ladder. Then, through grace, we press on in docility to the call of the Holy Spirit. To reach purity of heart, the sixth beatitude, we gradually and patiently ascend the ladder laid out through the gifts, aligned with the virtues and leading to the practice of the Beatitudes. This formation is present in the theology of the body as well. We will not find it extensively laid out in the same words as Augustine, but the image of the wellspring that John Paul employs has similar characteristics.

The vision of the Christian life set forth in these images corresponds better with experience. To present the Christian life primarily as a matter of duty and obligation leaves little room for understanding how the Holy Spirit acts. Ordinarily, Catholics do not stop practicing their faith in a grinding halt. They may still identify with "being Catholic," but their commitment wanes due to a few factors. Frustration is high on the list. The secular culture has conditioned us to look for returns on our investment. The perfect storm, laid out in the first chapter, leads us to count and measure our buying and spending. If we practice faith, we think, then God should deliver. This is often the culprit behind the decline in receiving the sacrament of Penance. People still believe in sin and that God forgives sin. They can see little reason for confessing their sins to receive this forgiveness. Why? Because early on, they discovered that when they do confess their sins, they still sin. We think confession should be like disinfectant spray that not only kills germs, but also keeps them away. We often think that going to confession should not only bring forgiveness of our sins, but also keep any further sinful inclination completely away. We reason that if we take the trouble to confess our sins and take responsibility for them, then we should get a measurable return. But the bad moods, cursing, unruly appetites, and myriad other faults all come knocking soon after we receive absolution, stand up, and leave the confessional.

The perfect storm of industry, pleasure, and technology, when absorbed by our psyches, translates into high expectations and a utilitarian standard: If we can't see immediate returns, then we abandon the effort and move on. God's sacramental actions are reduced to being automatic moments one step removed from magic. God rarely chooses to act in automatic ways, however, because love, while often immediate, is rarely automatic. The Christian life includes living within the tension that while we may be forgiven and live justly, the "lingering effects" of the "old self" still leave disordered appetites.[88] The gifts of the Holy Spirit strengthen believers to cling steadfastly in faith to Christ so that virtue may preserve them from giving in to disordered passions.[89]

The tradition demonstrates that God works in the way of love. The ordinary way of love is by way of the gift. God's gift to man is the Holy Spirit, who is often referred to as the Person-Gift:

> In his intimate life, God "is love," the essential love shared by the three divine Persons: personal love is the Holy Spirit as the Spirit of the Father and Son. Therefore he "searches even the depths of God," as *uncreated Love-Gift*. It can be said that in the Holy Spirit the intimate life of the Triune God becomes totally gift, an exchange of mutual love between the divine Persons, and that through the Holy Spirit God exists in the mode of gift. It is the Holy Spirit who is *the personal expression* of this self-giving, of this being-love. He is Person-Love. He is Person-Gift.[90]

Moral theology must recapture and convey the manner in which the Holy Spirit, who is Person-Gift, works through his seven gifts in the life of the believer. God does not simply set out a series of laws that we must obey, and then measure us with a stopwatch and chart from the sidelines. The Holy Spirit has often been too easily forgotten. Saint Gregory the Great, in his teaching on moral theology, repeatedly emphasizes that God acts in the world through the Holy Spirit. In turn, the Holy Spirit acts only in seven distinct ways: the seven gifts.

The seven gifts are enumerated in Isaiah 11:2: "The spirit of the Lord shall rest upon him: a spirit of wisdom and of understanding, a spirit of counsel and of strength, a spirit of knowledge and of fear of the Lord and his delight shall be the fear of the Lord." While the fear of the Lord is mentioned twice, the first is a reference to the gift of piety.

---

88. Cessario, *The Moral Virtues and Theological Ethics*, 120.
89. Ibid., 121.
90. John Paul II, *Dominum et Vivificantem*, 10.

The gifts are not measured out, like laws corresponding to some obligation for the believer. They are not rewards we earn, but gifts we receive through the action of the Holy Spirit. As noted, the gifts operate in our lives like an ascending ladder, as Saint Augustine notes in *Our Lord's Sermon on the Mount*. While seen as a series of stages, the gifts are not so much separate levels to be attained as steps that overlap one another.

The gifts are infused into the Christian in Baptism and strengthened in Confirmation. Worthy reception of the Eucharist nourishes the gifts in the Christian, who is led to prayer that heightens the reception of the gifts. The danger is that the gifts have tended to be overlooked in more recent approaches to moral theology because they were understood as data for sacramental theology.

You may remember memorizing the list of the gifts while preparing for Confirmation. I recall that the week prior to Confirmation, members of my class were required to bring several things to school: a large red felt banner, a medium banner of white felt, an unused drinking straw, thirty inches of string, scissors, and glue. The class activity was to cut letters out of white felt and spell the gifts of the Holy Spirit by gluing the letters to the large red felt banner. Then we placed the drinking straw on the top reverse of the banner, folded some of the felt over the straw and glued it down. We then fed the string through the straw and tied a knot to make a loop. Finally, we took the banners to the church and hung them along the wall.

The problem was, after the ceremony, it was easy to forget the gifts of the Holy Spirit and leave them in church. God chooses to act in the world in and through the actions of the Holy Spirit. Unfortunately, the seven gifts have been treated in an abstract way in theology in general, and moral theology in particular.

They have also been somewhat misunderstood in the work of more recent moral theology. Many Christians think of the virtues only as a program of ideal yet burdensome actions. Further, they see them as a repressive or unhealthy type of self-control used to suppress temptations.[91] Repression is always about escape through aggression, which bides its time.[92] Virtue, on the other hand, is about freedom. Unless they

---

91. Cf. Cessario, *The Moral Virtues and Theological Ethics*, 50, 75.
92. Cf. Bachelard, *The Poetics of Space*, 112.

understand this, people will think of virtue as what they cannot do instead of what they may do.

The tradition is rich in its teaching on virtue, however, and it starts with what virtue is. Saint Augustine, Saint Bonaventure, and Saint Thomas Aquinas all teach that virtue is "a good quality of mind by which one acts rightly, of which no one can make bad use, which God works in us without us."[93] The last seven words of that definition are often left off. Many of us are familiar with a self-focused understanding of the first two parts of the definition, but the third never quite made the black-board, much less the heart. "It is characteristic of God to work quietly, without a fuss."[94] The Holy Spirit does not try to control us or override our will, but acts in us through influence by repeatedly surging toward us with the gentle yet persistent presence of a tide. The Spirit attempts to transfer to us the movements of God's own heart and place the design of his shaping deep within.[95] Both the acquired and infused virtues work to shape the character so we can live righteously.[96] A virtue is not a technique but "a talent or genius for doing good human action...."[97] God intervenes through the gifts of the Holy Spirit and perfects our capacities in a way that changes our very nature. Virtue becomes an internal principle of action that transforms the powers of the soul, the reason, the will, and the appetites. It helps them to incline toward the true and the good, and thus effectively change human behavior for the better through authentic self-mastery.[98]

The names of the virtues are found in Scripture. For example, Saint Paul refers to the theological virtues of faith, hope, and love (1 Cor 13:13). The cardinal or moral virtues are found in the Book of Wisdom: prudence, justice, fortitude, temperance (Wis 8:7). While the ancients were aware of virtuous ways of acting, they did not create the virtues per

---

93. Augustine, *De Libero Arbitrio* ii, 19; Aquinas, *Summa Theologiae*, Ia IIae q. 55, a. 4; Bonaventure, *Collations on the Seven Gifts of the Holy Spirit*, 28. Peter Lombard includes *Deus solus*, "by God alone" in the definition (Book II, d. 27, c. 1 in *Sententiae in IV Libris Distinctae*, Tom. I. Pars II. Liber I et II, Third Edition, *Spicilegium Bonaventurianum* 4 [Grottaferrata: Collegium S. Bonaventurae, 1971], 480).

94. Tugwell, *The Beatitudes*, 42.

95. La Potterie and Lyonnet, *The Christian Lives by the Spirit*, v, vii, 8.

96. Cessario, *The Moral Virtues and Theological Ethics*, 53.

97. Ibid.

98. Ibid., 57.

se. Neither do we somehow conjure up the virtues only from our good will, persistent training, and behavior. The first thing about virtue concerns to whom it first belongs. All virtue is first God's. He forms the capacity to live the virtues within us. God does so through the seven gifts of the Holy Spirit. Each virtue is associated with a particular gift that disposes the person to receive the inspiration from God to act in a new way, a way that is beatitudinal.[99] Saint Thomas, in his treatment of the virtues, includes the particular gift that builds that virtue within the believer.

The ladder, or wellspring, is modeled on the chart below. It begins at the bottom left, with the Spirit's gift of fear of the Lord. The explanation in the following pages is a general description of the work of the gifts, virtues, and Beatitudes.[100]

SEVEN GIFTS (Is 11:2)	VIRTUES (1 Cor 13:13 / Wis 8:7)	BEATITUDES (Mt 5:1–10)
Wisdom	Love	Blessed are the peacemakers
Understanding	Faith	Blessed are the pure of heart
Counsel	Prudence	Blessed are the merciful
Courage	Fortitude	Blessed are those who hunger and thirst
Knowledge	Faith	Blessed are those who mourn
Piety	Justice / Temperance	Blessed are the meek
Fear of the Lord	Hope / Temperance	Blessed are the poor in spirit

99. Pinckaers, *The Pinckaers Reader*, 15–16.

100. For a more detailed development of the gifts, virtues, and Beatitudes, see the various works cited in the bibliography.

2. Purity of Heart

If we look at the Beatitudes as a ladder that begins with the poor in spirit, we find purity of heart six rungs up. So often the struggle for purity of heart in terms of sexual purity is seen as a matter of personal will and effort. Personal efforts toward purity have their place within a structure. In the schema of the Beatitudes, purity is the outcome of poverty of spirit, meekness, steadfast realism, endurance, and mercy. Any other outline for purity is deficient. Before the Beatitudes are actions, they are "a habitual condition of the spirit, a state of being...."[101]

Purity is the transformation that emerges when the gifts of the Holy Spirit join with the virtues. The chief virtue directed to purity is temperance:

> Purity consists in temperance.... Through such reverence, which is owed to the human body, purity as a Christian virtue is revealed ... as an effective way of detaching oneself from what is a fruit of the concupiscence of the flesh in the human heart ... purity is an *"ability"* *centered on the dignity of the body*, that is, on the *dignity of the person* in relation to his or her own body, to the masculinity or femininity that shows itself in that body. Understood as "ability," purity is precisely an expression and fruit of life "according to the Spirit" in the full sense of the term, that is, as a new ability of the human being in whom the gift of the Holy Spirit bears fruit.[102]

Growth in the life of virtue under the inspiration of the gifts of the Holy Spirit has certain features. The following section will describe the operation of the gifts together with the virtues and beatitudes that correspond to them.

Gift	Virtue	Beatitude
Fear of the Lord	Hope / Temperance	Blessed are the poor in spirit

---

101. Leiva-Merikakis, *Fire of Mercy, Heart of the Word*, vol. 1, 199.
102. John Paul II, *Man and Woman He Created Them*, 349.

a. *Fear of the Lord*

According to Saint Thomas Aquinas, temperance flows from the gift of fear of the Lord. In Saint Augustine's schema, the gift of fear of the Lord is the first gift that begins to form believers within their life experience. Filial fear is the gift of the Holy Spirit known as fear of the Lord: "Filial fear holds the first place, as it were, among the Gifts of the Holy Spirit, in the ascending order.... "[103] Through the gift of fear of the Lord, the Holy Spirit transforms the believer from worldly fear to the fear of God.

The Holy Spirit begins his work in each of us by working on our fears. He does this because fear is so common that everyone experiences it. Aquinas says there are four types of fear.[104] The first type is worldly fear. This fear results when we drift away from God to focus more readily on things of the world. This fear can concern even incidental things, such as fear of public speaking, fear of loss, fear of not knowing the answer, or even fear of being picked last for a team. Worldly fears from phobias to anxieties to worries can keep us in a state of unhealthy tension that makes us try to conform.

Worldly fear is born of inordinate self-love and arises ultimately from sin. This fear is like a net. The more we struggle when caught within it, the tighter it becomes. We can allow it to become a way of life so it affects our education, politics, work, and recreation. It is the law of the jungle. Our efforts are laden with "jockeying for position, striving to get ourselves into a more influential and powerful place" so that we may competitively impress others.[105] We want to have the last word, to interrupt others, and portray ourselves in the best light. God's mercy is far from our minds when we are under the sway of worldly fear.

Fear is one of the seven steps of sin, and as such forms the central pivot of every evil. It counters and negates the gift at the center of our identity. Worldly fear is love for the world and trust in the world's tactics and schemes. The Holy Spirit passes into this pivot point and seeks to reverse the motion by restoring the gift.

---

103. Aquinas, *Summa Theologiae*, IIa IIe q. 19, a. 9.
104. Ibid., a. 2.
105. Tugwell, *The Beatitudes*, 42.

As the Holy Spirit begins to move within us as we are caught in worldly fear, the nature of the fear begins to shift. Still drawn to the worldly pursuit of status and achievement, we quietly feel a new sense emerging in our consciousness. We begin to experience small movements of Aquinas' second type of fear, servile fear: we fear punishment from God. This second level of fear is actually charity beginning to shift the way we live according to worldly fear. Self-love begins to diminish. Instead of worldly fear guiding our daily decisions, the fear of punishment begins to move us in a different way. This transition is rooted in the fear of evil and the knowledge that sin is punished because it is a disorder. The world does not bring what it promises. The gap between promise and experience leads us to consider God from the standpoint of his power rather than of his goodness. Still caught in selfish concerns stemming from worldly fear, we can at first see God's action only under the aspect of punishment. The fear of loss predominates in servile fear. We fear the loss of goods, health, objects, friends, and also heaven. Still, this level of fear is more mature and advanced than worldly fear. Servile fear admits there is more than the world.

Servile fear remains caught in the world's residue and thus retains self-interest. But the self-interest has begun to look beyond the self. Another—the Holy Spirit—has intervened and shown that the world is not enough. The ways of the world are being revealed as limited. As the Holy Spirit begins to prove the world false, we experience the way of the world as flawed. Servile fear motivates us to avoid sin and is enough to make us ready for heaven. The danger is when servile fear is understood as the goal rather than a stage. If unduly cultivated, this fear can become a fixation and an encumbrance by which we seek to get others to heaven by scaring them. Something more is needed.

The Holy Spirit seeks to move us beyond servile fear to Aquinas' third level, initial fear. We now experience a mixture of fear of punishment and the fear of committing a fault against God. While we continue to seek to avoid sin because of fear of punishment, we slowly begin to realize that besides fearing the punishment of God, we may also love God. We may vacillate between avoiding sin because we fear punishment and avoiding sin because we love God. This balancing act is common to initial fear. Charity has moved us to the beginning of filial fear. The Holy Spirit has helped us mature beyond the fear of punishment to sense that

God's power is more than retribution. It is always a profound gift of love. As we realize this, we still sense the fear of hell, but the fear is due more to separation from love, and we move beyond our preoccupation with avoiding punishment.

The Holy Spirit then gradually introduces us to an awareness of a relationship with God pervaded more and more by love. We do not want to separate from God by sin because we fear punishment, but because we are growing in the love of God. Far from being a mere mental construct, this love becomes evident in our actions through charity. We begin to see sin as banal and unattractive. The old ways of worldly fear are seen as a futile maze that leads to a dead end. We wonder how we could have navigated the paths of worldly fear for so long.

But even this awareness quickly vanishes as we experience God more and more as a loving Father. The fourth level of fear, filial fear, is the love of a child before the father, but it is not a trembling worry of being overrun or overpowered. It is, rather, the fear of hurting the father because we love him. Filial fear realizes that we are the son or daughter, and so we move forward with a constancy that does not depend on the world.

One of my earliest memories captures the image of filial fear. When I was very young, before I could even walk steadily, I used to sit at my father's feet. I have a picture of myself doing just this, wearing blue overalls and sucking on a pacifier. With one hand on my father's shoe, I was looking up at the camera, wondering what that mysterious flash was. My father was six feet, four inches tall. He routinely wore good black leather shoes with thin shoelaces. He also wore good businesslike pants with a perfect crease. One of my first, repeated memories of my father is sitting at his feet playing with those thin laces, wrapping them, tugging at them, and twisting them. After about five minutes of this I would get distracted, or my father would stand up because it was time for us to leave for home or to move to the yard. Because I was only starting to walk, it was easier for him to carry me. When he stood up and I looked up at him, my gaze would travel up the pant leg, along that perfect crease stretched along the better part of a six-foot, four-inch expanse. The same thought would always come into my mind, and I can feel it in my ribs to this day, one of my original thoughts: "He goes on forever." That is filial fear. My father goes on forever. It is "that healthy fear which prevents us from living for ourselves alone and compels us to pass on the hope we hold to others."[106] It is only from this vantage point that we can have the hope necessary to say, "Blessed are the poor in spirit."

The Holy Spirit wishes to accomplish something in our lives by changing our daily fears into a strong feature of the inner life of virtue. He does this as his gift of fear of the Lord infiltrates the tendency to fear and helps the believer to understand the nature of God's merciful power that fortifies our innermost places.

b. Hope

The virtue of hope is not mere optimism. So often we look for God in outcomes and results. If we feel good or content, we assume that God is somehow present. If all turns out well, we feel that God is clearly at work. The virtue of hope is different, however. Through his gift of fear of the Lord, the Holy Spirit inspires the Christian to reach out in hope toward the future. A Christian can have many particular hopes: for the well-being of a family member, for gainful employment, for easing of stress, for emotional relief, for the return of a son or daughter to the faith. All of these are understood as good things, but they may be hard to attain due to some difficulty. The perceived difficulty can stall us and immobilize our hope. We must approach the object of our hope, and our very way of hoping, with filial fear.

The mature fear of a son or daughter is not preoccupied with the timing of an effect. Filial fear realizes that to reach for *a* true good is to reach in some way for *the* true good, God himself. To reach for and rely upon God is to already be *united* to God. The moment we hope, in the virtuous sense, we have entered the presence of God himself, no matter what the gauges of our life may read.[107] God himself is the proper object of hope.

Hope looks to a true good that is difficult for us to attain as we anticipate the future. In our decision to hope, we rely on God not as if he will automatically give us whatever we want, but in the sense that we trust in God's help for some aspect of life. The moment we rely on God, we are in the presence of God. Aquinas says, "When it is the case, then,

---

106. Benedict XVI, *Spe Salvi*, 29.
107. Aquinas, *Summa Theologiae*, IIa IIae q. 18, a. 1.

of hoping for something as possible to us precisely through God's help, such hope, by reason of its very reliance upon God, reaches God himself."[108] By hoping in the first place we have relied on God and bound ourselves in union with God. This reminds us that our ultimate hope of eternal life is in God. We learn from this that hoping in God is more vital than hoping for anything from God that we may intensely desire: "And now, LORD, what is there to wait for? In you rests all my hope" (Ps 39). In hoping for a particular future good from God we learn that our future completely resides in God alone: "... a distinguishing mark of [Christians] is that they have a future: it is not that they know the details of what awaits them, but they know in general that their life will not end in emptiness."[109] The learning that Christians receive from hope actually molds them to adjust and moderate their desires, so that they want what God wants through a kind of assimilation. Our desires themselves begin to change by our hoping in God, and our very disposition regarding the world and daily circumstances is made new and recreated. The concrete things we hope for are subsumed into hope itself. Thus, we sort our desires through God first, so that we train our desires to pursue the good and the true as God knows them to be. We are taught that the One on whom we rely for a particular good is the One in whom all good resides, in particular the good of perfect happiness in eternal life. Our hopes lead us to hope.

By hoping for something, then, we are caught up and transformed by the same hope to hope in Someone. Benedict XVI writes that Christians are not just rewarded by hope, but hope transforms them: "We see how decisively the self-understanding of the early Christians was shaped by their having received the gift of a trustworthy hope, when we compare the Christian life with life prior to faith, or with the situation of the followers of other religions."[110] From the transformation afforded by such hope, inspired as it is by the gift of fear of the Lord, the Christian message is "not only 'informative' but 'performative.'"[111] Hope begins to shape and extend the actions of Christians beyond their ordinary capac-

---

108. Ibid., q. 17, a. 1.
109. Benedict XVI, *Spe Salvi*, 2; cf. Aquinas, *Summa Theologiae* IIa IIe q. 18, a. 4.
110. Benedict XVI, *Spe Salvi*, 2.
111. Ibid.

ity: "[the Christian message] is one that makes things happen.... The one who has hope lives differently."[112]

We are hoping more and more in a Person rather than things. Our appetite for things is now changed and placed in a more proper perspective. The one who truly hopes also learns to hold fast not simply to an optimistic outlook on the future, but to the truths taught by the One who holds the future. Hope reveals our human appetites as futile and illusory. Instead, we rely on the hope afforded by God. The disposition of the one who hopes is changed. Hope transforms the believer to courageously move into the future despite difficulties.

c. Temperance

Fear of the Lord inspires hope in such a way that hope begins to transform our inner selves, including our appetites, drives, needs, instincts, emotions, and tendencies.[113] The appetites are born from the basic needs associated with physical life. We experience a strong inclination to pleasure. Temperance inclines us to engage the appetites with reason. "Temperance, by moderating the instinctive impulses of eager desire, which tends to devour everything immediately, makes room for listening and for hearing the word. 'Not by bread alone does man live, but by every word ...' (Deut 8:3)."[114] Temperance guards us from desiring pleasures that are against reason, and moderates our approach to reasonable pleasures.[115] The pleasures that food and sex bring to the sense of taste and touch strongly attract us. We are inclined to turn repeatedly to what assures us of continuance of the species, closeness to the other, and sustenance of our own life.[116] We are willing to fight to assure these needs are satisfied. These appetites require integration based on a proper understanding of how to reasonably satisfy them. Relying on God for who he is, not just for what he can do, brings to birth, through fear of the Lord, a truth about the human person and his actions. Since we are in relation to a God who loves us as Father, our activity can flow

---

112. Ibid.

113. Aquinas, *Summa Theologiae*, IIa IIe q. 141, a. 1, ad. 3.

114. Melina, *Sharing in Christ's Virtues*, 18–19.

115. Aquinas, *Summa Theologiae*, IIa IIe q. 141, a. 2.

116. Ibid., a. 5.

from a new source within us. Our conduct can now be aligned with his will in a natural and spontaneous way, rather than a burdensome and constraining way. We see the authentic good more clearly. We can put our strong reactions to sensible goods in a proper perspective and in the light of a new strength.

Due to the effects of sin the appetites subtly influence the intellect and will to choose a good in a disordered way. Flirting with food, drink, or sex shows this subtlety. Flirting is ordinarily first visual, then verbal, and then tactile. Fantasy accompanies flirting through the entire process. The temptation to pleasure is graphically portrayed in sexual temptation. Already sexual fantasy alleviates tension. The subject is always the star of the fantasy, in control of everything as the producer, director, and viewer. The buildup is alluringly immaterial and as such is sensational, because it seems like the fantasy will have no consequences. But such indulgence changes one's spirit. These fantasies leave us less prepared for what is real, and encourage us to treat the real with contempt. The faculties themselves become predisposed to favor the apparent good of the self rather than the authentic good of the other.

Temperance and purity aid us to confront such temptations from within and respond in practical and effective ways. We can take four concrete measures in the midst of sexual temptation: first, do not panic; second, ask, "Where is this coming from?"; third, make an act of confidence in God; and fourth, do something creative. This plan is supported by traits associated with temperance. *Verecundia* is a trait directly influenced by temperance that helps the temperate person naturally shy away from what is morally ugly. This is a sense of healthy avoidance based on the aversion to dishonor and disgrace. The trait of *verecundia* shows itself as a modest reserve, which restrains action and helps the person avoid what is immoral as regards the appetites. This trait makes us averse to what is morally repulsive. A second trait, *honestas*, is a positive sense of honor that sustains gracefulness.

Temperance leads us to practice chastity as regards sexual pleasure, abstinence as regards food, and sobriety as regards drink. Temperance helps us respect these appetites, because an ordered way of life reflects the divine design. Vices such as fornication, cohabitation, adultery, masturbation, and homosexual acts are curbed through temperance and the transformation it evokes in our hearts.

The invitation to live Christian purity is not merely a matter of white-knuckled, clenched-teeth chastity. John Paul teaches that purity arises from the virtue of temperance, which the Christian cultivates through the direct action of the Holy Spirit. The virtues are not ways of acting that we must keep trying until we "get it right," hoping the virtues will become automatic through sheer willpower. This point of view encourages us to see chastity as a line separating purity from impurity and to think that all we have to do is remain on the purity side of the line. The question immediately becomes one of "how far can I go" without being impure. This leads to a legalistic minimalism and focus on self. John Paul does not favor this approach to Christian morality: "Jesus shows that the commandments must not be understood as a minimum limit not to be gone beyond, but rather as a path involving a moral and spiritual journey toward perfection, at the heart of which is love (cf. Col 3:14)."[117] The Christian seeks to imitate Christ through the help of the Holy Spirit who changes our hearts through grace. Our actions then become signs of the new life to which all are called.

The manuals of moral theology focused on making us aware of our duty and obligation regarding chastity. The message was "Don't cross the line," and chastity became more of a standoff than a standing for something. As a result, many chose to live near the line, tricking themselves into thinking they would not cross it. Along came a strong wind, a strong drink, or a tilted set of life-changing transitions, and they drifted over the line. When virtues are learned in a manualist mindset, the one crossing the line just tries harder to not cross it. Instances where the line was crossed are often kept secret, bringing about a deeper internalization of shame. Burdened with shame and secrets, the trail quickly loops back to the line, with the surface comfort or thrill of crossing it again. A double life is born. Sooner or later the life of virtue becomes what was deemed an idealist mindset, made for an unrealizable temperament, and the person abandons any realistic hope of purity.

d. Blessed Are the Poor in Spirit

Fear of the Lord inspires temperance, which transforms actions so the believer begins to see life and actions in terms of the first beatitude:

---

117. John Paul II, *Veritatis Splendor*, 15.

"Blessed are the poor in spirit, the Kingdom of heaven is theirs" (Mt 5:3). The beatitude is not merely a command, but a seed we see emerging in life, like a new shoot emerging from the soil in spring. The newness of life is a sign of how our lives progressively conform to Christ. We are drawn to self-emptying love, and with this poverty of spirit we take the first steps of a life of charity. The poor have an abundance because they are not limited to navigating life on the basis of negotiations that end only in success or failure.[118] The poor person knows that despite any circumstances, the infinite God always has a path to ample fruits.

The poverty in question goes deeper than material poverty. The meaning of "poor" is concrete, not abstract.[119] The poor have a long history in the people of Israel. Jesus was aware of the poor and his mission to the world: Worship in the Jerusalem temple was not valid unless it was linked to social justice "founded on the memory of the slavery in Egypt," when Israel was poor.[120]

Wealth is not simply a calculation based on a financial portfolio, but often carries a proud superiority.[121] The wealthy who imbibe a sense of superiority draw a certain lift from the numbers, and the attitude that the numbers allow. They depend on the bottom line, and cravings easily drive them to seek even more money.

Conversely, the poor know they need God and his help.[122] Poverty may take the form of a lack of good health, loneliness, age, fear of the future, or even living in error and sin.[123] Poverty means that one has drilled down into the experiences of life and arrived at what Servais Pinckaers terms the "fundamental emptiness which lies at the depths of our being."[124] Buoyed by worldly standards, the rich person feels possessive about wealth, and this naturally affects his sense of self and attitude toward others.[125] The Christian who is obsessed with material wealth risks becoming less authentic in this world. Driven by the urge for

---

118. Tugwell, *The Beatitudes*, 40.
119. Pinckaers, *The Pursuit of Happiness*, 40.
120. Pontifical Biblical Commission, *The Bible and Morality*, 52.
121. Pinckaers, *The Pursuit of Happiness*, 40.
122. Ibid., 41.
123. Ibid., 44–45.
124. Ibid., 46.
125. Ibid., 47.

worldly success, we cannot get too far without compromising fidelity to God:[126] "There is a widely attested belief that this world, as we know it, is subject to the 'Ruler of this world' [Satan] (cf. Jn 14:30). There goes with it a sense of the real danger that prosperity in this world can be had only on the terms of the Ruler of this world."[127] Therefore, the Christian faces practical decisions in the world: "It is a real question for all of us, how far we can expect to achieve worldly success of any kind at all without compromising our fidelity to God[?]"[128]

The possessiveness of the world is always far from God's generosity, on which the life of the Christian is centered. Possessiveness is never far from activism and "the tyranny of immediacy."[129] God's generosity supplies us so that our arms may be empty to bear the self-gift of the cross.

When in poverty one moves away from the facades and temporary promises of the world, one can then learn true love. This process does not entail simply a positive feeling or appreciation of a secret knowledge. Instead, it springs from a begging for life from the deep places within the heart. The poor do not merely not want the things of the world, they live for something more important than the things of this world. This drive in the poor is not an illusion of those who "have not made it" or a remedy for some unconscious exclusion they may feel. Rather it is a true knowledge: "People who are on the edge of things have a mysterious knowledge."[130] Like Sheriff Pangborn in *Needful Things*, the poor see "too much." They know the world better than those who seem to control the world.

In speaking of the "poor in spirit," "we should understand 'spirit' here in the strong, literal sense of 'breath.'"[131] When the Holy Spirit inspires hope and temperance through the gift of fear of the Lord, the person's attitude becomes a begging for one's very life breath, such as humility. "What Jesus here intends is most likely not a neatly spiritualized attitude of interior detachment, but an existence (πνευμα [pneuma]: one's breath,

---

126. Tugwell, *The Beatitudes*, 18.
127. Ibid., 17. See also Daniélou, *Advent*, 106.
128. Tugwell, *The Beatitudes*, 19.
129. Ibid., 48.
130. Bly, *The Sibling Society*, 99.
131. Leiva-Merikakis, *Fire of Mercy, Heart of the Word*, vol. 1, 188.

each moment we inhale air) wholly dependent upon God's mercy and providence."[132] The poor depend on God not out of mere duty, but because, "When we encounter the trial of poverty, Christ mysteriously draws near to us and plumbs its depths together with us, asking the decisive question: Here at this point of your life, do you or do you not believe?"[133] The poor in spirit realize that they "depend on God in the same way our lungs and our voice depend on air."[134] The poverty of the beatitude depends on quality, not quantity: The man who "expands and embraces reality" expresses the greatest of riches because he reaches out to anticipate a fullness when he "discovers that of himself he can never attain this fullness"—this is his "constitutive poverty."[135] The poor have a kingdom that surpasses and does not depend on the things of this world.

Concretely, this poverty takes the form of a childlike attitude. The believer is blessed, and this blessedness is not threatened by weakness and suffering. It is actually enlivened to address such frail and perilous experiences. This is because something about God is revealed more in helplessness than in strength. The child is the one who is ultimately helpless. The child is naturally poised to live in the present.

One weekday I went to have lunch with a family who are good friends of mine. The two older boys were in school, and their youngest son, a three-year-old, was at home. When I stopped to get gas, I bought a soda and a candy bar. I then realized that if the little boy saw my candy bar, he would want one. So I purchased two. I arrived at their house about 11:15 and greeted the mom and dad. Their three-year-old came in wearing sweatpants. He was playing and running, jumping into his mother's arms. It was his heaven. I showed him the candy bar. His eyes lit up and as his smile widened he began to reach for it. But then he turned and spontaneously called over his shoulder, "Mom … Mom … is it after lunch yet?" He was so excited that he had forgotten the time of day. He had forgotten the sequence of events in his little heaven. So rather than figure it out he asked his mom. He knew the rule of no

132. Ibid., 186.
133. Pinckaers, *The Pursuit of Happiness*, 52.
134. Leiva-Merikakis, *Fire of Mercy, Heart of the Word*, vol. 1, 186.
135. Melina, *Sharing in Christ's Virtues*, 49.

candy before lunch, but the rule fit in joyously to a wider schema: This candy was his, preferably sooner, but for sure later. He was in the kairos time of his home. Time passed for him in such a way that time itself was immeasurable.

Children live in the emphatic present. They have no past that makes them want to somehow "program the future."[136] In this sense hope makes us young: Augustine says, "newer than all things."[137] Our society turns to creams, laser treatments, and injections to find youth. Youth is found only in the hope and spontaneity afforded by God.

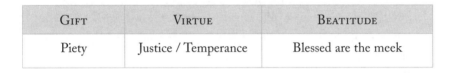

Gift	Virtue	Beatitude
Piety	Justice / Temperance	Blessed are the meek

e. Piety

The gift of piety is a habitual disposition that makes the soul receptive to the movement of the Holy Spirit by which we show affection to God the Father.[138] Meekness removes the obstacles to piety.[139] The person who is being transformed from worldly fear to filial fear is no longer at the mercy of the things of the world. Market sectors, prices, and profits—or lack of them—no longer dominate the person's interior world. Previous maps are abandoned, and we follow the direction of hope. We live from a hope beyond ourselves. The gift of the Holy Spirit enables us to be less driven by appetites for worldly things, and to become more temperate. More and more our lives and relationships are overtaken by poverty of spirit, which rejoices in freedom from the things of the world. Such freedom is the creative place over which God readily hovers to create a new kingdom.

---

136. Tugwell, *The Beatitudes*, 7.

137. Augustine, *De Genesi ad Litteram Libri Duodecim*, bk. VIII, ch. 26, 48, col. 392 PL 34.

138. Aquinas, *Summa Theologiae*, IIa IIe q. 121, a. 1.

139. Ibid., a. 2.

In this atmosphere, the gift of piety begins to inspire us. For John Paul, piety arouses the virtue of justice in a way that makes the virtue of temperance flourish. John Paul notes that temperance is wrought through the gift of piety, which develops our capacity for the virtue of justice:

> The link of purity in love, and the link of the same purity in love with piety as gift of the Holy Spirit, is a little known guiding thread of the theology of the body, but nevertheless deserves particularly deep study.[140]

As such,

> Purity as a virtue or ability of "keeping one's body with holiness and reverence," allied with the gift of piety as a fruit of the Holy Spirit's dwelling in the "temple" of the body, causes in the body such a fullness of dignity in interpersonal relations that *God himself is thereby glorified.*[141]

Notice that the teaching of Aquinas and John Paul, taken together, show temperance as the work of two gifts of the Holy Spirit, fear of the Lord and piety. As such, the virtues of hope and justice strengthen the human quest for holiness as regards temperance: "*Purity in the sense of temperance* matures in the heart of the human being who cultivates it and who *seeks to discover and affirm the spousal meaning of the body* in its integral truth."[142] Fear of the Lord and piety, aligned with hope, justice, and temperance, are the initial movements of Augustine's ascending ladder. They are the initial movements of transformation as we begin to be poor in spirit and meek.

f. Justice

The theology of the body is not simply a private quest to win the battle of purity. In its most clear light, the theology of the body is action in *communio*, for it takes places relationally. Piety, like all the other gifts of the Holy Spirit, is relational. As I recognize my own poverty through the work of the gifts and virtues, I must also see that my neighbors, too, are called to be poor in spirit. Whether or not they have reached that

---

140. John Paul II, *Man and Woman He Created Them*, 353.
141. Ibid. See also John Paul II, *Pilgrim to Poland* (Boston: St. Paul's Editions, 1979), 76.
142. John Paul II, *Man and Woman He Created Them*, 283–284.

goal, however, does not determine the way I treat them. In my relationship with my neighbors I simply cannot misuse their bodies or my own because they, like me, are children of God. I have a devotion that wells up from a source within me, rooted in God, that inspires and develops respect for my neighbor and his or her body as well as my own body. My pleasure can never be private because it always involves my body or the body-person of another in some way.

Instead of a self-centered justice and overt concern for one's own rights, a just person begins to see justice as other-centered. Justice is ordinarily understood as giving another his due. The Holy Spirit's gift of piety strengthens us to render justice to God, neighbor, self, and the created world. As such, justice can be a complex topic that takes various forms, such as distributive or retributive justice. The principles of justice underlie professional and personal relationships, and they animate and protect relationships and commitments such that I always render others their due.[143]

g. Blessed Are the Meek

As we are developing the Beatitudes to this point, we are cultivating a sense of filial love before God. That love inspires hope and temperance and allows us to live from the deep source of poverty of spirit. The things of the world look different when viewed from the margins. This new vision inspires the virtue of piety in the believer's heart. Piety takes the form of an authentic, positive, and loving regard for God, others, and self. The Christian is thus led to deepen his poverty by meekness. Modern translations of the Gospel of Saint Matthew list "Blessed are those who mourn" as the second beatitude. The "western textual tradition, including the Latin Vulgate Bible, places second in the list of the beatitudes the one about the meek."[144]

Meekness is not the hunched, protective shoulders of a nagged husband. It is not insipid resignation, embarrassing sentimentality, or a too-easy temperament.[145] Nor is it passivity, constraint, or tameness.[146] Jesus

---

143. Aquinas, *Summa Theologiae*, IIa IIe q. 58, a. 1.
144. Tugwell, *The Beatitudes*, 29; cf. Pinckaers, *The Pursuit of Happiness*, 73.
145. Pinckaers, *The Pursuit of Happiness*, 55, 57, 58.
146. Leiva-Merikakis, *Fire of Mercy, Heart of the Word*, vol. 1, 193–194.

proclaims that he is "gentle and humble of heart" (Mt 11:29). The meek person is the one who can stand strong and firm because his heart responds from its abundance. This abundance is the

> outcome of a long struggle against the disordered violence of our feel-
> ings, failings, and fears ... [and this] implies tremendous inner
> strength and merits the praise of the Book of Proverbs: "He who is
> slow to anger is better than the mighty, and he who rules his spirit
> than he who takes a city" (16:32).[147]

The meek person has seen much. He knows that the world's craving for possessions continues and appears to be rewarded time and time again. But he sees beyond the world's tactics. He knows that even while all the greedy people prosper "there is no future for the wicked. And therefore there is no occasion for us to interfere ... indignation and officiousness are inappropriate reactions."[148] The meek man learns how to respond to the wicked from the Lord's example. The wicked seem to prosper, but Psalm 37 shows the Lord's response: "The wicked man plots against the just and gnashes his teeth against him; but the LORD laughs at the wicked, for he sees his day is at hand." When the wicked appear "what the Lord does is simply laugh ... for all their threats and preten-sions, there is really nothing to them. To react to them with anger and outrage is to ascribe to them more substance than is their due."[149]

The meek person knows that God has led him thus far, to the extent of adopting him as a son or daughter. The meek one can thus refrain from the tactics of the world and can receive all as a gift.[150] The meek one is the person who recognizes how God acts. The Lord routinely leads us through poverty of spirit to show us the way of the kingdom. The scars of learning poverty sketch the map that leads to meekness. As such, the meek man knows that "God loves the meek and takes their part against the powerful."[151] Meekness is steadfastness learned through suffering. This meekness must ground our conscience and displace sin and self-interest. As such, authentic meekness can arise only from the

---

147. Pinckaers, *The Pursuit of Happiness*, 61.
148. Tugwell, *The Beatitudes*, 30.
149. Ibid.
150. Leiva-Merikakis, *Fire of Mercy, Heart of the Word*, vol. 1, 194.
151. Pinckaers, *The Pursuit of Happiness*, 56.

passion of Christ: "the inexhaustible source of God's mercy and sweetness is opened up in Christ."[152] The meek person learns that God favors the unexpected and takes the part of the underdog: those who "stand no chance" are the ones who receive the promise of the Lord.[153]

GIFT	VIRTUE	BEATITUDE
Knowledge	Faith	Blessed are those who mourn

h. Knowledge

The gift of knowledge is not directed toward acquiring knowledge in a worldly sense. The sacraments of Baptism and Confirmation do not give infused knowledge about algebra, for example, so that our mathematics grade will rise from C to A. The gifts of hope and piety have begun to direct us to the love of knowledge. This sanctifies the intellects of Christians, and we begin to read inwardly the true nature of things, especially the actions of Christ. The world is obsessed with knowing trivia: the lives of Hollywood stars, political personalities, and the minutiae of people's personal lives. The gift of knowledge leads us to the things that really matter. We begin to digest the truths of faith on a personal level through union with God. The gift of knowledge moves us away from utilitarian knowledge to knowledge as a right judgment about what is believed.[154] Knowledge grows into discernment in a twofold way: knowing what to believe, and knowing what not to believe.[155] The Holy Spirit enlightens our minds to grasp how faith applies to human or created things.[156] Looking at the world and relationships from God's perspective, we better understand the true nature of things: "I muse on all your works and ponder your mighty deeds. Your ways, O God, are holy" (Ps 77). Such knowledge is not mere confidence in our own opinion, but truly relates to

---

152. Ibid., 71.
153. Tugwell, *The Beatitudes*, 31.
154. Aquinas, *Summa Theologiae*, IIa IIe q. 9, a. 1.
155. Ibid.
156. Ibid., a. 2.

things in themselves. Through supernatural assistance we are led to authentic judgments about the faith. The gift of knowledge leads to practical reliance on God's providence, and proclaims in realistic fashion the words of Psalm 43: "O send forth your light and your truth; let these be my guide." Because the believer has learned justice he is open to the knowledge of God: "Light shines forth for the just...." (Ps 97). We learn to understand in a new light the things we have been taught earlier in life. Then we can more easily make determined judgments about daily life. We begin to see more clearly the reasonableness of faith and authentic Church teaching. We can more quickly see the connection from creation to Creator to God as Father, and begin to understand reality from God's point of view. This knowledge leads to practical applications in daily life because it concerns temporal matters.[157] It helps us learn speculation in the true sense of the word: Speculation is not a random reading of the environment based on our fancies and hunches. Speculation in the true sense is gazing upon the world, patterns, and relationships in a way that brings the deep meaning of such practical matters to light.[158] The gift of knowledge enables us to unite knowledge of faith with our personal daily actions.[159] The mind senses the inner structure of reality more clearly and can make right judgments about the world based on the supernatural assistance of knowledge.

i. Faith

Faith is a particular type of belief. Faith concerns all the things we believe about God and the mystery surrounding his life. Faith differs from opinions and predictions about the weather, our favorite sports team, or political candidates.[160] Religious faith is an act of the intellect. While parents and family play a fundamental and profound role in handing on faith, the act of faith itself does not arise exclusively from our parents' influence in telling us from an early age what to believe.

---

157. Ibid., a. 2, ad. 1. See also Wojciech Giertych, O.P., "The Dominican Order's Intellectual Service," *The Thomist* 73 (2009), 138.

158. Aquinas, *Summa Theologiae*, IIa IIe q. 9, a. 3.

159. Ibid., a. 3, ad. 3. See also, John Corbett, O.P., "The Functions of Paraclesis," *The Thomist* 72 (2009), 96.

160. Cessario, *The Virtues, or the Examined Life*, 44.

Along with external assistance, the act of faith is inspired by the Holy Spirit's gift of knowledge in the mind of the believer. Each of us has the capacity for intellectual operations that take place on the level of the mind. As such the mind has recourse to reason, affections, logic, and education as it is presented with the truths of faith. These all influence our natural intellectual aptitude. Our intellectual level resides at a more profound depth than logic, reason, or education itself. Knowledge presumes those things. Then it clears the way for us to see more nimbly how the truths of faith interconnect.

While God makes use of the ordinary means of catechesis, the direct action of the Holy Spirit works in the mind of the believer at a more profound level. Created in the image and likeness of God, human persons also have a supernatural capacity to know the truths about God in the mind. Through this capacity, enlivened by the gift of knowledge, the Holy Spirit inspires the mind of the believer to make an act of faith. In a progressively profound manner, the intellect adheres not just to the belief *that* there is a God, or to trust the truths *about* this God, but *in* God himself. The act of faith is understood in light of the three meanings of religious faith as outlined by Saint Augustine: "But it makes a great deal of difference whether someone believes that Jesus is the Christ, or whether he believes in Christ."[161] Aquinas teaches that the act of faith is appropriately distinguished into "believing about God" (*credere Deum*), "believing God" (*credere Deo*), and "believing for the sake of God" (*credere in Deum*).[162]

At the first level, we learn the beliefs about this God who exists, *credere Deum*. This ordinarily takes place through catechetical moments in early life. As the child begins to discern the world, he or she is led to practice prayer, to worship, to hear Bible stories, and to learn practical notions about God and daily life. This turn to belief in God may occur or accelerate later in life due to a transition or profound experience. Each person has a faith history that may draw upon an experience, an encounter, a word, a phrase from a book, a special thought, or a reflection that spurs a decisive turn to faith.[163] The fundamentals are often first: The existence of

---

161. Augustine, *Sermones ad Populos* 144, no. 2 (PL 38, 788).
162. Aquinas, *Summa Theologiae*, IIa IIae q. 2, a. 2.
163. Kasper, *Transcending All Understanding*, 33.

God includes basic concepts of the strength and love God has for his people, God's power over the created world, and God's justice and mercy.

The second level consists of a movement within us. The belief of trust, *credere Deo*, moves the relationship with God to a new level. We go from simply believing general things about God to trusting that these truths concern us personally, as well as God personally. God is reliable. The third level gives a special impetus to the previous two. *Credere in Deum* is the act of faith that reflects the seasoned belief of those who journey toward God within the Church. From simply believing about God, and then trusting in what God has revealed, we go on to believe for the sake of God himself as a Person. The act of faith has transformed us so much that we rely on it for direction with realistic and mature energy.

Thus, when a Christian says, "I believe God exists," something more is at work than a settling prediction, pious sentiment, or a reasoned estimate. Regarding the existence of God, the Apostle James writes, "Even the demons believe this, and tremble" (Jas 2:19). The Christian proclaims God's existence with certainty when he claims this on faith. "[T]rust ... is based on the completely determined content of faith ... faith in God's history with mankind, on the Incarnation of God, on the cross and Resurrection of Jesus Christ and on the efficacious presence of God's Holy Spirit in the word and sacraments of the Church."[164]

Faith is not simply a certain prediction that it will rain because the clouds are gathering and the pressure is rising. The probability of rain in such a case is a well-informed opinion. Faith is also not simply a blind regard for authority. Faith in God is categorically different from a self-assured rationale about whether a supreme being exists.[165] Faith in the Christian God is very different from assurance regarding spiritual techniques, spiritualism, astrology, reincarnation, or the tenets of the New Age.[166] The Christian faith moves a person immediately beyond sociological, personal, or political experiences to the substance of the Person of Christ. Faith is to be lived as a witness that is directly related to reflection on the mystery of Christ.[167] This is belief in a Person.[168]

---

164. Ibid., 17.
165. Ibid., 33.
166. Ibid., 36.
167. Ibid., 15.
168. Ibid., 16.

Faith has an "inner structure": "It is more than a case of turning to Jesus as a worker of miracles and relief; it is a question of believing in a salvation-giving God who reveals himself in Christ."[169] In faith, the gift of knowledge transforms our capacity to perceive the depth of the truths of the faith. The human powers of knowing themselves are sharpened and receive renewed life "from the contact with Jesus" and gain "strength from his person."[170] Such knowledge grounds us in God. This knowledge transcends personal experience or a logical proof of God's existence. Through the gift of knowledge, faith is strengthened in that we learn the concrete depth of what it means to rely upon God. Belief brings us to a close union with God. "When anyone acknowledges that Jesus is the Son of God, God dwells in him, and he in God" (1 Jn 4:15). Grace takes the believer beyond what reason alone provides and past whatever the believer himself expected. Faith is never simply a private system of beliefs.[171]

j. Blessed Are Those Who Mourn

A person being inspired by the gifts of the Holy Spirit is a person being transformed. The believer detects a newness that emerges from beyond him. He does not approach God as a severe rule maker or a soft pushover of his own making. Rather, he approaches God who is veiled in mystery. The believer steps forward each day on the basis of trust in God. This trust does not waver even before those circumstances that appear most barren and unfriendly. The believer who acts under the influence of the gifts of the Holy Spirit is led to an attitude of mourning, which abides as a kind of inverse jealousy. When he sees others, he does not seek to obtain their good. He does not wish that the world would share his own good, but the goodness of God in greater measure. The just one takes on the disposition expressed in Psalm 39: "A mere breath the man who stood so firm, a mere shadow the man passing by, a mere breath the riches he hoards, not knowing who will have them" (Ps 39). He mourns because he wishes for more time and space where the goodness of God

169. Rudolf Schnackenburg, *The Moral Teaching of the New Testament*, 38.
170. Ibid.
171. Kasper, *Transcending All Understanding*, 14.

could be revealed. He is blessed then because he mourns. The mourner also grieves because he himself was once caught in worldly ways and mastered by evil. He grieves more because he thought these disordered ways were good.[172] He experiences this grief not so much as nagging regret but as unfortunate nostalgia. He becomes aware of the loss and thus has a kind of knowledge that reaches beyond the loss.[173] Knowledge comes through loss and sorrow.

We all experience at some time the loss of a loved one. But the acceptance of the loss itself tends to elude us. We protect ourselves by denial of the deep pain and by avoiding it, which may lead to depression and anger. As we work through this, we finally come to the point of true grief over the death of a loved one. Such a loss "designates the keenest of sufferings, experienced when someone we love has died and there is nothing more we can do but weep."[174] Grief is the land we enter when we are "afflicted interiorly above all because of the death of someone [we] love, and show such keen grief exteriorly by signs."[175] We do not hide in activity, addiction, work, or a series of new relationships. Grieving is a plateau that opens a new world before us. The one who truly grieves "learn[s] to trust not in himself but in God, who raises up the dead."[176]

Authentic grief means recognizing love as the other side of grief. It is necessary to experience our authentic grief for as long as we need to. If we bypass the grief, we miss the full extent of the love we feel for the one who has died. Love underlies death and stands at the end of the road of grief. Faith teaches this in a preeminent way. Our faithfulness in facing the death of a loved one brings us to a connectedness to Christ, who alone is faithful. God's fidelity is not revealed in prosperity, but in adversity. This declaration is passed on from age to age: "Fathers declare to their sons, O God, your faithfulness" (Is 38:19). We are then faithful in facing death because we have learned through the most pivotal of losses that "life is sovereign over death."[177]

---

172. Aquinas, *Summa Theologiae*, IIa IIe q. 9, a. 4.
173. Ibid.
174. Pinckaers, *The Pursuit of Happiness*, 73.
175. Leiva-Merikakis, *Fire of Mercy, Heart of the Word*, vol. 1, 190.
176. Pinckaers, *The Pursuit of Happiness*, 75.
177. Leiva-Merikakis, *Fire of Mercy, Heart of the Word*, vol. 1, 190.

Grief reveals a layer of meaning in the last place we would expect to find it: on the other side of death and loss. Our daily life is filled with distractions, pursuits, and anxieties. "The solitude of suffering which accompanies the uniqueness" of each death interrupts those daily pursuits, and allows the person to acquire "a grateful eye."[178] The person who looks at the world through tears can perhaps "see things that dry-eyed" people do not.[179]

Losing a loved one prepares us for the losses of daily life: losing a job, everyday disappointments, routine problems and setbacks. When these things occur, the one who mourns is not surprised or shocked. He realizes that God is at work. Letdowns remind us that we are pilgrims on a journey. Our true home is the happiness that comes from God alone, not from the ways of the world. God enters at these moments and shows us the way of sacrificial love. The Christian mourns not because he cannot follow the way of the world, but because he wishes more people would find the way of sacrificial love.

Life's intense losses teach us how to cope with the smaller losses of daily life. Authentic grieving teaches us that the ways of the world often disappoint. We must go to the other who has been bitten by life and left by the wayside. Those who authentically mourn live an authentic life. They learn human truths in a much more direct fashion: "To know the truth of our human predicament is to know it as something that can be met only with mourning."[180] Therefore, once we have met our grief, a world of emotion opens up before us. Because we have faced the most tremendous loss, we can face any emotion. We emerge from grieving and see the truth that "a capacity for real enjoyment is inseparable from a capacity for real distress."[181]

The person who has been inspired by the gifts of the Holy Spirit and has lived the life of virtue and the Beatitudes advances through grief with a new courage, a courage learned with those who gather beneath the cross.

---

178. Nicholas Wolterstorff, *Lament for a Son* (Grand Rapids, MI: Wm. B. Eerdmans, 1987), 10, 13, 24.
179. Ibid., 26.
180. Tugwell, *The Beatitudes*, 63.
181. Ibid., 61.

Gift	Virtue	Beatitude
Courage	Fortitude	Blessed are those who hunger and thirst

k. Courage

So far we have discussed how the Holy Spirit inspires the believer with the gifts of fear of the Lord, piety, and knowledge. Those gifts foster the virtues of hope, temperance, justice, and faith. Next comes the virtue of fortitude, which is inspired by the gift of courage and fortifies the believer.

As he lives the Christian mystery, the believer realizes that the world is often hostile to the Good News. His example and spirit do not immediately attract those who still live within the confines of worldly fear. They are not ready to give up the ways of the world. As a result the meek person experiences trials and hardships in daily life. He sees the backroom deals, power plays, and gossip. He is accustomed to greed and vice exerting continued influence. In the midst of the ways of the world, the Holy Spirit's gift of courage inspires a firmness of mind to do good and endure evil.

The meek person will meet much difficulty as he seeks to do good. But that shouldn't make him forsake the path to goodness. He need not seek out trials, for these will find him if he truly tries to be just. The world cannot abide true justice for long. The just person must be strengthened by a deep love of good, especially when evil consequences come. The Holy Spirit strengthens us to persist to the end of the good work we have begun, despite any setbacks we may meet along the way. The gift of courage inspires practical confidence so that we can persist despite trials. We are not always successful, but we are called to remain faithful. Our strength is meant to last beyond this world to everlasting life. Courage is not reckless abandon. It is a confidence that expels fear and perfects the just person to overcome all dangers standing between him and eternal life.[182]

---

182. Aquinas, *Summa Theologiae*, IIa IIe q. 139, a. 1.

l. Fortitude

Courage strengthens the virtue of fortitude in the believer. This virtue enables us to remain dedicated and resist difficulties while pursuing what is truly good.[183] Fortitude is bravery that enables us to stand firm in the face of infirmity, danger, and assault.[184] The Christian life challenges the world. But the believer is tempted through fear to compromise the Christian way and give in to the world. When a Christian is shy or apologetic about the faith, the virtue of fortitude can strengthen the believer to resist the fear.[185] Psalm 92 testifies that God well knows our fear and will assist us: "To me you give the wild-ox's strength; you anoint me with the purest oil."

At the other extreme, fortitude moderates the temptation to proclaim the Christian message in an overzealous way. A too aggressive campaign disrespects the full depth of human nature by reducing Christianity to force. In such cases, fortitude introduces moderation. John Paul recalls Saint Gregory the Great's teaching that fortitude actually inspires the Christian to heroically love the difficulties of this world for the sake of the next world.[186] Fortitude inspires us to endure and remain steadfast under all kinds of dangers, including death, with confidence in God.

m. Blessed Are Those Who Hunger and Thirst

The poor in spirit know the true character of hope because they know they have to depend on God. The believer can be meek and steadfast because he walks in justice, strengthened by the gift of piety. As such, he grows in a mature faith that knows the way the world ought to be. He longs for this justice, all the while mourning that many more do not enter the way of life. So he relies on the courage that comes from the Holy Spirit and stands firm in fortitude so that his witness may proclaim the kingdom for which he hungers and thirsts.

Hunger moves us quickly.[187] But the believer's hunger and thirst is not a mere physical craving. It is a refusal to be satisfied with anything

---

183. Ibid., q. 123, a. 1.
184. Aquinas, *Summa Theologiae*, IIa IIe q. 123, a. 2.
185. Ibid., a. 3.
186. John Paul II, *Veritatis Splendor*, 93.
187. Pinckaers, *The Pursuit of Happiness*, 92.

less than God.[188] The believer conducts his life of hope, justice, and faith with an insatiable desire. That hunger and thirst[189] only becomes more patient in the face of long delay.[190] The Christian hungers and thirsts not for convincing arguments or for everyone to think the way that he does. His hunger is much more insatiable than that. As Isaiah says: "He who practices virtue and speaks honestly ... he shall dwell on the heights ... his food and drink in steady supply" (Is 33:15–16). The courage to persist in waiting on the Lord shows that "there exists in our depths a yearning for God as vigorous as any bodily hunger or thirst ... the chief purpose of the beatitude is to form in us that spiritual appetite...."[191] This beatitude shows that virtue is no mere tranquilizer of those who settle for just being good. The tension between craving and contentment is very real for those who long to follow Jesus. The resolution of this tension in trust makes the Christian more mysterious and elusive to the world. In doing so it brings him down to earth. He can wait in patience for the Lord; his patience itself is a kind of hunger.

The gift of courage enables us to get down to the basics of life. This is why "the very foundation of the spiritual life must be a basic realism about what it means to be human."[192] The Christian knows that the good he has chosen in faith seems foolish to the world. Through courageous perseverance, he has found that behind every no lies a richer yes: "It is more important, eventually, to know how to say 'yes' to a desire than to know how to say 'no.'"[193] What desires do Christians says yes to? It is their steadfast affection for the way of love made visible in Jesus and attained in charity. As such they may appear foolish to the world. They will stop to feed the poor, pray while others rush to the parking lot after Mass, forgo the shopping spree at Christmas so they can give 10 percent to the Christmas food drive. This apparent foolishness does not drive them to practice this faith as if it were private. Instead, the apparent foolishness is converted to a positive energy that can only be released as humility. By modest disposition the Christian startles the world into new

188. Leiva-Merikakis, *Fire of Mercy, Heart of the Word*, vol. 1, 195.
189. Aquinas, *Summa Theologiae*, IIa IIe q. 139, a. 2.
190. Ibid., a. 2, ad. 3.
191. Pinckaers, *The Pursuit of Happiness*, 95.
192. Tugwell, *The Beatitudes*, 73.
193. Ibid., 80.

ways of thinking and living.[194] His simplicity intensifies his reserve, and he learns in a deep way that "holiness is defined, not by any mysterious aura or hidden powers, but by the conformity of the mind and the actions of a man to the objective truth of which God is the source."[195]

Those who hunger and thirst for righteousness take desires, needs, and satisfactions and turn them toward the last things the world would want. The believer realizes when he encounters the appetites that "there is more than physical hunger and thirst at stake here."[196] In serving the true and lasting good, Christians try to deal with desires by responding to everyday needs with integrity. If we have a headache we do not tell the whole world, much less blame the last five people we had to deal with. We do not feel the need to study the guests at the party to size up who's who. We respond to our needs by relying on what God has provided in this moment. As we do this we learn the true character of the intangible needs of ourselves and others.[197] We begin to discover the true nature of need: it is a sign that points to God, not to our own frustration. The hunger of the Christian is natural and learned through virtue under the inspiration of the Holy Spirit.

Gift	Virtue	Beatitude
Counsel	Prudence	Blessed are the merciful

n. Counsel

The person who lives as a child of God and treats others as such lives by a distinct knowledge of faith in a spirit of courage. His fortitude, however, must be guided in daily actions so that his witness is directed and led according to God's plan. The Holy Spirit's gift of counsel inspires us to live the virtue of prudence so that the knowledge of the faith may be applied in particular circumstances. Through his reason, the believer

194. Ibid., 70.
195. Leiva-Merikakis, *Fire of Mercy, Heart of the Word*, vol. 1, 195.
196. Pinckaers, *The Pursuit of Happiness*, 91.
197. Tugwell, *The Beatitudes*, 75.

can grasp rational principles as directed by God, who comprehends all things. Counsel is not a secret hotline to God. Rather, under the influence of counsel, all our actions are directed as though counseled by God.[198] In particular, this concerns matters necessary for salvation.[199] God's goal is the salvation of humanity. Therefore God arranges the world such that the Good News of redemption is always close by.

The gift of counsel guides the Christian directly to the moral good, especially through the choppy water of the passions. When inflamed by the passions, the appetites can easily tilt us in the wrong direction. So the journey to God requires special aid. This help is not a secret divine revelation that immunizes or numbs us from the passions themselves. Rather, counsel transforms us, making our hearts familiar with the things of God through grace. God knows all things, and he helps us in our particular circumstances, while never overriding our freedom. The world is tricky, and it often sets traps. Counsel supplies God's guidance to the docile heart by a gentle teaching. God teaches the heart, especially when we turn to God often and await his guidance.

o. Prudence

Counsel inspires prudence in the Christian. Prudence is not simply a cautious reserve. Prudence is a long-range virtue that concerns the results of our actions. When we act, various things happen. Prudence scans these and looks for the true end for which we act. It seeks the ultimate thing we are doing and weighs it to ask: is this a true and good action? Prudence tells us what to seek and what to avoid.[200] This virtue helps us understand the past and present and learn from our experience.[201] The goal is to direct our choices and actions by right reason as we pursue what is truly good.[202]

The virtue of prudence transforms the knowledge of moral truth into concrete choices and actions that are ultimately simple to do. This is not a kind of robotic, rule-based functioning. Rather, it is a judgment based

---

198. Aquinas, *Summa Theologiae*, IIa IIe q. 52, a. 1, ad. 1.

199. Ibid., IIa IIe q. 52, a. 1, ad. 2.

200. Ibid., IIa IIe q. 47, a. 1, *sed contra*.

201. Ibid., a. 1.

202. Ibid., a. 2.

upon knowing the rational nature of reality and how God intends it to be fulfilled. Prudence often must enter into conflicts caused by concupiscence and the uproar of the appetites. Prudence steps in to assist reason as it navigates the unpredictable waters of human interiority and action. Prudence brings moral truth within the believer's reach, so that he or she may choose and act in accord with truth and goodness.

The believer thus turns inward in prudence in the movement of *synderesis* and finds the first principles of practical reason. *Synderesis*, a term used in moral theology, refers to the knowledge we have of the principles of moral action. The believer also turns outward to the nature of things and decides whether a particular choice is a morally good action. Thus *synderesis* and *intellectus* come together as the Christian grasps the principles that will guide a proposed action. Several factors must be considered: history, appetites, passions, short-sighted reasons, poor training, short time span, physical stress, apparent goods, and habit. We must integrate memory, simple intuition, docility, reason, and experience and submit these to the light of God's counsel. Then they themselves will become progressively transformed. We must further take a true good and discern how to find it and bring it about in a particular situation.

Prudence guides us to navigate through the appetites. Prudence directs us to the true and the good through careful deliberation in both ordinary matters and in complex cases. Prudence brings a moral clarity so that we can choose the true good. This will authentically fulfill our nature through practical acts carried out in the concrete world.

p. Blessed Are the Merciful

Counsel enables us to act with prudence in concrete situations. Prudence always looks like mercy. Counsel seeks the ultimate reason for a practical action. An action can have many motives: higher status, good effect, beneficial outcome, or sustained security. We can have many reasons for acting, and usually our motives are mixed regarding our practical choices. Vacations are good decisions because they allow us to slow down, rest, and renew our energy. Vacations also give us time away from people who may annoy us. So we may have mixed motives for spending a few days away. Our mixed motives often bother us and can pester us to do only those things for which we have a pure motive. This perfectionism disguises itself as an examination of conscience: "Self-justification is one of fallen man's favorite occupations."[203] In the final analysis, however, mercy is the form of the ultimate human act. Unless an action has the interior form of mercy it is not yet completely Christian. Counsel therefore directs mercy.[204] Through counsel, God inspires us to a mercy that always invites us to "move beyond our initial reactions."[205] When we do move past our knee-jerk conclusions and pause, mercy opens up options we never knew existed. We begin to see the world with a new clarity, and the true nature of concrete daily life opens up to our consciousness. We find ourselves capable of a new action: "the spontaneous, creative movement of life-bestowing love that bends down wherever it detects misery."[206] Mercy is the only theorem that leads to newness:

> Mercy is no soft option.... It is the only really hard-headed response to evil, faced frankly and judged accurately for what it is. It is the only power which can face evil and not flinch, because it knows a power stronger than evil, the power of God's Word, in which the promise of creation still stands, and in which, therefore, the seed of new creation waits to germinate.[207]

Counsel gives the heart a new horizon of action. It makes the heart capable of a more direct response to each moment of the day. The heart desires to find a real relationship to the other, which can be an occasion to renew the gift of love. This gift of love takes the form of mercy: "The movement of the heart (*cor*) that is shaken at the sight of another's plight (*miseria*) and moves to do something, going out of itself toward the other."[208] The other is not held to the high criterion that always accompanies the false goods of the world.

As the merciful action moves toward the other, it prompts an undetected return action, which deepens prudence in the one who acts with mercy. In giving, we receive the gift we gave and more: "The act of mercy we perform toward our neighbor in the name of Christ, however humble

---

203. Tugwell, *The Beatitudes*, 86.
204. Aquinas, *Summa Theologiae*, IIa IIe q. 52, a. 4.
205. Pinckaers, *The Pursuit of Happiness*, 116.
206. Leiva-Merikakis, *Fire of Mercy, Heart of the Word*, vol. 1, 197.
207. Tugwell, *The Beatitudes*, 90.
208. Leiva-Merikakis, *Fire of Mercy, Heart of the Word*, vol. 1, 197.

and hidden, is precisely the key which opens our hearts to the divine Trinity."[209] The merciful person finds mercy is not an isolated action of goodwill or momentary charity. Mercy is a passport into the world by which one goes further into the world and finds a deeper way to be human. This is why "forgiveness … is the dogged refusal to settle down in such a world of discord."[210] Mercy is the only action that has or can change the world for good after sin.

Gift	Virtue	Beatitude
Understanding	Faith	Blessed are the pure of heart

q. Understanding

Inspired by hope, we approach life with an inbred simplicity. We navigate relationships under the influence of piety so that we abide by unaffected justice, which results from a great openness to the other. All this leads us to an authentic knowledge that prompts the virtue of faith. Then we spontaneously exude a genuine sense of balanced urgency that the things of God guide the world more and more. We are developing courage to make known our pressing concern in places and situations that are less than welcoming to the word of God. Under the impulse of the Holy Spirit, we act courageously to apply the things of God in prudence to daily life situations. Doing so, we are always aware that mercy embraces all—no situation can have too much mercy. As such, our faith is deepened even further by the gift of understanding.

The Spirit's gift of understanding inspires us to follow the light of understanding. It enables us to read within the nature of a thing or situation so as to gain an intimate knowledge beyond the ordinary. God allows us to see the meaning, the nature, the causes of things via a supernatural light. The true nature of circumstances are thus revealed as part

209. Pinckaers, *The Pursuit of Happiness*, 124.
210. Tugwell, *The Beatitudes*, 90.

of God's plan.[211] We are led more directly to see that plan behind the incidentals. Worldly ways begin to lose their luster, and the ways of God shine forth in the mundane events of daily life. We find ourselves drawn to love the plan of God. This does not mean that we have any kind of secret knowledge about the will of God. Rather, we listen spontaneously for the voice of God that leads toward salvation, discerning it carefully. Meditation on the mysteries of Christ in Scripture helps us to sense God's ways in daily life.

r. Faith

Aided by the gift of understanding, the virtue of faith forms the Christian to personally see God as the ultimate truthful One. The Holy Spirit so forms us interiorly that the truths of revelation never fade into abstraction. The Spirit leads the believer to understand them in view of the importance of union with Christ. This relationship with Christ is central in a practical way, not an ideological one. Christ is understood as the Mediator in such a way that his mysteries are united to the believer in a personal way. The teaching of Blessed Columba Marmion thoroughly developed this approach.[212] The gift of understanding inspires an original understanding of the cross and resurrection. It is the culminating, all-important event that accomplishes the *exitus-reditus* in the life of the believer through the Church's mediation in the sacraments. This is uncomplicated in the faith of the one who is blessed with understanding.

Sin dulls and obscures our union with Christ, leading us to seek union with other things. When this happens, the gift of understanding steps in. It helps us to turn to the mysteries of Christ out of devotion to his Person, rather than from an attachment to the law. In this way our faith, far from being simply utilitarian or nostalgic, grows from a new, more interior place. Regular practice of a sacramental life is based on a strong devotion to the mystery of Jesus in his sacrifice on the cross. The believer's devotion arises from much more than duty and obligation. Grounded

---

211. Aquinas, *Summa Theologiae*, IIa IIe q. 8, a. 1.

212. For further consideration of his thought see: Blessed Columba Marmion, *Christ, The Life of the Soul*, trans. Alan Bancroft (Bethesda: Zaccheus Books, 2005).

in the gift of understanding, God's plan is not narrowed down to our plans. Instead, our plans grow by being formed on the plan of God alone. The heart opens to receive the designs of God.

s. Blessed Are the Pure of Heart

John Paul highlights the call to purity in light of the beatitude, "Blessed are the pure of heart, for they shall see God." Purity of heart, especially sexual purity, cannot be reduced to tight repression that aims to eliminate sexual feelings. The heart stands for the "'inner man,' and in particular for the mind and the will."[213] The mind and the will naturally experience a wide range of affections that are part of the sexual appetite. Purity of heart is built upon virtue that is tested in the world and knows two things in particular: First, it knows what God is not in terms of inner experiences, and so it seeks to keep the inner person free of inordinate affections. Second, purity of heart looks for who God is, and so it seeks to keep the pathways of the inner person clear. Then the heart can receive God's truth, which travels along legitimate affections.[214]

When the human heart is free from inordinate affections and open to receive proper affections, the person's actions have their foundation in an original spontaneity.[215] This spontaneity is proper to a heart "that has been removed from the realm of the profane and consecrated to the service of God, a heart in some sense made into a vessel to receive the presence of God."[216] This is the authentic basis of human transformation. The Christian's demeanor and conduct can then originate not from unpredictable moods or wrangling, but from an even and natural foundation. The transformed life is not skin deep nor based on appearance. Purity of heart allows the Christian to have

> a life which wells up in us from a source too deep for us to plumb. To have a pure heart is to have a heart that is not just created by God and then abandoned to us for us to make the most of it; it is to have a heart

---

213. Tugwell, *The Beatitudes*, 94.
214. Aquinas, *Summa Theologiae*, IIa IIe q. 8, a. 7.
215. Tugwell, *The Beatitudes*, 95.
216. Leiva-Merikakis, *Fire of Mercy, Heart of the Word*, vol. 1, 199.

which is constantly being created and sustained by the newness of life in God.[217]

Purity of heart is not the result of unaided firmness of intention, strict ascetical practices, fervent aspirations, experience, naïveté, or stringent attitudes. Purity is an outcome and an aftermath as much as it is an intention. Purity is the fruit of engaging the deep places of humanity and not settling for easy or automatic answers. To recognize the way of the gift calls for careful discernment that struggles with the deepest energies of love and life:

> Purity does not reach full maturity without having fought a spiritual battle, without having confronted, in the depths where spirit and flesh are joined, the obscure forces which draw us to impurity in its multiple forms. The one who has known how to overcome his adversary in a long struggle and to drag all his ruses and evasions into the light of day—do we not say this one has taken the measure of evil?[218]

The striving for purity of heart always retains an air of combat because we are so strongly attracted to pleasure. Therefore the heart must stay awake and channel our energies into the experience of the heart. It would be false to reduce purity to control of genital sensations. This is only part of the battle. Christians use various methods and strategies to diminish the intensity of the struggle. Techniques that are limited simply to controlling behavior are not enough for authentic self-mastery. The persistent urge of the energy for life and love requires measures that fill up the heart rather than merely ward off feelings. In fighting this battle for self-mastery, we first learn much about their inner terrain, such that "the organ for seeing here is the heart rather than the eyes."[219] If the struggle for purity of heart dwindles to self-analysis and continued self-reproach, falls will be more frequent. Purity of heart is not found primarily in what we turn away from, but in Whom we turn toward: "The pure heart *sees* God because it turns its gaze away from everything else."[220] Purity of heart emerges as we ascend the ladder and guard the hidden wellspring.

---

217. Tugwell, *The Beatitudes*, 97.
218. Pinckaers, *The Pursuit of Happiness*, 138.
219. Leiva-Merikakis, *Fire of Mercy, Heart of the Word*, vol. 1, 199.
220. Ibid., 199–200.

Gift	Virtue	Beatitude
Wisdom	Love	Blessed are the peacemakers

t. Wisdom

The sense of being a child of God is infused through the gift of fear of the Lord. An interior gift, our childhood before God becomes visible as we show justice to others through the gift of piety. Moved by justice, we maintain a steadfast devotion in our interior and exterior world. Meekness fuels a steady determination, sustained by freedom that grows in the knowledge of the things of God. The trivial things of the world do not ensnare the believer who is renewed by God's mysteries. Perseverance in the things of God leads to persistence and fortitude when faced with the things of the world. The Christian can rejoice that the things of the world reflect their original creation and, more, their re-creation in Christ. The believer knows the mysteries of Christ will overtake the puzzles of the world as surely as the tide covers the shoreline. We long for the sudden onrush as the mystery of God pours out upon new places. The longing matures into prudence as we realize that our time must expand to be God's. Mercy enlarges the action of Christians. We learn the true path of deliverance by enduring even God's delay. Endurance pries our categories open even wider, so that we can replenish our faith in the gift of understanding. Our hearts dilate as the Holy Spirit opens wide the mysteries of the Son. Through this special visitation of the gift of wisdom, we consider the highest cause and can now judge every other cause by the vantage point of faith.[221] Daily annoyances, rather than weighing us down, now become secret passageways to the Scriptures and to the natural contours of mercy. We do not have to grapple with regret or frivolous expectations, because the present opens in a unique way. The Church's teaching is now much more accessible to the Christian's interior sense. Doctrine is aligned so closely to the believer's heart that he or she can barely tell

---

221. Aquinas, *Summa Theologiae*, IIa IIe q. 45, a. 1.

the difference between meditation and thinking.[222] God's truths are revealed as being accessible and practical without jettisoning any degree of their transcendence.[223]

u. Love

Despite its claim to favor diversity, the world will only tolerate one essential definition of love: Love is characterized as a free-floating, sensation-based energy that exists as long as it enhances one's individuality. As long as it does so, no particular private act associated with this "love" can be deemed contrary to it. As such, love is the most imitated reality in time and space. Real love can never be reduced to one of its parts. Its counterfeits go by many names: permissiveness, promiscuity, infatuation, control, use, validation, eroticism, or neediness. Tolerance masquerading as love seeps into society's ideas of education, occupation, business, politics, economics, religion, and entertainment. But true love is too sublime and authentic for caricatures. The simple complexity of love cannot be easily duplicated.

Charity, or agape, is the love that resides in God alone. "… it is clear what Jesus meant by love of God: not a feeling, an emotional rapture, nor yet mystical bliss, but only obedience and service."[224] In the Christian sense, charity is a heroic, selfless love. Charity has never gazed into a mirror, because it is reflected in God alone. As such, the ability to love comes to us as a pure gift that dwells within our very being. Love as charity or agape is an inheritance born from communion with God himself. It comes to us and makes a unique home in the deepest places of our being. The action of Jesus on the cross communicates authentic selfless love, a love made visible.

Love is the cause and sign of the believer's participation in the love of God himself. The one who loves selflessly through the authentic gift of self has met the fountain of undiminished love poured out only through the Holy Spirit. This love, then, creates ways of unity among persons: marriage between a man and a woman, and the love of parents for their

---

222. Ibid., a. 2.
223. Ibid., a. 3.
224. Schnackenburg, *The Moral Teaching of the New Testament*, 98.

children. The family is the most original natural institution where we can find unconditional love.

The mysteries of Christ are immediately bound up with marriage and family: The incarnation takes place in the midst of the marriage of the Virgin Mary to Joseph. The crucifixion of the Son takes place before the first cell of the Church, the Blessed Mother and Saint John. He is entrusted to her as son, and she to him as mother. These moments of love give birth to actions of love within the human family. Communion begets communion. In the final analysis, love has no ingredients. It is never abstract or anonymous. In its complexity it is the most simple reality in existence. Love is the only cause of love.

v. Blessed Are the Peacemakers

Love is more present the more it is hidden. Love as charity and agape fills without limiting; it surrenders without diminishing; it increases without calculating. As such, the peace that flows from love is not an outcome or a product, but only an effect. The peace that abides in Christians does not come from their living on a different plane from everyone else. Peace is not a denial or escape from the world's pain and suffering. Peace is not serene repose, avoiding controversy, or unblinking passivity as alarm bells go off in the world. Peace is the serenity of the one who engages all the world has to offer, but does so on God's terms: "The spiritual man does not seek peace because he is not hampered by the lack of peace."[225] A steadied resolve arises in myself and in others from setting due order in things by participation in the likeness of the Son of God.[226] It emerges only from the cross: "But this peace is wrought on the Cross."[227]

---

225. Tugwell, *The Beatitudes*, 114.
226. Aquinas, *Summa Theologiae*, IIa IIe q. 45, a. 6.
227. Tugwell, *The Beatitudes*, 114; cf. Leiva-Merikakis, *Fire of Mercy, Heart of the Word*, vol. 1, 201.

Conclusion

Karol Wojtyla was used to stepping into the middle. He was born into the middle of a loving family. He stood in the middle of culture. He withstood German Nazism, Soviet Communism, and Western secularism, all from the vantage point of his dynamic personalism. He understood the Second Vatican Council as the key to the third millennium. He stood in the middle between faith and reason, and he patiently insisted that beauty unites the two. John Paul invited us along as he followed Jesus, who stood in the middle between the legalism of certain Pharisees and the beauty of Genesis.

To be in the middle is to be in the heart of life. From regimes that resided at the bleakest margins of death throughout the twentieth century, John Paul led the way to the middle, to the heart. More so, he embodied the *middle*. He did not begin with extremes, but stood secure in the truth available in the experience of existence itself. He stood within the middle of human experience and the revelation of God. His proclamation of the culture of life through his teaching, most notably in the theology of the body, has pointed the way toward a civilization of love through life according to the Spirit. His sustained and innovative teaching on the identity of the human person has been an exercise of faithful originality. In it he attends to both the signs of the times and the revelation of God's wise and loving plan. From his unique vantage point, John Paul has mapped out the path for the new evangelization, taken the first steps toward the renewal of moral theology, and embraced the human race. As we turn again to those we love, and even those whom we find difficult to love, we follow the steps of the young man from Krakow who changed the world.

Bibliography

Sources mentioned in the text and notes

Anderson, Carl A. *A Civilization of Love*. New York: HarperOne, 2008.

Aquinas, Thomas. *Summa Theologiae* in *Basic Writings of St. Thomas Aquinas*. Edited by Anton C. Pegis. New York, NY: Random House, 1945.

Asci, Donald P. *The Conjugal Act as a Personal Act: A Study of the Catholic Concept of the Conjugal Act in the Light of Christian Anthropology*. San Francisco: Ignatius Press, 2002.

Athanasius. *The Life of Antony and the Letter to Marcellinus*. Translated by Robert C. Gregg. New York: Paulist Press, 1980.

Augustine. *De Libero Arbitrio*. Available in many printed editions and on the Web.

_____. *De Trinitate*. Available in many printed editions and on the Web.

_____. *On Genesis: Two Books on Genesis Against the Manichees*. Translated by Roland J. Teske, SJ. Washington, DC: The Catholic University of America Press, 1991.

_____. *Our Lord's Sermon on the Mount*. Available in many printed editions and on the Web.

_____. *Sermones ad Populos*. Available in printed editions and on the Web.

Bachelard, Gaston. *The Poetics of Space: The Classic Look at How We Experience Intimate Places*. Boston: Beacon, 1994.

Balthasar, Hans Urs von. *The Christian State of Life*. San Francisco: Ignatius Press, 1983.

———. *Explorations in Theology II: Spouse of the Word*. San Francisco: Ignatius Press, 1991.

———. *Explorations in Theology IV: Spirit and Institution*. San Francisco: Ignatius Press, 1995.

———. *The Glory of the Lord: A Theological Aesthetics II: Clerical Style*. San Francisco: Ignatius Press, 1984.

———. *The Glory of the Lord: A Theological Aesthetics VII: Theology: The New Covenant*. San Francisco: Ignatius Press, 1989.

———. *Mysterium Paschale*. Grand Rapids, MI: Wm. B. Eerdmans, 1993.

———. *Theo-Drama II: Dramatis Personae: Man in God*. San Francisco, Ignatius Press Press, 1990.

———. *Theo-Drama IV: In the Action*. San Francisco: Ignatius Press, 1994.

———. *Theo-Drama V: The Last Act*. San Francisco: Ignatius Press 1994.

———. *Theo-Logic I: Truth of the World*. San Francisco: Ignatius Press, 2001.

———. *Theo-Logic II: Truth of God*. San Francisco: Ignatius Press, 2004.

Benedict XVI, *Spe Salvi*. Boston: Pauline Books & Media, 2007.

Berrigan, Daniel, SJ. *Genesis: Fair Beginnings, Then Foul*. Lanham, MD: Rowman & Littlefield, 2006.

Bishops of Pennsylvania, *Living Together: Questions and Answers Regarding Cohabitation and the Church's Moral Teaching*. Harrisburg: Pennsylvania Catholic Conference, 1999.

Blankenhorn, David. *Fatherless America, Confronting Our Most Urgent Social Problem*. New York: Basic Books, 1995.

Blazynski, George. *Pope John Paul II: A Richly Revealing Portrait*. New York: Dell, 1979.

Bly, Robert. *Iron John: A Book About Men*. New York: Addison-Wesley, 1990.

———. *The Sibling Society*. New York: Addison-Wesley, 1996.

Bonaventure. *Collations on the Seven Gifts of the Holy Spirit*. Translated by Zachary Hayes, OFM. Vol. 14 of *Works of St. Bonaventure*. New York: Franciscan Institute, 2008.

Boniecki, Adam, MIC. *The Making of the Pope of the Millennium: Kalendarium of the Life of Karol Wojtyla*. Stockbridge, MA: Marian Press, 2000.

Browning, Don S. *Marriage and Modernization: How Globalization Threatens Marriage and What to Do About It*. Grand Rapids, MI: Wm. B. Eerdmans, 2003.

Bunge, Gabriel, OSB. *Dragon's Wine and Angel's Bread: The Teaching of Evagrius Ponticus on Anger and Meekness*. New York: St. Vladimir's Seminary Press, 2009.

"CARA Reflections on the Pew Religious Landscape Survey." In *The CARA Report* 13:4, Spring 2008.

Cassian, John. *The Conferences*. Translated by Boniface Ramsey, OP. Mahwah, NJ: Paulist Press, 1997.

Cessario, Romanus, OP. *Introduction to Moral Theology*. Washington, DC: The Catholic University of America Press, 2001.

_____. *The Moral Virtues and Theological Ethics*. Indiana: University of Notre Dame Press, 1995.

_____. *The Virtues, or the Examined Life*. New York: Continuum, 2002.

_____. "What the Angels See at Twilight." In *Communio* 26:3, Fall 1999.

Cherlin, Andrew J. *Marriage, Divorce, Remarriage*. Cambridge, MA: Harvard University Press, 1992.

Christiansen, Drew, SJ. "Of Many Things." In *America*, May 19, 2008.

Climacus, John. *The Ladder of Divine Ascent*. Translated by Colm Luibheid and Norma Russell. Mahwah, NJ: Paulist Press, 1982.

Cloud, Henry, and John Townsend. *Safe People: How to Find Relationships that Are Good for You*. Grand Rapids, MI: Zondervan, 1995.

Congar, Yves. *Faith and Spiritual Life*. New York: Herder and Herder, 1968.

_____. *A Gospel Priesthood*. New York: Herder and Herder, 1967.

_____. *The Word and the Spirit*, San Francisco: Harper & Row, 1986.

Corbon, Jean. *Path to Freedom: Christian Experiences and the Bible*. New York: Sheed & Ward.

Crosby, John. *The Selfhood of the Human Person*. Washington, DC: Catholic University of America Press, 1996.

Curran, Charles. *The Moral Theology of Pope John Paul II*. Washington, DC: Georgetown University Press, 2005.

Daniélou, Jean. *Advent*. New York: Sheed and Ward, 1951.

_____. *The Angels and Their Mission: According to the Fathers of the Church*. Translated by David Heimann. Westminster, MD: Newman Press, 1957.

_____. *Christ and Us*. New York: Sheed & Ward, 1961.

_____. *God and the Ways of Knowing*. San Francisco: Ignatius, 2003.

_____. *In the Beginning ... Genesis I–III*. Baltimore: Helicon, 1965.

_____. *The Lord of History: Reflections on the Inner Meaning of History*. Chicago: H. Regnery, 1958.

_____. *Myth and Mystery*. New York: Hawthorne Books, 1968.

_____. *Origen*. New York: Sheed & Ward, 1955.

_____. *The Scandal of Truth*. London: Burns and Oates, 1962.

D'Antonio, William V., et al. *American Catholics Today: New Realities of Their Faith and Their Church*. Lanham, MD: Rowan & Littlefield, 2007.

Davies, Oliver. *A Theology of Compassion: Metaphysics of Difference and the Renewal of Tradition*. Grand Rapids, MI: Wm. B. Eerdmans, 2001.

de Lubac, Henri. *A Brief Catechesis on Nature and Grace*. San Francisco: Ignatius Press, 1984.

———. *At the Service of the Church: Henri de Lubac Reflects on the Circumstances that Occasioned His Writings*. San Francisco: Ignatius Press, 1989.

———. *History and Spirit: The Understanding of Scripture According to Origen*. San Francisco: Ignatius Press, 2007.

Dougherty, Nancy J., and Jacqueline J. West. *The Matrix and Meaning of Character: An Archetypal and Developmental Approach*. New York: Taylor & Francis, 2007.

Dulles, Avery, SJ. *The Splendor of Faith: The Theological Vision of Pope John Paul II*. New York: Crossroad, 1999.

Fairlie, Henry. *The Seven Deadly Sins Today*. Indiana: University of Notre Dame Press, 1995.

Forte, Bruno. *To Follow You, Light of Life; Spiritual Exercises Preached before John Paul II at the Vatican*. Grand Rapids, MI: Wm. B. Eerdmans, 2005.

Gawronski, Raymond, SJ. "The Distant Country of John Paul II." In *Creed and Culture: Jesuit Studies of Pope John Paul II*. Edited by Joseph W. Koterski, SJ, and John J. Conley, SJ. Philadelphia: St. Joseph's University Press, 2004.

Glendon, Mary Ann. *Abortion and Divorce in Western Law: American Failures, European Challenges*. Cambridge, MA: Harvard University Press, 1987.

Grabowski, John S. *Sex and Virtue: An Introduction to Sexual Ethics*. Washington, DC: The Catholic University of America Press, 2003.

Guigo II. *The Ladder of Monks: A Letter on the Contemplative Life and Twelve Meditations*. Translated by Edmund Colledge and James Walsh. Kalamazoo, MI: Cistercian Publications, 1981.

Hogan, Richard M., and John M. LeVoir. *Covenant of Love: Pope John Paul II on Sexuality, Marriage, and Family in the Modern World*. New York: Doubleday, 1985.

International Theological Commission. "Communion and Stewardship: Human Persons Created in the Image of God." In *Origins* 34:15, September 23, 2004.

Johnson, Paul M. *A History of the American People*. New York: HarperCollins, 1998.

Kasper, Walter. *Transcending All Understanding: The Meaning of Christian Faith Today*. San Francisco: Ignatius Press, Communio Books, 1989.

Kavanaugh, John F. "Autonomous Individualism." In *America*, January 15–22, 2007.

King, Stephen. *Needful Things*. New York: Signet, 1992.

———. *Salem's Lot*. Garden City, NY: Doubleday, 1975.

Knights of Columbus. *An American Perspective*. New York: Marist College Institute for Public Opinion, 2008.

Kreeft, Peter. *Ecumenical Jihad: Ecumenism and the Culture War*. San Francisco: Ignatius, 1996.

_____. *Making Choices: Finding Black and White in a World of Grays*. Ann Arbor, MI: Servant Books, 1990.

Kupczak, Jaroslaw. *Destined for Liberty: The Human Person in the Philosophy of Karol Wojtyla / John Paul II*. Washington, DC: The Catholic University of America Press, 2000.

Laffitte, Jean. "Love and Forgiveness." In *The Way of Love: Reflections on Pope Benedict XVI's Encyclical* Deus Caritas Est. Edited by Livio Melina and Carl A. Anderson. San Francisco: Ignatius, 2006.

La Potterie, Ignace de, SJ, and Stanislaus Lyonnet, SJ. *The Christian Lives by the Spirit*. New York: Alba House, 1971.

Leo the Great. *Sermons*. Available in printed editions and on the Web.

Leon-Dufour, Xavier. *To Act According to the Gospel*. Peabody, MA: Hendrickson, 2005.

Leiva-Merikakis, Erasmo. *Fire of Mercy, Heart of the Word: Meditations on the Gospel According to St. Matthew*, vol. 1. San Francisco: Ignatius Press, 1996.

Maher, Briget, ed. *The Family Portrait: A Compilation of Data, Research and Public Opinion on the Family*. Washington, DC: The Family Research Council, 2004.

Marengo, G., and B. Ognibeni, eds. *Dialoghi sul mistero nuziale*. Rome: Pontifica Universitá Lateranense, 2003.

Marquardt, Elizabeth. *Between Two Worlds: The Inner Lives of Children of Divorce*. New York: Crown, 2005.

Martin, Francis. "The New Feminism: Biblical Foundations and Some Lines of Development." In *Women in Christ: Toward a New Feminism*, edited by Michele M. Schumacher. Grand Rapids, MI: Wm. B. Eerdmans, 2003.

Martino, Steven C., et al. "Exposure to Degrading Versus Nondegrading Music Lyrics and Sexual Behavior Among Youth." In *Pediatrics* 118:2, August 2006.

McDermott, John M., ed. *The Thought of Pope John Paul II*. Rome: Editrice Pontificia Università Gregoriana, 1993.

McDermott, John M., and John Gavin, eds. *John Paul II on the Body: Human, Eucharistic, Ecclesial*. Philadelphia: Saint Joseph's University Press, 2007.

McIntosh, Mark A. *Discernment and Truth: The Spirituality and Theology of Knowledge*. New York: Crossroad, 2004.

McNerney, John. *Footbridge Towards the Other: An Introduction to the Philosophy and Poetry of John Paul II*. New York: T & T Clark, 2003.

Meeker, Meg. *Epidemic: How Teen Sex Is Killing Our Kids*. Washington, DC: LifeLine Press, 2002.

_____. *Strong Fathers, Strong Daughters: 10 Secrets Every Father Should Know.* Washington, DC: Regnery, 2006.

Melina, Livio. *Sharing in Christ's Virtues: For a Renewal of Moral Theology in Light of* Veritatis Splendor. Translated by William E. May. Washington, DC: The Catholic University of America Press, 2001.

Moehringer, J. R. *The Tender Bar.* New York: Hyperion, 2005.

Mugridge, Christian A., SOLT, and Marie Gannon, FMA. *John Paul II: Development of a Theology of Communication.* Rome: Libreria Editrice Vaticana, 2008.

Muller, Earl C. SJ. "The Nuptial Meaning of the Body." In *John Paul II on the Body: Human, Eucharistic, Ecclesial.* Philadelphia: Saint Joseph's University Press, 2007.

Muller, Gerhard. *Priesthood and Diaconate: The Recipient of the Sacrament of Holy Orders from the Perspective of Creation Theology and Christology.* San Francisco: Ignatius Press, 2002.

National Marriage Project. *The State of Our Unions 2003: The Social Health of Marriage in America.*

Pew Forum on Religion & Public Life. *U.S. Religious Landscape Survey.* Washington, DC: Pew Research Center, 2008.

Pinckaers, Servais. *Morality: The Catholic View.* South Bend, IN: St. Augustine's Press, 2003.

_____. *The Pinckaers Reader: Renewing Thomistic Moral Theology.* Edited by John Berkman and Craig Stevens Titus. Washington, DC: The Catholic University of America Press, 2005.

_____. *The Pursuit of Happiness: God's Way.* New York: Alba House, 1988.

Pontifical Biblical Commission. *The Bible and Morality: Biblical Roots of Christian Behavior,* 2008.

Pontifical Council for the Laity. *Woman and Man: The* Humanum *in Its Entirety.* Proceedings on the Twentieth Anniversary of John Paul II's Apostolic Letter *Mulieris Dignitatem* (1988–2008). International Congress, Rome, February 7–9, 2008.

Prendergast, Terrence. "'A Vision of Wholeness': A Reflection on the Use of Scripture in a Cross-Section of Papal Writings." In *The Thought of Pope John Paul II: A Collection of Essays and Studies.* Edited by John M. McDermott, SJ. Rome: Editrice Pontificia Università Gregoriana, 1993.

Quay, Paul M. *The Mystery Hidden for Ages in God.* New York: Peter Lang, 2002.

Ratzinger, Joseph. *God and the World: A Conversation with Peter Seewald.* San Francisco: Ignatius Press, 2002.

_____. "The New Evangelization: Building the Civilization of Love." http://www.ewtn.com/new_evangelization/Ratzinger.htm.

Rhoads, Steven E. *Taking Sex Differences Seriously*. San Francisco: Encounter Books, 2004.

Schmitz, Kenneth. *At the Center of the Human Drama: The Philosophical Anthropology of Karol Wojtyla/Pope John Paul II*. Washington, DC: The Catholic University of America Press, 1993

———. *The Gift: Creation*. Milwaukee: Marquette University Press, 1982.

———. *The Recovery of Wonder: The New Freedom and the Asceticism of Power*. Montreal: McGill-Queen's University Press, 2008.

Schnackenburg, Rudolph. *The Moral Teaching of the New Testament*. New York: Herder and Herder, 1971.

Scola, Angelo. "The Formation of Priests in the Pastoral Care of the Family." In *Communio International Catholic Review* 24:1, Spring 1997.

———. *The Nuptial Mystery*. Grand Rapids, MI: Wm. B. Eerdmans, 2005.

Seifert, Josef. "Philosophy and Science in the Context of Contemporary Culture." In *The Human Search for Truth: Philosophy, Science, and Theology / The Outlook for the Third Millennium*. Proceedings of the International Conference on Science and Faith, May 23–25, 2000. Philadelphia: Saint Joseph's University Press, 2002.

Shivanandan, Mary. *Crossing the Threshold of Love: A New Vision of Marriage*. Washington, DC: The Catholic University of America Press, 1999.

———. "Body-Soul Unity in Light of the Nuptial Relation." In *Dialoghi sul mistero nuziale*. Edited by G. Marengo and B. Ognibeni. Rome: Pontificia Università Lateranense, 2003.

Simpson, Peter. *On Karol Wojtyla*. Belmont, CA: Wadsworth Publishing, 2000.

Speyr, Adrienne von. *The Boundless God*. San Francisco: Ignatius Press, 2004.

———. *Light and Images: Elements of Contemplation*. San Francisco: Ignatius, 2004.

Svidercoschi, Gian Franco. *Stories of Karol: The Unknown Life of John Paul II*. Liguori, MO: Liguori, 2003.

Swetnam, James, SJ. "A Vision of Wholeness: Response." In *The Thought of Pope John Paul II: A Collection of Essays and Studies*. Edited by John M. McDermott, SJ. Rome: Editrice Pontifica Università Gregoriana, 1993.

Szulc, Tad. *Pope John Paul II: The Biography*. New York: Scribner, 1995.

Tiger, Lionel. *The Decline of Males: The First Look at an Unexpected New World for Men and Women*. New York: St. Martin's Griffin, 2000.

Tripoli, Martin R., SJ. "John Paul II: The Countercultural Pope." In *Creed and Culture: Jesuit Studies of Pope John Paul II*. Edited by Joseph W. Koterski, SJ, and John J. Conley, SJ. Philadelphia: Saint Joseph's University Press, 2004.

Torrell, Jean-Pierre, O.P. *Saint Thomas Aquinas: Spiritual Master* Volume 2. Washington, DC: The Catholic University of America Press, 2003.

Tugwell, Simon. *The Beatitudes: Soundings in the Christian Tradition.* Springfield, IL: Templegate, 1980.

Weigel, George. *Witness to Hope: The Biography of Pope John Paul II.* New York: HarperCollins, 1999.

Woznicki, Andrew N. *A Christian Humanism: Karol Wojtyla's Existential Personalism.* New Britain, CT: Mariel, 1980.

Wolterstorff, Nicholas. *Lament for a Son.* Grand Rapids, MI: Wm. B. Eerdmans, 1987.

Works by Karol Wojtyla

The Acting Person. Translated by Andrzej Potocki. Edited by Anna-Teresa Tymieniecka. *Analecta Husserliana* 10; New York: Reidel, 1979.

Fruitful and Responsible Love. New York: Seabury Press, 1978.

Love and Responsibility. Translated by H. T. Willetts. San Francisco: Ignatius Press, 1993.

Person and Community: Selected Essays. Translated by Theresa Sandok, OSM. Edited by Andrew N. Woznicki. Vol. 4 of Catholic Thought from Lublin. New York: Peter Lang, 1993.

Sign of Contradiction. New York: Seabury Press, 1979.

Sources of Renewal: The Implementation of the Second Vatican Council. Translated by S. Falla. San Francisco: Harper & Row, 1980.

Works by Pope John Paul II

Christifideles Laici. Boston: Pauline Books & Media, 1988.

Crossing the Threshold of Hope. New York: Knopf, 1994.

Dives in Misericordia. Boston: Pauline Books & Media, 1980.

Dominum et Vivificantem. Boston: Pauline Books & Media, 1986.

Evangelium Vitae. Boston: Pauline Books & Media, 1995.

Familiaris Consortio. Boston: Pauline Books & Media, 1981.

Fides et Ratio. Boston: Pauline Books & Media, 1998.

God, Father and Creator: A Catechesis on the Creed. Boston: Pauline Books & Media, 1996.

Jesus, Son and Savior: A Catechesis on the Creed. Boston: Pauline Books & Media, 1996.

Laborem Exercens. Boston: Pauline Books & Media, 1981.

Letter to Families. Boston: Pauline Books & Media, 1994.

Letter to Women. Boston: Pauline Books & Media, 1995.

Man and Woman He Created Them: A Theology of the Body. Introduction by Christopher West. Boston: Pauline Books & Media, 2006.

Memory and Identity: Conversations at the Dawn of a Millennium. New York: Rizzoli, 2005.

Mulieris Dignitatem. Boston: Pauline Books & Media, 1988.

Novo Millennio Ineunte. Boston: Pauline Books & Media, 2001.

Reconciliatio et Paenitentia. Boston: Pauline Books & Media, 1984.

Redemptoris Missio. Boston: Pauline Books & Media, 1990.

Sollicitudo Rei Socialis. Boston: Pauline Books & Media, 1987.

Tertio Millennio Adveniente. Boston: Pauline Books & Media, 1994.

The Trinity's Embrace: God's Saving Plan: A Catechesis on Salvation History. Boston: Pauline Books & Media, 2002.

Veritatis Splendor. Boston: Pauline Books & Media, 1993.

Other Magisterial Documents

Benedict XVI. *Deus Caritas Est.* Boston: Pauline Books & Media, 2006.

Catechism of the Catholic Church, Second Edition. Washington, DC: United States Conference of Catholic Bishops, 2006.

Code of Canon Law. Washington, DC: Canon Law Society of America, 1983.

Congregation for the Doctrine of the Faith. *Declaration on Certain Questions Concerning Sexual Ethics.* Washington, DC: United States Catholic Conference, 1976.

_____. *Donum Vitae.* Boston: Pauline Books & Media, 1987.

Leo XIII. *Arcanum.* In *The Papal Encyclicals 1878-1903.* Edited by Claudia Carlen. Wilmington, NC: McGrath, 1981.

Paul VI. *Evangelii Nuntiandi.* Boston: Pauline Books & Media, 1975.

_____. *Humanae Vitae.* Boston: Pauline Books & Media, 1968.

Pius XI. *Casti Connubii.* Boston: Pauline Books & Media, 1930.

Pontifical Biblical Commission. *The Interpretation of the Bible in the Church.* Boston: Pauline Books & Media, 1993.

_____. *The Jewish People and Their Sacred Scriptures in the Christian Bible.* Boston: Pauline Books & Media, 2002.

_____. *Preparation for the Sacrament of Marriage.* Boston: Pauline Books & Media, 1996.

_____. *The Truth and Meaning of Human Sexuality.* Boston: Pauline Books & Media, 1996.

_____. *Vademecum for Confessors Concerning Some Aspects of the Morality of Conjugal Life.* Boston: Pauline Books & Media, 1997.

Sacred Congregation for Catholic Education. *Educational Guidance in Human Love*. Boston: Pauline Books & Media, 1983.

Second Vatican Council. *Closing Speeches*. Boston: Pauline Books & Media, 1965.

————. *Dignitatis Humanae*. Boston: Pauline Books & Media, 1965.

————. *Gaudium et Spes*. Boston: Pauline Books & Media, 1965.

————. *Lumen Gentium*. Boston: Pauline Books & Media, 1964.

Vatican Commission for Religious Relations with the Jews. *Notes on the Correct Way to Present the Jews and Judaism in Preaching and Catechesis in the Roman Catholic Church*. June 24, 1985.

Other Sources

Albacete, Lorenzo. *God at the Ritz: Attraction to Infinity*. New York: Crossroad, 2002.

Allen, Prudence, RSM. "Integral Sex Complementarity and the Theology of Communion." In *Communio* 17:4, Winter 1990, 523-544.

————. *The Concept of Woman: The Aristotelian Revolution* 750 BC–1250 AD. Grand Rapids, MI: Wm. B. Eerdmans, 1997.

————. *The Concept of Woman: The Humanist Reformation* 1250–1500. Grand Rapids, MI: Wm. B. Eerdmans, 2002.

Augustine. Sermon LXIX, c. 2, 3. In *Patrologia Latina*, 38, 441.

Batut, Jean-Pierre. "The Chastity of Jesus and the Refusal to Grasp." In *Communio* 24:1, Spring 1997, 5–13.

Beigel, Gerard. *Faith and Social Justice in the Teaching of Pope John Paul II*. New York: Peter Lang, 1997.

Buttiglione, Rocco. *Karol Wojtyla: The Thought of the Man Who Became Pope John Paul II*. Grand Rapids, MI: Wm. B. Eerdmans, 1997.

Chesterton, G. K. *The Collected Works*, vol. 1. San Francisco: Ignatius Press, 1986.

de Haro, Ramón Garcia. *Marriage and the Family in the Documents of the Magisterium*. Translated by William E. May. San Francisco: Ignatius Press, 1993.

de Lubac, Henri. *The Drama of Atheistic Humanism*. San Francisco: Ignatius Press, 1995.

————. *The Mystery of the Supernatural*. New York: Crossroad, 1998.

de Montfort, Louis. *True Devotion to the Blessed Virgin*. Bay Shore, NY: Montfort Publications, 1993.

————. *The Secret of the Rosary*. Bay Shore, NY: Montfort Publications, 1998.

Derrick, Christopher. *Sex and Sacredness: A Catholic Homage to Venus*. San Francisco: Ignatius Press, 1982.

Elliot, Peter J. *What God Has Joined ... : The Sacramentality of Marriage*. New York: Alba House, 1990.

Fagan, Patrick. "A Culture of Inverted Sexuality." In *Catholic World Report*, November 1998, 57.

Freud, Sigmund. *New Introductory Lectures in Psychoanalysis*. Translated and edited by James Strachey. New York: Norton, 1966.

Giussani, Luigi. *The Religious Sense*. Translated by John Zucchi. Montreal: McGill-Queen's University Press, 1997.

Gneuhs, Geoffrey, ed. *The Legacy of Pope John Paul II: His Contribution to Catholic Thought*. New York: Herder and Herder, 2000.

La Potterie, Ignace de. *Mary in the Mystery of the Covenant*. New York: Alba House, 1992.

Lawler, Ronald, Joseph H. Boyle, and William E. May. *Catholic Sexual Ethics*, second edition. Huntington, IN: Our Sunday Visitor, 1998.

May, William E. *Marriage: The Rock on Which the Family Is Built*. San Francisco: Ignatius Press, 1995.

Prokes, Mary Timothy, FSE. *Toward a Theology of the Body*. Grand Rapids, MI: Wm. B. Eerdmans, 1996.

Other Books on the Theology of the Body

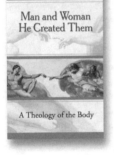

Man and Woman He Created Them
John Paul II
A new translation of the complete text of John Paul II's monumental work, which he himself called "theology of the body." Includes a comprehensive introduction, translator's footnotes, and a detailed index.

0-8198-7421-3 $29.95

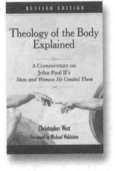

Theology of the Body Explained
A Commentary on John Paul II's
Man and Woman He Created Them
Christopher West
Unpacks the entire work of the theology of the body. Revised and expanded to reflect the improved translation and new scholarship.

0-8198-7425-6 $29.95

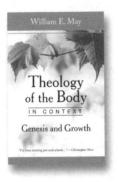

Theology of the Body in Context
Genesis and Growth
William E. May
The zenith of John Paul II's thought on the human person, marriage, and the family is found in his "theology of the body." For the first time, William E. May provides a comprehensive yet readable overview of this work in the context of several other key writings of Karol Wojtyla/John Paul II, providing rich insights into its development.

0-8198-7431-0 $16.95

The Theology of the Body Made Simple

Anthony Percy

A simple introduction to the theology of the body.

0-8198-7419-1 $9.95

God's Plan for You

Life, Love, Marriage, and Sex

David Hajduk

John Paul II's theology of the body made accessible for teens, answering their questions about life, relationships, and sexuality.

0-8198-4517-5 $16.95

Theology of the Body

Some Thoughts and Reflections

Karen Doyle

Some basic reflections on key ideas of Pope John Paul II's ground-breaking work, the Theology of the Body.

0-8198-7427-2 $10.95

The Genius of Womanhood

Karen Doyle

A collection of thoughts and reflections on what it means to be a woman, the qualities that mark the feminine, and why it is so crucial that women embrace these qualities that are unique to their gender.

0-8198-3109-3 $10.95

auline
BOOKS & MEDIA

A mission of the Daughters of St. Paul

As apostles of Jesus Christ, evangelizing today's world:

We are CALLED to holiness
by God's living Word and Eucharist.

We COMMUNICATE the Gospel message
through our lives and through all
available forms of media.

We SERVE the Church
by responding to the hopes and needs
of all people with the Word of God,
in the spirit of St. Paul.

For more information visit our website: www.pauline.org.

Pauline
BOOKS & MEDIA

The Daughters of St. Paul operate book and media centers at the following addresses. Visit, call, or write the one nearest you today, or find us at www.pauline.org.

CALIFORNIA
3908 Sepulveda Blvd, Culver City, CA 90230	310-397-8676
935 Brewster Avenue, Redwood City, CA 94063	650-369-4230
5945 Balboa Avenue, San Diego, CA 92111	858-565-9181

FLORIDA
145 S.W. 107th Avenue, Miami, FL 33174	305-559-6715

HAWAII
1143 Bishop Street, Honolulu, HI 96813	808-521-2731
Neighbor Islands call:	866-521-2731

ILLINOIS
172 North Michigan Avenue, Chicago, IL 60601	312-346-4228

LOUISIANA
4403 Veterans Memorial Blvd, Metairie, LA 70006	504-887-7631

MASSACHUSETTS
885 Providence Hwy, Dedham, MA 02026	781-326-5385

MISSOURI
9804 Watson Road, St. Louis, MO 63126	314-965-3512

NEW YORK
64 W. 38th Street, New York, NY 10018	212-754-1110

PENNSYLVANIA
Philadelphia—relocating	215-676-9494

SOUTH CAROLINA
243 King Street, Charleston, SC 29401	843-577-0175

VIRGINIA
1025 King Street, Alexandria, VA 22314	703-549-3806

CANADA
3022 Dufferin Street, Toronto, ON M6B 3T5	416-781-9131

¡También somos su fuente para libros,
videos y música en español!